WHICH PSYCHOTHERAPY?

WHICH PSYCHOTHERAPY?

Leading Exponents Explain their Differences

Edited by
COLIN FELTHAM

SAGE Publications
London • Thousand Oaks • New Delhi

First published 1997

SAGE Publications Ltd
6 Bonhill Street
London EC2A 4PU

SAGE Publications Inc
2455 Teller Road
Thousand Oaks, California 91320

SAGE Publications India Pvt Ltd
32, M-Block Market
Greater Kailash - I
New Delhi 110 048

British Library Cataloguing in Publication data

A catalogue record for this book is
available from the British Library.

ISBN 0 8039 7478 7
ISBN 0 8039 7479 5 (pbk)

Library of Congress catalog card number 96-072588

Typeset by Type Study, Scarborough
Printed in Great Britain by Biddles Ltd, Guildford, Surrey

Contents

List of Contributors

Jerold D. Bozarth is emeritus professor of the University of Georgia and president of Person-Centered International in the USA. He is editor of the international publication, *The Person-Centered Journal*, and has published over 200 articles and book chapters concerning the theory and practice of the Person-Centered Approach, psychotherapy effectiveness and qualitative and quantitative inquiries in the fields of counselling, mental health and rehabilitation. He is currently writing two books, one of them being a compendium of his papers which examine the evolving nature of the Person-Centered Approach over the past decade.

Petruska Clarkson, Fellow of the BAC, is a Consultant Chartered Counselling and Clinical Psychologist, a psychotherapist, supervisor and organizational consultant. She is a visiting lecturer at a number of universities in the UK and abroad, and the author/editor of 12 books and 90 professional papers which have been translated into 12 languages to date. She is a Supervisor and Teaching Member of Archetypal Jungian, Transactional Analysis, Gestalt, Integrative Psychotherapy and Group Psychotherapy organizations and for trainee and qualified BPsS Psychologists (Counselling, Clinical and Occupational). She was the founder and first Chair of the British Institute for Integrative Psychotherapy and is Honorary Reader in the psychology of supervision at Surrey University. She is Chair of the Board of Examiners for the British Psychological Society Diploma in Counselling Psychology.

Albert R. Elllis is the President of the Albert Ellis Institute for Rational Emotive Behavior Therapy in New York. He is the founder of Rational Emotive Behavior Therapy (REBT) and the 'grandfather' of Cognitive Behavior Therapy (CBT). He has written more than 60 books and 700 articles on psychotherapy and counselling.

Colin Feltham is Senior Lecturer in Counselling in the School of Education at Sheffield Hallam University, where he leads the MA in Counselling and Psychotherapy and a postgraduate supervision course. He is a Fellow of the British Association for Counselling. He edits two books series, *Professional Skills for Counsellors* and *Perspectives on Psychotherapy* for Sage Publications. His publications include *Psychotherapy and Its Discontents* (with

Windy Dryden, Open University Press, 1992), *What is Counselling?* (Sage, 1995) and *Time-Limited Counselling* (Sage, 1996).

John M. Heaton is a founder member of the Guild of Psychotherapists and a member of the training committee of the Philadelphia Association (founded by R.D. Laing). He was Chair of the Guild of Psychotherapists and of the Psychotherapy section of the The British Psychological Society and a Visiting Professor at Duquesne University, Pittsburgh. His works include *The Eye: Phenomenology and Psychology of Function and Disorder* (1968), *Wittgenstein for Beginners* (1994) and many articles on the relation of psychotherapy to philosophy. He is engaged in private practice in psychotherapy and is writing a book on Wittgenstein and psychotherapy.

Robert Langs, MD is the author of 36 books and some 125 papers on psychotherapy and related subjects. He is a classically trained psychoanalyst and holds positions as Visiting Professor of Psychiatry at the Mt Sinai Medical School in New York and Visiting Research Scientist at The Nathan S. Kline Institute for Psychiatric Research in Orangeburg, New York. His most recent books include *A Clinical Workbook for Psychotherapists* (1992), *Science Systems and Psychoanalysis* (1992), *Empowered Psychotherapy* (1993), *Doing Supervision and Being Supervised* (1994), *Clinical Practice and the Architecture of the Mind* (1995), *The Evolution of the Emotion Processing Mind: With an Introduction of Mental Darwinism* (1996) and *Death Anxiety and Clinical Practice* (1997), all published by Karnac Books. For Alliance Publishing he has written *The Dream Workbook* (1994), *The Daydream Workbook* (1995) and *The Cosmic Circle: The Unification of Mind, Matter and Energy* (with A. Badalamenti and L. Thomson, 1996). Dr Langs is a practising psychoanalyst and psychotherapist, primarily in the form of empowered psychotherapy.

Alvin R. Mahrer, PhD, is professor of psychology at the University of Ottawa and has been in private practice since 1954. From 1954–67 he was director of psychotherapy training and research in hospitals, and was professor and director of the clinical psychology program at Miami University from 1967–72 and professor of psychology at the University of Waterloo from 1972–77. He is on the editorial board of 10 professional journals and has authored 11 books and approximately 200 articles, mainly on his experiential psychotherapy, on psychotherapy theory, research, training and practice, and the philosophy of science. He is a fellow of the American Psychological Association.

Stephen Palmer is Director of the Centre for Stress Management in London. He is on the editorial board of 7 professional journals and has written numerous articles on counselling and stress management. His most recent books are *Counselling: The BAC Counselling Reader* (with Dainow and

Milner, Sage, 1996), *Dealing with People Problems at Work* (with Burton, McGraw-Hill, 1996), *Stress Management and Counselling: Theory, Practice, Research and Methodology* (with Dryden, Cassell, 1996), *Stress Counselling: A Rational Emotive Behaviour Approach* (with Ellis, Gordon and Neenan, Cassell, 1997), and *Client Assessment* (with McMahon, Sage, 1997). He is a fellow of the British Association for Counselling and the Royal Society for Health. He is the editor of *Counselling Psychology Review*, co-editor of *The Rational Behaviour Therapist* and former editor of *Counselling*.

John Rowan is the author of a number of books, including *The Transpersonal in Psychotherapy and Counselling* (Routledge, 1993) and most recently *Healing the Male Psyche: Therapy as Initiation* (Routledge, 1996). He is on the editorial board of *The Transpersonal Review*, and is a founder member and on the Board of the Association of Humanistic Psychology Practitioners. He is a Fellow of the British Psychological Society, and has been helping to bring into being a Transpersonal Section within the BPS. He is a qualified psychotherapist (AHPP) and an accredited counsellor (BAC), and practises Primal Integration, which is a holistic approach to therapy. He also teaches, supervises and leads groups at the Minster Centre in London.

Kleinians think that you get to have a personality disorder because your mother looks at you cross-eyed at the age of six months. . . .

Melanie Klein ... and most of the other object relations analysts . . . write brilliant garbage.

(Albert Ellis, in Palmer and Ellis, 1993: 172–3)

I don't see Jungian therapy as therapy at all. I see is as some art form, some mystical encounter, some religious experience. . . . I don't think of this as therapy in the sense of helping people in distress, effecting change, overcoming problems or anything like that.

There are certainly no data that the person-centred approach alleviates tics, phobias, compulsions, habit disorders, obsessions, panic disorders, or any host of other complaints, but what it does, and certainly does well, is to facilitate the passage of young college students into the next phase of their identity. . . . I see person-centred therapy merely as a useful backdrop.

(Arnold Lazarus, in Dryden, 1991: 47–8)

Even to the most sincere and convinced psychoanalyst, there is something grotesque about a book like *Psychotherapy: A Basic Text* by the highly respected psychoanalyst and teacher Robert Langs. . . . Rules as rigid as these must be mad.

(John Rowan, 1990: 113–15)

There is . . . an erroneous assumption underlying psychoanalytic theory – and, unfortunately, psychoanalytic practice – which we may call 'pandeterminism'. By this I mean any view of man which disregards or neglects the intrinsically human capacity of free choice and interprets human existence in terms of mere dynamics.

(Viktor Frankl, 1985: 67)

Some self-designated 'eclectic' or 'integrative' counsellors are, in actuality, practising *syncretism*: an arbitrary and unsystematic blending of concepts of two or more of the 400 plus 'schools' of psychotherapy. . . . Their pluralistic intentions are to be commended, but their haphazard hybrids are an outgrowth of pet techniques and inadequate training.

(Norcross and Tomcho, 1993: 81–2)

In their attempt to avoid ideological rigidity, integrationists try to meld disparate ideas and conflicting schools into a co-operative and harmonious whole. . . . The main problem here is that, upon close scrutiny, what seems to be interchangeable among different theories, often turns out to be totally irreconcilable.

(Arnold Lazarus, 1989a: 248–58)

In most cases the theory and practice of brand name therapies are far from being the patiently accumulated knowledge of an industrious academic community, but represent rather the hastily elaborated ideas of one more or less charismatic figure who developed personal therapeutic style into a pseudotechnical blueprint for all (who join the club) to follow.

(David Smail, 1993: 14)

Nor would I on any account recommend someone in need of help to begin analysis as even a temporary solution, because the ensuing damage could be irreversible. This insight led me to resign from the International Psychoanalytical Association. . . . The *only* therapy concept I do recommend is the one developed by J. Konrad Stettbacher and described by him in his book *Making Sense of Suffering*.

(Alice Miller, 1992: 43–50)

If you are at all open-minded, then any closed system of therapy becomes difficult to practise. For example, I saw many people who did not respond well to behavioural methods. . . . Having done dynamic therapy, having read widely in psychoanalysis, I have also seen some of the worst of that, too, which is the excessive interest in and dependence on speculation, inference and subjectivity.

(John Marzillier, in Dryden, 1992: 95)

Note: For full references, see References section at the end of Chapter 1.

1

Introduction: Irreconcilable Psychotherapies?

Colin Feltham

This is a book about comparative psychotherapy, which takes and juxtaposes the views of eight distinguished practitioners who espouse quite different theories and methods of psychotherapy. These particular practitioners represent eminent contributions to the field of psychotherapy and demonstrate some of its diversity, but it is of course impossible to have *all* or even most psychotherapeutic orientations represented, for obvious reasons. Each writer has been asked to address twelve questions in their own way (these are reproduced in Appendix 1). Some have done so explicitly, others implicitly or rather obliquely. The purpose of asking such questions is to highlight the distinctive properties of each orientation and also to demonstrate in most cases how and why the practitioner of each approach came to this position and why he or she, for the most part, cannot tolerate or integrate with other approaches.

This is a book about sincerely held views, and a presentation that does not shy away from raising the possibility of utter non-consensus! Few, if any, of the writers have made outright attacks on each other in this book, but perhaps it does not take much reading between the lines to realize how sympathetically or otherwise each one regards the views of other practitioners in the field of psychotherapy generally. There is a disingenuous tendency in many psychotherapy textbooks to present a number of mainstream therapeutic orientations as if they all co-exist in a civilized therapeutic community and as if any frictions between them are minor, unimportant affairs, the subject of occasional genteel debate. I suggest they are anything but minor and unimportant; rather, it is arguable that the field of twentieth-century psychotherapy has been fundamentally characterized by serious disagreement on views of human nature, aetiology of psychological dysfunctions, treatment rationales and goals.

Radical questioning of the tenets of the schools of psychotherapy is naturally often disliked or found irritating. Counter-critiques of therapy's critics (see, for example, Dryden and Feltham, 1992) sometimes pose the suggestion that doubt and challenge are empty exercises. We should all be more interested in advancing therapeutic knowledge, and the kind of sophistry indulged in by critics does nothing to help clients, some would say. Criticism is thereby swept away by ostensibly compassionate clinical preoccupations. Although I partly share this view, my own belief is that our tendency to erect and defend divisive therapeutic ideologies is itself part and parcel of human sickness. In some important but difficult to articulate sense, our theories and methods are divisive, wasteful and signify an unwillingness or inability to collaborate seriously in understanding and addressing human distress. Members of each school may passionately believe themselves to hold the answer, or the best available approximation to the answer, or the best cluster of clues. Yet it is quite conceivable that the widespread human tendency towards attachment to prized beliefs (in religion, politics, psychology and other areas of endeavour) is one of the main roots of individual and social conflict.

I may sincerely believe that my particular religious, political or psychotherapeutic beliefs are truer than others, or that they can co-exist with others. A counter-argument, however, is that such beliefs cannot be innocuous. From a certain perspective it can be argued that any fixed therapeutic ideology is ultimately as insane and damaging as any personal delusional belief. If there is any truth in this, then the attempt to understand and eliminate conflicts and delusions among therapeutic ideologies is itself a kind of therapeutic activity, a therapeutic scepticism if you will (Heaton, 1993). It seems to me that we are at least as resistant to examining our therapeutic truth claims as our clients often are to examining their longstanding and unproductive scripts and narratives. Can we really deny that the world of psychotherapy is a circus of colourful beliefs and practices? Positively, we can certainly try to claim that it resembles an understandable collection of tribes (Hart et al., 1975) or expresses the subpersonalities within the field (Rowan, 1990), for example. Or we might say that it reflects a healthy postmodernist respect for diversity. Or simply that it reflects the diversity found historically and in current human sciences when human nature itself is under scrutiny (Stevenson, 1987).

Arthur Janov, claiming to have found 'the cure for neurosis' (primal therapy) which renders all other approaches meaningless, and which has purportedly cured many people who found no help elsewhere, argued:

> The great majority of psychologists are eclectic in their approach, meaning that they have no special approach to the patient. In eclecticism, the practitioner pays total allegiance to no one theory of personality, yet employs 'useful information' from all of them. If this situation appeared in any other branch of science, it would be ludicrous. Can you imagine ten different theories about the same phenomenon in nuclear physics? . . . Eclecticism is . . . hardly an auspicious way to treat a sick person.
>
> (Janov, 1982: 138)

Now look at what Arnold Lazarus, founder of multimodal therapy (a form of systematic eclecticism) has to say about one of his own clients, who was successfully helped by multimodal therapy:

> By the time he was referred to me, he had received – in addition to psychoanalysis and his brief bout with behavior therapy – drug therapy, electroconvulsive therapy, primal therapy, transactional analysis, transcendental meditation, and

existential therapy. He still suffered from agoraphobia and numerous other phobias, bathroom rituals and other obsessive-compulsive problems. . . . Because Janov claims that primal therapy is 'the *only* cure', which 'renders all other psychologic theories obsolete and invalid' (Janov, 1972: 19), we are entitled to ask why our client was not cured by primal therapy. Similarly, did he just happen to see a poorly trained transactional analyst, a half-baked existentialist, an unqualified behavior therapist, and so forth?

(Lazarus, 1989b: 20–1)

These are public statements making diametrically opposed claims. What are funders and potential clients to make of them? If we accept the sincerity with which they are made and accept that Janov and Lazarus give truthful accounts of their own clinical work, where are we led by logic? Perhaps to the trite conclusion that people are individuals and respond differently to different treatments, that timing often plays a part in successful therapeutic outcome, as does chance. However, this hardly brings us nearer to explaining psychotherapy as in any way systematically effective. It seems only to affirm the view that the field contains too many variables to ever, perhaps, be adequately assessed (Kline, 1992).

Psychotherapy, which is dedicated to understanding and ameliorating human distress, is a pluralistic endeavour. Some 300 or 400 different theoretical and/or clinical approaches are said to exist (Karasu, 1992a). According to Prochaska and Norcross (1994) this represents phenomenal and increasing growth since an estimated 36 distinct therapies in the 1950s. Herink (1980) counted around 250 therapies in his handbook. An abbreviated list of some of the different current brands is given in Appendix 2. Even allowing for exaggeration and error in compilations of the number and spread of therapies, there are obviously more than any potential client could hope to research and probably many more even than most therapists themselves could hope to be familiar with.

Historically, there have of course been many bitter schisms and also many attempts to compare therapeutic orientations rationally or coolly. The rifts between Freud, Adler and Jung are among the earliest and best documented. Feuds between Anna Freud and Melanie Klein and between Karen Horney and the New York Psychoanalytical Institute are well documented. Indeed, the history of psychoanalysis alone is peppered with personal, professional and ideological rifts. Within the Melanie Klein schism, Edward Glover is said to have referred to the 'heretical deviation' and 'pious opinions' of Kleinian sympathizers (Brome, 1982: 206). Battegay (1996) suggests that all such splitting of group members into good and bad objects, often based on the leaders' 'reciprocal narcissistic involvement', resembles the dynamics found in many religious cults. Buirski (1994) has made an interesting comparative study of therapies confined exclusively to analytic approaches.

The *British Journal of Psychotherapy*, basically devoted to psychoanalytic psychotherapy, has examined some comparisons and has also contained one writer's attack on rational emotive behaviour therapy (Clarke, 1990), followed by rebuttal by correspondence. In the same journal Michael Pokorny reported on the progress of the (then) United Kingdom Standing Conference for Psychotherapy (now UKSCP) and its efforts at unity:

> When I spoke here last year, I made the point that we did not have to respect each other's form of therapy. But that it is essential that we should respect each other's right to practise and teach that form of psychotherapy that we, as individuals, hold to be valid and reasonable and effective. . . . No one form or kind of therapy has any right to dominate the scene or hold itself out to be superior to any other psychotherapy.
>
> (Pokorny, 1991: 305)

It is often clear in some private conversations just how little psychotherapists do in fact respect approaches other than their own. Pokorny's public admission is revealing but its further implications, if explorable, would be fascinating. Almost certainly, at least some psychotherapists consider the approaches of others to be nonsense, but they are obliged to defend each other's right to practise. They are not obliged, apparently, to air exhaustively what they believe not to deserve respect within the profession.

One of the best-known pieces of comparative psychotherapy is the film (or rather series of films – *Three Approaches to Psychotherapy*) showing different therapists working briefly, one after another, with the same client. Gloria, for example, is shown discussing her concerns with Carl Rogers (person-centred therapy), Fritz Perls (Gestalt therapy) and Albert Ellis (rational emotive behaviour therapy) sequentially. She is questioned afterwards by Everett Shostrom and gives her views on each practitioner and his way of conducting therapy. One of the main values of this film is that it allows us to see three very experienced and very different therapists in action. We see not only three different clinical approaches but three different personalities in action, allowing us to compare what they say they do with how they actually do it. It is evident from this film, I think, that each does work quite differently and each has something distinctive to offer. One can imagine Gloria benefiting from consulting each practitioner further (although according to Ellis, Gloria felt cruelly upset by Perls (Palmer and Ellis, 1993: 173)).

Various attempts have been made in edited texts to compare clinical responses of therapists from different orientations, including Naftulin et al. (1975) and Saltzman and Norcross (1990). Corsini (1991) invited five therapists to respond to the same imaginary case. The British psychotherapist and counsellor Michael Jacobs has published similar exercises, inviting therapists from different theoretical perspectives to suggest how they might respond clinically to an actual client (e.g., Jacobs, 1995) and has also extended this to examples of how supervisors from different orientations might supervise Jacobs' work with an actual client (Jacobs, 1996). Bellack and Hersen's (1990) *Handbook of Comparative Treatments for Adult Disorders* examines the likely efficacy of various psychotherapies (understood as simply psychotherapy) compared with behaviour therapy, cognitive therapy, social skills training and pharmacotherapy in the treatment of depression, panic and agoraphobia, obsessive-compulsive disorder, post-traumatic stress disorder, anorexia and bulimia, and so on. Frank (1974) is of course well known for a perspective on comparative psychotherapy which includes examples from non-Western societies and which seeks to identify common factors.

Certain theoretical and empirical comparisons have also been made. Lomas (1968), for example, compared the merits of Freudian psychoanalysis with those of existential analysis and, while pointing out the real differences, urged that these schools should grow together rather than apart. Appelbaum (1979), from the position of a committed psychoanalyst, sampled many of the humanistic therapies and wrote about them generously. Wachtel (1977) is well known for his belief in the possibility of integrating behaviour therapy and psychoanalysis, a project considered doomed by many others.

Some like to assert that the differences between the therapies are merely skin-deep, each using a different language to say essentially the same thing, or each in practice resembling all others in spite of their theoretical rhetoric. In recent years the fashion for integrationism has elevated the appealing and convenient hypothesis that all or most therapies are or should be converging at some level: perhaps it is simply a matter of time before all theoretical orientations join hands. A 1996 psychotherapy book catalogue tells us somewhat hopefully that 'there is a new sense of openness to cross orientation learning'. In the present book, the reader is invited to consider the idea that integrationism or integrative psychotherapy may be a myth or, in spite of good intentions, simply another orientation or group of orientations in the making. Unlike Prochaska and Norcross's (1994) venture in comparative psychotherapy using a transtheoretical analysis and attempting *rapprochement*, this book focuses on differences, not commonalities. According to Samuels (1989), psychotherapeutic pluralism may be seen as complementing the psychological diversity of persons and our argument here can consequently be interpreted as representing a productive moral force.

Looked at in *any* depth, it becomes clear that the proponents of each of the distinctive orientations holds his or her own approach dear, inevitably sees it as in some way superior to others and, implicitly or explicitly, regards at least some other approaches as nonsense, ineffective or dangerous. You cannot have your cake and eat it (can you?). Either you possess some distinctively truthful and potent understanding and approach, or you merely describe what you do *as if* it is distinctive when in reality it is just another, differently packaged brand of the same product. Of course you may (and no doubt our present contributors do) sincerely believe that one product is better than another, even in the absence of convincing evidence. Or you may simply, more modestly, find one approach more appealing than others on aesthetic grounds.

It has been argued that a deep commitment to an approach is an essential ingredient of psychotherapy:

> Therapists must strongly believe in themselves and what they practice, and they must find a method that is most congenial to their personal needs and style. The more passionate a therapist is about his or her theories and personal healing

powers, the more likely he or she is to have an impact on patients. One of the
enduring ingredients of effective psychotherapy is transmitting one's beliefs, which
do not have to be correct – just convincing. Indeed, the therapist's conviction is
the basis for 'doctrinal compliance'.

(Karasu, 1992b: 27)

Langs (1980) at one time argued that communicative therapy was 'truth
therapy' while all other approaches were 'lie therapy'. The distinction made
by Langs in his chapter in this book is between manifest content therapies
and therapies which deal with the deep unconscious system. Smith has soft-
ened Langs' views on truth and lie therapy along the following lines:

We have to *work* at the truth, evaluating competing hypotheses against objective
evidence and discarding those that do not stand up to the test. . . . Another form
of intellectual dishonesty – a form of Lie Therapy if you will – is expressed in the
refusal to even consider the relative virtues of rival theories in an objective fashion.
Such a person then clings dogmatically to a point of view which he or she makes
no effort to question. Thus, the mere fact that a person advocates a certain *type*
of therapy does not automatically mark them out as a Lie or Truth Therapist. The
crucial variable is one's readiness to bring beliefs before the higher court of evidence.

(Smith, 1991: xii)

How are therapies born? Somewhat tongue in cheek, I have toyed with
the idea of launching a new therapy myself, called eschatonics or eschatonic
therapy. (It is essential to use impressive-sounding neologisms when creating
a new psychotherapy.) This is based on a fusion of ideas from theology
(eschatology – the doctrine of the last things) and medicine (a tonic being,
of course, something which restores a healthy tone). Since a great deal of
psychotherapy rests on developmental theories (understanding the past in
order to correct present problems), it seems high time that someone suggested that our problems are caused by faulty perceptions of the future and
faulty aetiological views generally. (Of course, this is not really a new idea
at all.) Essentially, by accepting as profoundly true the view that the present
is the only time we have, that tomorrow or even the next moment may end
the life of any one of us by accident or other mortal despatch mechanism,
we are invigorated, freed from the illusion that we must solve the problems
of the past and perhaps even from the illusion that there are any real problems besides hunger and physical pain.

Not only is there ample biblical and philosophical endorsement for this
view, but we can find pertinent traces in psychotherapeutic literature. Unfin-
ished business and other Gestalt concepts, for example, point towards
eschatonics. Eschatonics embodies therapeutically the being-unto-death discussed by some existentialists. Ultimately, most psychological problems are
about people refusing to come to terms with the past and their own limitations and refusing to face concretely present fears. By dealing with your
problems and neuroses unflinchingly *now*, you are released from the misery
narrative. Each session of eschatonics might begin with the question to the
client 'What are you refusing to face yourself by coming to this session?'
By facing responsibility and mortality we resolve our myriad minor

anxieties. Eschatonics could even be promoted as 'the death of psychotherapy' (and the dawn of a new honesty-driven era of psychological health).

Now, what would it take for me to elaborate eschatonics into a psychotherapy package? I would need to spell out a rationale, to write some case studies explained in eschatonic terms, to link it with other literature, perhaps to conduct some sort of limited favourable research, to found an institute and recruit trainees, and to launch a journal. Above all, I would need to believe in and embody the principles of eschatonics. It could be done. What, if anything, would distinguish this from other extant therapies? The name, certainly, and the rationale. Perhaps I could be accused of cynically constructing an approach merely for the sake of amusement. But suppose I actually did it and found that it worked? Perhaps if I really believed in it, owned it, and perceived a glimpse of immortality to be within my grasp, I might energetically operationalize it in such a way that my clients improved dramatically. My early acolytes would also be suffused by my enthusiasm and probably achieve similar successes. This hypothetical psychotherapy has, at least, illustrative powers. Interestingly, after having written the above, I began within my own clinical work to 'see' traces of eschatonics actually at work, and to wonder if I had in fact stumbled on some grand new insight!

Presumably the founders of clinical approaches enthusiastically create or modify practices based on the genuine ambition to understand and reduce distress. But, according to Norcross and Newman:

> Unfortunately professional reputations are made by emphasizing the new and different, not the basic and similar. In the field of psychotherapy, as well as in other scientific disciplines, the ownership of ideas gets far too much emphasis. Although the idea of naturally occurring, co-operative efforts among professionals is engaging, their behavior, realistically, may be expected to reflect the competition so characteristic of our society at large.
>
> (Norcross and Newman, 1992: 23)

Readers are invited to consider the contents of the following chapters and their subjective appeal, but also to try to get a feeling for the construction of clinical theories – where they come from, why their proponents are motivated to construct or modify them – and to weigh up carefully the arguments involved. Why do psychotherapists often come to quite different conclusions about human suffering and how best to address it? Are theoretical, clinical and professional conflicts themselves in some way implicated in our widespread failure to achieve higher levels of mental health in society (Adams, 1984)? Or is the inevitable entrenchment associated with theoretical affiliations and the ensuing diversity of schools itself healthy (Norcross, 1985)? Can psychotherapy credibly and effectively continue as the pluralistic field it is today? Goldfried (1982) argued that paradigm strain was naturally and perhaps inorexably leading to forms of eclecticism and integration but, years later, there is no sign that the number of named therapies is declining. Are specific therapies indicated for specific problems

Table 1.1   Reasons for theoretical allegiances

1 *Original training.* Was my orientation simply the only one available at the time and in the geographical area where I trained? (It was a pragmatic choice at best.)

2 *Personality fit.* Did/does it appeal to me because it suits my personality? (It has often been suggested that founders of new therapies create systems that reflect or bolster their own personalities, for example.)

3 *Truth appeal.* Does it strike me as truest to reality? Allied to this question, of course, are judgements about whether the approach seems well grounded, close to commonsense, or far-fetched and even weird.

4 *Selecting the best.* I looked around carefully and decided on what I considered best – best pedigree, best researched, etc. 'The best' is interpreted by some using aristocratic (snob) criteria, for example how long has it survived, how prestigious is it, etc.?

5 *Accepting research evidence.* Have I objectively digested available evidence on outcomes and chosen the best supported approach?

6 *Clinical experience.* Have I found myself forced or wanting to adapt, modify, integrate or even reject my original views in the light of trying to help different clients?

7 *Retraining.* Have I decided restlessly or conscientiously to be retrained in another method, either to complement or to replace my original orientation?

8 *Eclecticism.* Do I value the ability to utilize techniques from different approaches without necessarily subscribing to overarching theoretical structures?

9 *Relationship factors.* Have I decided on the basis of clinical experience, research or simply subjective preference that the (idiosyncratic in each case) client–therapist relationship is more significant than any theoretical allegiance?

10 *Conservatism.* Am I wary of new approaches? Do I judge them on the basis of prejudice (e.g., they seem gimmicky, unproven, too shallow, etc.) or that I just do not like change?

11 *Novelty.* Am I always on the look out for new approaches and techniques because I easily get bored or observe that many clients need innovative techniques?

12 *Theoretically consistent eclecticism.* In spite of my tendency to use a variety of interventions, I think it is crucial to adhere to one main, supporting theoretical framework.

13 *Certitude.* I know that my approach is the only valid one and that others represent diversions or even defences against the necessary work involved in (my) true approach.

14 *Respect.* I value all approaches and believe that we all probably arrive at the same ends by different means.

15 *The atheoretical/agnostic stance.* I do not or cannot decide or settle on any one approach, or combination of approaches. I do only what I can, modestly, in each therapy hour.

(Howard et al., 1995)? It is with these kinds of questions in mind that this book has been constructed.

Those approaching the field for the first time as students or consumers wishing to be well informed, or those reflecting on their involvement as practitioners are certainly advised not to regard commitment to a clinical orientation lightly. There is increasing concern for the variables implicit in practitioners' choice of orientation (Vasco and Dryden, 1994). Some of the variables facing newcomers to the field as well as experienced practitioners seeking understanding of their current position include those given in Table 1.1. To complicate matters, it has been argued, variously, that we need to develop an explicit training model (Horton, 1996), a personal (practitioner) model (Elton Wilson, 1993) and that we should perhaps be wary of carrying theory into the consulting room at all (Tame, 1996).

We should also pause to consider to what extent clients have an informed choice. Many agencies still operate exclusively on the basis of a single theoretical orientation, which is quite often not declared or explained to clients. Thus, a psychodynamic practitioner has written in the following terms:

> Nearly everyone who comes to see us brings a reality problem to be sorted out and an unconscious to be explored, an anxiety to be relieved and a phantasy to be untangled, an acute need to be helped and a transference relationship to be tested out.
>
> (Noonan, 1983: ix)

Such statements are by no means rare in the literature. Increasingly, and necessarily, clients are advised whenever possible to prepare themselves for what they need, what their goals are, and exactly what agencies or therapists will be offering them (Engler and Goleman, 1992; Dryden and Feltham, 1995). It is hoped that all psychotherapists, inspired by an ethical commitment to client welfare above all other considerations, will transcend their own allegiances sufficiently to be able to advise potential clients of alternative approaches when these are indicated. Perhaps in the long run we may harbour the hope that clients' needs, in tandem with commonsense and research indications, will always take precedence over our own enthusiasms. Perhaps we must also, in all humility, consider that therapists and clients alike may be susceptible to passing or fixed enthusiasms, helpful or unhelpful guiding fictions, personal and cultural blind spots and the shifting balance of ignorance and understanding embedded in the human condition.

References

Adams, H.E. (1984) The pernicious effects of theoretical orientations in clinical psychology. *The Clinical Psychologist*, 37, 90–3.

Appelbaum, S.A. (1979) *Out in Inner Space: A Psychoanalyst Explores the New Therapies*. New York: Doubleday.

Battegay, R. (1996) Group leaders: charisma and possible dangers in religious congregations, political movements and psychotherapy schools. *International Journal of Psychotherapy*, 1 (1), 35–43.

Bellack, A.S. and Hersen, M. (eds) (1990) *Handbook of Comparative Treatments for Adult Disorders*. New York: Wiley Interscience.

Brome, V. (1982) *Ernest Jones: Freud's Alter Ego*. London: Caliban.

Buirski, P. (ed.) (1994) *Comparing Schools of Analytic Therapy*. New York: Aronson.

Clarke, L. (1990) Rational emotive therapy. *British Journal of Psychotherapy*, 7 (1), 86–93.

Corsini, R. (1991) *Five Therapists and a Client*. Itasca, IL: Peacock.

Dryden, W. (1991) *A Dialogue with Arnold Lazarus: 'It Depends'*. Buckingham: Open University Press.

Dryden, W. (1992) *The Dryden Interviews: Dialogues on the Psychotherapeutic Process*. London: Whurr.

Dryden, W. and Feltham, C. (eds) (1992) *Psychotherapy and Its Discontents*. Buckingham: Open University Press.

Dryden, W. and Feltham, C. (1995) *Counselling and Psychotherapy: A Consumer's Guide*. London: Sheldon.

Elton Wilson, J. (1993) Towards a personal model of counselling. In W. Dryden (ed.), *Questions and Answers on Counselling in Action* (pp. 95–102). London: Sage.

Engler, J. and Goleman, D. (1992) *The Consumer's Guide to Psychotherapy*. New York: Simon & Schuster.

Frank, J.D. (1974) *Persuasion and Healing: A Comparative Study of Psychotherapy* (Rev. edn). New York: Schocken.

Frankl, V.E. (1985) *Psychotherapy and Existentialism: Selected Papers on Logotherapy*. New York: Washington Square Press.

Goldfried, M.R. (ed.) (1982) *Converging Themes in Psychotherapy: Trends in Psychodynamic, Humanistic and Behavioral Practice*. New York: Springer.

Hart, J., Corriere, R. and Binder, J. (1975) *Going Sane: An Introduction to Feeling Therapy*. New York: Delta.

Heaton, J. (1993) The sceptical tradition in psychotherapy. In L. Spurling (ed.), *From the Words of My Mouth: Tradition in Psychotherapy* (pp. 106–31). London: Routledge.

Herink, R. (ed.) (1980) *The Psychotherapy Handbook*. New York: New American Library.

Horton, I. (1996) Towards a model of counselling. In R. Bayne, I. Horton and J. Bimrose (eds), *New Directions in Counselling* (pp. 281–96). London: Routledge.

Howard, K.I., Orlinsky, D.E. and Lueger, J. (1995) The design of clinically relevant outcome research: some considerations and an example. In M. Aveline and D.A. Shapiro (eds), *Research Foundations for Psychotherapy Practice* (pp. 3–47). Chichester: Wiley.

Jacobs, M. (1995) *Charlie: An Unwanted Child?* Buckingham: Open University Press.

Jacobs, M. (1996) *In Search of Supervision*. Buckingham: Open University Press.

Janov, A. (1972) *The Primal Revolution: Toward A Real World*. New York: Simon & Schuster.

Janov, A. (1982) *Prisoners of Pain*. London: Abacus.

Karasu, T.B. (1992a) The worst of times, the best of times. *Journal of Psychotherapy Practice and Research*, 1, 2–15.

Karasu, T.B. (1992b) *Wisdom in the Practice of Psychotherapy*. New York: Basic Books.

Kline, P. (1992) Problems of methodology in studies of psychotherapy. In W. Dryden and C. Feltham (eds), *Psychotherapy and Its Discontents* (pp. 64–86). Buckingham: Open University Press.

Langs, R. (1980) Truth therapy/lie therapy. *International Journal of Psychoanalytical Psychotherapy*, 8, 3–34.

Lazarus, A.A. (1989a) Why I am an eclectic (not an integrationist). *British Journal of Guidance and Counselling*, 17, 248–58.

Lazarus, A.A. (1989b) *The Practice of Multimodal Therapy*. Baltimore, MA: Johns Hopkins University Press.

Lomas, P. (1968) Psychoanalysis – Freudian or Existential. In C. Rycroft (ed.), *Psychoanalysis Observed* (pp. 116–44). Harmondsworth: Pelican.

Miller, A. (1992) *Breaking Down the Wall of Silence*. London: Virago.

Naftulin, D., Donnelly, F. and Wolkon, G. (1975) Four therapeutic approaches to the same patient. *American Journal of Psychotherapy*, 29, 66–71.

Noonan, E. (1983) *Counselling Young People*. London: Methuen.

Norcross, J.C. (1985) In defence of theoretical orientations for clinicians. *The Clinical Psychologist*, 38, 13–17.

Norcross, J.C. and Newman, C.F. (1992) Psychotherapy integration: setting the scene. In J.C. Norcross and M.R. Goldfried (eds), *Handbook of Psychotherapy Integration* (pp. 3–45). New York: Basic Books.

Norcross, J.C. and Tomcho, T.J. (1993) Choosing an eclectic, not syncretic, psychotherapist. In W. Dryden (ed.), *Questions and Answers on Counselling in Action* (pp. 81–5). London: Sage.

Palmer, S. and Ellis, A. (1993) In the counsellor's chair: Stephen Palmer interviews Dr Albert Ellis. *Counselling*, 4(3), 171–4.

Pokorny, M. (1991) United Kingdom Standing Conference for Psychotherapy. Conference January 1991: Chairman's Address. *British Journal of Psychotherapy*, 7 (3), 303–6.

Prochaska, J.O. and Norcross, J.C. (1994) *Systems of Psychotherapy* (3rd edn). Pacific Grove, CA: Brooks/Cole.

Rowan, J. (1990) *Subpersonalities: The People Inside Us*. London: Routledge.

Salzman, N. and Norcross, J.C. (eds) (1990) *Therapy Wars: Contention and Convergence in Differing Clinical Approaches*. San Francisco: Jossey-Bass.

Samuels, A. (1989) *The Plural Psyche: Personality, Morality and the Father*. London: Routledge.

Smail, D. (1993) *The Origins of Unhappiness: A New Understanding of Personal Distress*. London: HarperCollins.

Smith, D.L. (1991) *Hidden Conversations: An Introduction to Communicative Psychoanalysis*. London: Routledge.

Stevenson, L. (1987) *Seven Theories of Human Nature* (2nd edn). Oxford: Oxford University Press.

Tame, J. (1996) The seductiveness of theory: thinking about dyads and triads in a case history. *Psychodynamic Counselling*, 2 (1), 39–54.

Vasco, A.B. and Dryden, W. (1994) The development of psychotherapists' theoretical orientation and clinical practice. *British Journal of Guidance and Counselling*, 22 (3), 327–41.

Wachtel, P.L. (1977) *Psychoanalysis and Behavior Therapy: Toward an Integration*. New York: Basic Books.

2

The Person-Centered Approach

Jerold D. Bozarth

Carl R. Rogers presented to the world of therapy and interpersonal relationships a paradoxical theory and schema. He presented a different paradigm (Bozarth, 1984; Rogers, 1959) to the therapeutic community. At the same time, he offered a schema for an integrative statement (Stubbs and Bozarth, 1996; Rogers,1957) for all therapies and situations that involve interpersonal relationships that have as a goal constructive personality change. Unfortunately, Rogers' works are vastly misunderstood and dismissed by notable scholars of therapy and even by those who identify themselves as 'person-centered' (Bozarth, 1995). Rogers' message is incredibly simple and at the same time remarkably complicated. Simply put, the basic client/person-centered value is that the authority about the person rests in the person rather than in an outside expert. The therapist's only goal is to be a certain way by embodying certain attitudes that will nurture a natural constructive process in the client.

The foundation block of the approach in client-centered/person-centered therapy is that of the actualizing tendency. In Rogers' words:

> Practice, theory and research make it clear that the person-centered approach is built on a basic trust in the person . . . [It] depends on the actualizing tendency present in every living organism's tendency to grow, to develop, to realize its full potential. This way of being trusts the constructive directional flow of the human being toward a more complex and complete development. It is this directional flow that we aim to release.
>
> (Rogers, 1986: 198)

It has often puzzled me why belief in this assumption is so functionally true for some therapists and so difficult to assimilate for other therapists. Although there must be many reasons for this, one of the most prevalent reasons seems to be that many therapists do not experience the true potency of trusting those inner resources of other individuals. This is, of course, most likely related to many factors, including training, personal experiences and basic assumptions about life and people. My person-centered stance consists of having an abiding faith in the inner resources of people which, seemingly, stems from my personal experiences which were later buttressed by my experiences as a therapist. A brief autobiographical statement may elucidate why I believe I have held a person-centered stance for many years.

Personal statement

My recollection of any semblance of a person-centered stance is that somehow as a teenager it was important for me to understand and accept the views that others had about life. One of the things that I noticed about my elementary and high school years is that I never belonged to any particular social norm group. Yet, I was accepted by most groups. I could be a welcome guest with the 'jocks', the 'intellectual nerds', or the 'delinquents'. Later, I worked my way through college involved in many activities. I poked hoppers, carried whiskey barrels, cleaned boilers, and worked construction jobs in more than a dozen industries. In addition, I stocked women's attire in a department store, ushered at a theater and sold furnace repair orders door to door. I was an elder, Sunday School Superintendent and church janitor in a Second Reformed Church in my early twenties. In the US Army, I was attached to a Special Category of Army With Air Force (SCARWAF) in France and lived with a variety of individuals from various cultures.

All of these activities entailed a wide variety of social and work relationships with those who held diverse views of the world. I somehow learned early to be empathic and to trust and acknowledge the views of others while accepting that their worlds and lives were the most relevant ways for them. In retrospect, my early experiences seemed to place me in diverse situations that nudged me towards a respect for the frames of reference of other individuals. Years later, this view permeated my involvement with others as a professional counselor and therapist.

My person-centered stance as a professional counselor and therapist was formed, I believe, during my first position as a Psychiatric Rehabilitation Counselor working with chronic long-term psychotics in Illinois State Mental Hospitals. I had no experience or supervision as a therapist or counselor, no formal group experience and had never heard of Carl Rogers. The job, however, turned out to involve mostly doing therapy but having an added action dimension of assisting individuals with obtaining training, finding jobs and settling out of the hospital. Concomitantly, I worked on my master's degree in counseling and studied a 'general counseling' model (which included Rogers' ideas) with the guidance of the project director of the state mental health program.

The long-term hospitalized psychotics with whom I worked turned out to have a high success ratio in terms of hard criteria for hospital release, small attrition rate, employment and independent living. My discovery of Carl Rogers' theory of therapy provided me with a basis for the way that I had learned to operate as a therapeutic counselor with hospitalized mentally ill individuals. My model, however, was not necessarily tied to the response forms (primarily reflection of feeling) which were often associated with client-centered therapy at that time. Rather, I adapted the necessary and sufficient conditions hypothesized by Rogers as a meta-model along with my development of an exceptional trust in the client's actualizing tendency. My general mode of operation was that the individuals with whom I worked simply had the opportunity to talk (or not talk) about anything. No rules, directions, or orientation were ever given.

Although all of my formal training emphasized other models of therapy, I had discovered that reliance on the client was the most potent approach for me. Ironically, while critics were condemning the person-centered approach as one which would never work with 'psychotics', I was learning the approach from those same individuals who were considered severely disturbed long-term hospitalized 'patients' and finding high success rates based on hard criteria. My formal training, however, did not include this approach. I attended the Adlerian Institute in Chicago, studied Psychodynamic Psychotherapy and assessment-oriented counseling in my master's program, and was inundated with behaviorism in my doctoral program. Even though many tried, it was too late for anyone to change my person-centered stance. I had experienced the potency of the client when the client was allowed to be his/her own best expert and found myself gravitating towards experiences that allowed me to explore the nuances of the approach. Every year from 1974, I was a participant in groups of one or two weeks duration with Rogers and his various colleagues. I became, in effect, a participant/observer of person-centered encounter groups and large community groups. My views, however, are predicated not only upon these experiences, but upon attending to the basic assumptions of the theory emanating and evolving from Rogers' basic works.

One conclusion which I have reached is that Rogers' theory is a different paradigm from other theoretical conceptualizations of therapy and human relationships. At the same time, his conceptualization of the core conditions for all therapy is a basic explanation for the success or failure of all therapies.

The paradigmatic difference

There is a fundamental difference between client-centered/person-centered therapy and nearly any other therapy in that *trust in the power resting in the individual is so extensively central to the theory*. Elsewhere, I have suggested that the person-centered approach 'offers a paradigm consistent with the fundamental model of modern physics and with the parallel assumptions of the writings of mystics' (Bozarth, 1985: 180). Rogers' (1980) hypothesis of the formative, directional tendency in the universe is similar to the systems theory underlying modern physics. In his words:

> This is an evolutionary tendency toward greater order, greater complexity, greater inter-relatedness. In humankind, this tendency exhibits itself as the individual moves from a single cell origin to complex organic functioning, to knowing and serving below the level of consciousness, to a conscious awareness of the organism and the external world, to a transcendent awareness of the harmony and unity of the cosmic system including humankind.
>
> (Rogers, 1980: 139)

In Rogers' theory, there is one natural motivational force in human beings that is constructive and growth directed; that is, the actualizing tendency. This natural growth tendency may be thwarted by the conditional positive regard individuals receive, perceive and introject from significant others. An individual then develops conditional positive regard towards him or herself and, concomitantly, the actualizing tendency is thwarted. It is when the individual perceives unconditional positive regard that he or she develops unconditional positive self-regard and, concomitantly, the process of actualization is promoted (Rogers, 1959). The process of actualization is a functional construct in client-centered therapy (Bozarth and Brodley, 1991) which assumes an individual as well as a general process in that there is a striving for each person to meet one's potentialities. Each individual is his or her unique process. Concomitantly, extrapolation of Rogers' theory (Van Belle, 1990) suggests that each individual is also part of the unitary phenomenon of the universe. This idea was also promoted by Rogers (1980) in his reference to the formative tendency of the universe as the macro-concept of his theory.

Rogers (1957, 1959, 1986) hypothesized the necessary and sufficient conditions for therapeutic personality change as *part of the client-centered framework and as central in all types of constructive interpersonal relationships*. In this formulation, he said that if the client perceived the therapist to be congruent and to be consistently experiencing empathic understanding and unconditional positive regard towards the client that therapeutic personality change would ensue.

Rogers (1961, 1980, 1986) discussed these conditions and speculated upon variations (Baldwin, 1987) throughout his life. However, Rogers' openness to new ideas and change never necessitated that he alter his basic theory and practice. His dedication to change did not alter his disciplined and rigorous delineation of the theory (Rogers, 1959) in which *the bedrock of therapeutic change is the client's experiencing of unconditional positive regard*. I (Bozarth, 1996) have suggested that Rogers' (1959) major theoretical statement poses the conditions of congruence, empathic understanding, and unconditional positive regard as being highly interrelated. However, the importance of therapist congruency (or genuineness) in Rogers' model is primarily that of enabling the therapist to better experience the other two conditions towards the client. Moreover, empathic understanding viewed as a separate condition would be better considered as the most pure way for the communication of unconditional positive regard. Nevertheless, the reality of Rogers' conceptualization of empathy is part and parcel of unconditional positive regard. Empathy and Unconditional Positive Regard are essentially the same in Rogerian empathy (Bozarth, in press).

It is when the therapist can consistently hold these facilitative attitudes in relationship with the client that the natural constructive direction is promoted. This is the primary difference between person-centered theory and other approaches to therapy. In nearly all other prominent therapeutic approaches the therapist is viewed as an expert who intervenes at some point. Rogers insisted that it is the individual who best knows the problems and direction to take. In his words: '. . . it is the client who knows what hurts, what directions to go, what problems are crucial. . . . I would do better to rely upon the client for the direction of movement in the process' (Rogers, cited in Kirschenbaum, 1979: 89). One of Rogers' interrogators aptly pointed out the politics of the client-centered approach in a way which exemplifies the paradigmatic difference:

> I spent three years of graduate school learning to be an expert in clinical psychology. I learned to make accurate diagnostic judgments, I learned the various techniques of altering the subject's attitudes and behavior. I learned subtle modes of manipulation under the labels of interpretation and guidance. Then I began to read your material, which upset everything I had learned. You were saying that the power rests not in my mind but in his (the client's) organism. You completely reversed the relationship of power and control which had built up in me over three years. And then you say there is no politics in the client-centered approach.
>
> (Rogers, 1977)

In essence, *the paradigmatic difference of person-centered therapy is the extent to which the power and direction is centered in the client* (Bozarth and Brodley, 1984). It is this paradigmatic difference which differentiates the person-centered approach from other approaches. The failure to acknowledge this difference ultimately results in misunderstandings of the approach. It is somewhat confounding since Rogers poses the core therapist attitudes as a central part of his theory of client-centered therapy and as also being the necessary and sufficient conditions for therapeutic personality change in all therapies. It is, thus, that Rogers' hypothesis of the attitudinal conditions permeates all theories of therapy. *In his theory of therapy, they are the central therapeutic focus in relation to the individual's actualizing tendency that creates a functionally different paradigm of therapy.*

The Integrative Statement

Carl R. Rogers' (1957) formulation of a revolutionary hypothesis that there are certain necessary and sufficient conditions for therapeutic personality change is a statement that is *not* about client-centered therapy, as is often assumed. Rather, it is a statement that is meant to integrate therapies and helping relationships through assumptions of common therapeutic variables. Rogers' search for core foundations in therapy seemed to lead him towards the development of his theory of therapy. The major difference between Rogers' 1957 integrative and 1959 theory statements has vast implications for the assessment of studies purporting to study research on client-centered therapy and, as well, for determinations of the modes of communication of the conditions. This difference is that in 1957, Rogers considers the conditions as essential in all theories of therapy and, indeed, of all helping relationships. In 1959, the hypothesis is presented as a core and integral part of client-centered theory. The central therapist conditions are embedded within the context of the foundation block of the theory, the actualizing tendency. Additionally, the 1959 statement included the importance of the self-concept, implied non-directivity and the 'technical' forms (e.g., reflection, restatement rule, empathic understanding responses) for implementation of the theory as part of the package. This focus is not necessarily so in 1957 where Rogers is quite clear that he is not referring to conditions that are essential for only client-centered therapy. His statement refers to 'conditions which apply to *any* situation in which constructive personality change occurs, whether we are thinking of classical psychoanalysis, or any of its modern offshoots, or Adlerian psychotherapy, or any other' (Rogers, 1957: 230). Rogers hypothesized, 'that effective psychotherapy of any sort produces similar changes in personality and behavior, and that a single set of preconditions is necessary' (1957: 231). The 1957 statement is truly meant as an integrative medium for all psychotherapies and, even for integration of helping relationships into everyday life. As Rogers stated: 'It is not stated that psychotherapy is a special kind of relationship, different in kind from all others which occur in everyday life' (1957: 231). Rogers further explains: 'Thus the therapeutic relationship is seen as a heightening of the constructive qualities which often exist in part in other relationships, and an extension through time of qualities which in other relationships tend at best to be momentary' (1957: 231).

Rogers even refers to the hypothesis being relevant to programs that are aimed at constructive personality change and mentions programs of leadership, educational programs, and 'community agencies aim[ed] at personality and behavioral change in delinquents and criminals' (1957: 233). He suggests that if the hypotheses are supported, 'then the results, both for the planning of such programs and for our knowledge of human dynamics, would be significant' (1957: 233). Thus, Rogers' integrative statement is referring to conditions which are qualities for therapists in all therapies and for helpers in all situations which have as a goal the development of personality change.

Studies of the conditions have taken on a decided focus on communication and have focused attention on the forms of behavior that are then considered to be the manifestations of the attitudinal qualities. These studies are further complicated by the operational definitions necessary for measuring the conditions. The therapists' specific behavior responses are assessed with varying degrees of behavioral specificity *rather than with examination of the therapists' experiences of the attitudinal qualities towards clients as well as the clients' perceptions of the therapists' attitudes.* When he responds to the theoretical usefulness of his hypothesis, Rogers explicitly cites a variety of techniques that he viewed as having 'essentially' no value to therapy; such as, interpretation of personality dynamics, free association, analysis of dreams, analysis of transference, hypnosis, interpretation of lifestyle, and suggestion. However, Rogers adds:

> Each of these techniques may, however, become a channel for communicating the essential conditions which have been formulated. An interpretation may be given in a way which communicates the unconditional positive regard of the therapist.

A stream of free association may be listened to in a way which communicates an empathy which the therapist is experiencing. In the handling of the transference an effective therapist often communicates his own wholeness and congruence in the relationship. Similarly for the other techniques. But just as these techniques *may* communicate the elements which are essential for therapy, so any one of them may communicate attitudes and experiences sharply contradictory to the hypothesized conditions of therapy.

(Rogers, 1957: 234)

An implication of Rogers' integrative statement and of his comments is reflected in his revelation that 'the techniques of the various therapies are relatively unimportant except to the extent that they serve as channels for fulfilling one of the conditions' (1957: 233).

Rogers' statement is really quite astounding. He suggests that a person may perform a technique that is conceptually antithetical, for example, to the concept of empathic understanding (e.g., interpretation) while still *experiencing* and *communicating* empathic understanding and/or unconditional positive regard. Although some forms, such as the restatement rule (Teich, 1992) and empathic understanding responses (Brodley, 1988; Brodley and Brody, 1994), may be less interfering and purer channels to allow for client perceptions of therapist experiencing, *they are not necessarily called for in either the theory or the integrative model.*

As far as the integration conceptualization is concerned, it is speculated (Stubbs and Bozarth, 1996) that therapists must achieve their own congruence, including the use of their own 'technique system' in order to maximize their capacity for experiencing empathic understanding and unconditional positive regard for the client. It is asserted that Carl Rogers' (1957) statement concerning the necessary and sufficient conditions of therapeutic personality change is an integrative statement for psychotherapy and helping relationships that is separate from his statements concerning the conditions in client-centered therapy. The failure to consider this statement as integrative has resulted in additional misunderstandings and misdirection of investigation for both the theory and Rogers' hypothesis of integration.

Misunderstandings

I believe that misunderstandings abound among advocates and adversaries of the person-centered approach (Bozarth, 1995). The training models in many of our university training programs, as well as many clinical textbooks, de-value and/or trivialize Rogers' contributions and, worse, communicate inaccurate understandings of the approach. Most of the students who take my person-centered seminar are stunned by their misunderstanding of the approach after they have read some basic articles concerning client-centered/person-centered therapy. They make comments such as: 'I was taught that the Egan Model was Client-Centered Therapy'; 'I thought that the therapist was *not* involved in client-centered therapy'; 'We learn a

completely different thing'; I didn't realize the effectiveness of the approach
. . . thought it was preliminary to doing something else . . .'.

Egan (1994), who is clear that he is focusing on a problem-management
approach of a helping skills model, offers a classic statement that leads to
the misunderstanding of client-centered therapy. In a discussion of assessment, he states:

> Client-centered assessment is the ability to understand clients, to spot 'what is
> going on' with them, to see what they do not see and need to see, to make sense
> out of their chaotic behavior and help them make sense out of it – all at the service
> of helping them manage their lives and develop their resources more effectively.
>
> (Egan, 1994: 143)

Egan's statement, which exemplifies the expertise and directivity of the
therapist, is reflective of much of the inaccurate dissemination of literature
about 'client-centered' concepts.

Several relevant quotes from noted authors in the field of psychotherapy
concerning views of person-centered therapy further illustrate misunderstandings:

> What if at core there are other urges as motivational, urgent and powerful as the
> actualizing tendency?
>
> (Quinn, 1993: 11)

> The positing of universally applicable factors is the product of myopic schoolism
> and violates the principle of tailor-making the therapy to the needs of the patient.
>
> (Fay and Lazarus, 1992, abstract)

> . . . if Rogers were correct, there would be no point in bothering to learn any
> specific techniques – be warm, genuine, congruent and empathic and establish a
> good therapeutic alliance – period!
>
> (Fay and Lazarus, 1992: 3)

> At its worst, Rogers' contentions perpetuated simplistic formulations and singu-
> lar treatments for all clinical encounters.
>
> (Norcross, 1991, cited in Norcross, 1992: 2)

> . . . the potential of client-centered counseling is severely limited because of the
> relative paucity of information that is being incorporated.
>
> (Cain, 1993: 135)

These quotes are indicative of a process and position taken by authors to
criticize the theory and hypothesis formulated by Carl R. Rogers. The
process is, in essence, that of dismissing or ignoring the fundamental
assumption of the approach (that of the actualizing tendency and the self-
authority of the client) as untenable or questionable and proceeding with
criticism of the theory from other theoretical frames of reference. The position taken by these authors is embedded, to varying degrees, on the assumption of the therapist as the expert for the treatment and behavior change of
the client. Hence, their theoretical argument is a *non sequitur* from the
actual meaning of Rogers' theory (Bozarth, 1995).

Quinn (1993), who identifies himself as a client-centered therapist, provides a classic example of dismissing the fundamental assumption and the subsequent implications for growth. He decides, while recognizing that fundamental assumptions are 'ultimately unprovable', that we might ask whether or not there are 'other urges as motivational, urgent and powerful as the actualizing tendency' (Quinn, 1993: 11)? This may, of course, be a viable dialogue and one which Ford (1994) has discussed from an empirical perspective. However, Quinn simply dismisses Rogers' assumption as untenable. With that dismissal of the basic assumption of client-centered theory, he proceeds to conclude from his clinical experience that confrontation is 'absolutely necessary to successful outcomes' (Quinn, 1993: 11). In short, he communicates his lack of trust in the assumption and then finds anecdotal support in his clinical work which verifies that one cannot trust the assumption.

Others exemplify the inaccuracy of viewing Rogers' theory from the perspective of different frameworks when they conclude that Rogers is suggesting a 'unitary case formulation and universal treatment plan' (Norcross, 1992: 8) and that Rogers 'violates the principle of tailor-making the therapy to the needs of the patient' (Fay and Lazarus, 1992: abstract). The perceptual stance of these authors that the clinician is an artful director of prescriptive matching for tailoring treatment to the individual is radically different from Rogers' assumption of the client knowing what is best in his or her life. They demonstrate an ironic misunderstanding of person-centered therapy. They somehow do not understand that the practice of person-centered therapy is focused on individual differences and not predicated on 'doing something to the client that is predetermined by an authoritative therapist who takes responsibility for the treatment and behavior of the client' (Bozarth, 1991: 467). The experiencing of certain attitudes towards a person is not the same as prescribing 'relationship stances and technical interventions for each situation' (Norcross, 1992: 8). Fay and Lazarus are replete in their amazement of a different way of relating to people when they sarcastically state: 'if Rogers were correct, there would be no point in bothering to learn any specific techniques – be warm, genuine, congruent and empathic and establish a good therapeutic alliance – period!' (Fay and Lazarus, 1992: 3). *This is exactly correct.* What one does as a person-centered therapist is what emerges in the relationship with the client. In the context of client-centered theory, it is creating an atmosphere of unconditional positive regard that enables the person to develop unconditional positive self-regard and, subsequently, to resolve his or her specific problems. The theory is not one which applies certain conditions the way one applies dosages of drugs to a person in an effort to finalize a treatment plan. *The therapy is a human endeavor that trusts the growth of each individual, and wherein the therapist resonates person to person with the other individual.*

Why is there such a lack of understanding or acceptance of person-centered therapy? Why do eminent scholars with high integrity, including those who identify themselves as client-centered, fail to understand and/or accept the foundation block of client-centered theory? The primary factor appears to me to be that their perceptual stance does not permit them to understand a theoretical base that so radically trusts the client (Bozarth, 1990). Thus, they summarily dismiss the position and misconstrue the meaning. Person-centered therapy lies in the basic trust of this drive towards growth. It *is the client who knows best where to go and how to get there.* Since this is an unacceptable position to many practitioners and scholars, they re-integrate it into their own perceptual scheme.

Even major contributors to the person-centered approach take the stance that the client's capacity of finding his or her own direction can be helped by the non-interventive expertise of the therapist using various forms of encouragement. For example, Cain concludes that Rogers' theory is of 'little help in understanding the wide varieties of disturbing and pathological behaviors (e.g., depression, obsessive-compulsive behavior, disturbed body image) that render people dysfunctional to varying degrees' (Cain, 1993: 136). *This reaction simply ignores Rogers' theoretical position that such labels are meaningless and that as the person develops increasing positive self-regard, the 'dysfunctional' problems are dealt with by the person.* Cain, like Quinn and others, assesses the theory from other theoretical frameworks which have assumptions that are predicated upon the expertise and authority of the therapist. The focus is, thus, shifted from the client's frame of reference to the expert's assessment of the 'client's problem' and to the 'doing' of the therapy rather than the embodiment of the therapist's attitudes in the relationship with the client (Bozarth, 1992). Actions which emerge from the therapist's empathic stance with the client are considerably different from those initiated by the therapist's assumed *armamentarium* of knowledge.

An example of the type of question frequently directed to person-centered therapists might be: 'If I am a practicing therapist and I hear about a new method (e.g. eye movement desensitization and reprocessing-EMDR) which many colleagues tell me seems extremely effective for certain conditions, what am I to do? Should I say, No, this does not fit my theory/practice?'

My initial personal response to such information is that I usually find that the validity of such alleged effectiveness is questionable. This is especially true when the client has the locus of control. The next section on research discusses this position at greater length. Even so, I agree with my colleague, Dr Barbara Brodley (personal communication, November, 1995), that as client-centered therapists we often respond with interest to such information and consider it as something to share with a client in case the person asks for techniques. When operating from the person-centered paradigm, the emphasis is on the client's frame of reference. Dr Brodley, a clinical psychologist with over thirty years of therapeutic practice, echoes my view when she states:

> I have responded to clients' requests for techniques (information plus referrals) or given explicit support for their search for techniques or practitioners, and I've also told clients about them when there seemed to be an interest although not an

explicit request, and I've given information when clients asked if I know anything about a specific technique. While working with me, clients have gone to other practitioners for eye movement desensitization, massage therapy, relaxation therapy, yoga, hypnotherapy, anger therapy, behavior and cognitive therapy, shamanism, fortune tellers, focusing, sex therapy, Gerbode's repetition therapy for trauma, Week's techniques for panic attacks, and to psychiatrists and pharmacologists for medication. The only instructions I've given, a few times, are for relaxation, yogic deep breathing and some cognitive techniques.

(Personal communication, November, 1995)

Dr Brodley offers more clarification on this question from her extensive clinical experience as a client-centered therapist:

I do think it part of being responsive to clients' own leads and inclinations to inform them of techniques and treatments that exist when they are asking or seem to be asking. I think it has helped people to have my support (or at least no sign of lack of support along with my empathic understanding of their interests) in trying some of these techniques. It seems to be part of the therapy process for some clients to search for techniques just as they search for partners, schools that are right for them, medical doctors and so forth. . . . In fact, relaxation and some of the things that are simple self-help techniques do help relieve symptoms sometimes, and give the person a way of helping themselves besides the therapy.

(Personal communication, November, 1995)

My experience is that when I can trust the client enough, he/she always finds the best way to help her/himself anyway. Raskin (1988) clarifies this point when he refers to the trust of both the therapist's and client's self-directed capacities. He suggests that the trust of the therapist 'might bring into play different ways of expressing empathy, the use of intuition, or self-disclosure . . . while maintaining the same basic respect for the self-directive capacities of the client' (Raskin, 1988: 1). He adds: 'The therapist may go further and, in a spontaneous and non-systematic way, offer reactions, suggestions, ask questions, try to help the client experience feelings, share aspects of his or her own life, etc., while maintaining a basic and continuing respect for the client as architect of the process' (1988: 1). Raskin suggests that this unsystematic therapist activity 'may represent person-centered therapy at its optimal level, with a freely functioning therapist accepting the client as leading the way while not being bound by a set of rules' (1988: 1). Systematic and unsystematic therapist activities are differentiated by the view that systematic approaches: 'may have a preconceived notion of how they wish to change the client and work at it in systematic fashion, in contrast to the person-centered therapist who starts out being open and remains open to an emerging process orchestrated by the client' (1988: 2). Raskin's point has significant implications related to such questions as the previous one (as well as for the ideas of testing and assessment) as part of the 'unsystematic' emerging process orchestrated by the client.

My view is that the person-centered therapist is flexible depending upon the idiosyncrasies of the client, counselor, and situation (Bozarth, 1984). Such activities are consistent with the theory in that they may occur as unsystematic actions that are decided upon by the client from the client's frame of reference. When the trust is there, the therapist's behavior might entail giving the client information about a process or 'treatment'. As an emergence from the therapist's interaction with the client's world, such information might range from discussing EMDR, herbal treatment or polka dancing as possible actions by the client. I resonate with Rogers' comment *that if I thought that I knew what would help, I'd tell the person.* Since I seldom think that I know another person's best directions, I am seldom tempted to offer such advice. This position is reflective of the person-centered paradigm.

Another example of a question that perplexes many individuals about the person-centered stance is the following type of question: 'If I am an ordinary person feeling somewhat depressed or lost or panicking and I am looking for a therapist, should I rely on my feelings about the therapist I happen to find regardless of their acclaimed orientation or profession?' The client is the decision-maker and the best judge for him/herself. Who can better make that decision?

Advocates and adversaries alike perpetuate the misunderstandings of Rogers' theory by missing the point that it is the client who knows best about him/herself.

The current related research

The most popular research paradigm is directed by the specificity question: 'What treatment by whom is most effective for this individual with that specific problem under what set of circumstances?' (Paul, 1967: 111) and is adhered to and promoted by professional leaders (Norcross, 1992) in spite of contradictory data (Stubbs and Bozarth, 1994). In fact, this primary foundation of the most prevalent therapy approach is more prone to empirical criticism than the criticism previously leveled at Rogers' conceptualizations (Bozarth, 1991; Bozarth and Stubbs, 1990; Patterson, 1984; Stubbs and Bozarth, 1994).

Stubbs' and Bozarth's qualitative study of psychotherapy research effectiveness reports that Rogers' hypothesis is the most stable major thread running through the effectiveness of psychotherapy throughout, at least, the last four decades. Of five emergent temporal categories of focus, the abiding relationships to outcome that emerged in *some form* are those that Rogers (1957) hypothesized in his classic integrative statement as core ingredients for therapeutic personality change (i.e., congruence, unconditional positive regard and empathic understanding). Stubbs and Bozarth also specifically note that the predominant temporal category that is the forerunner to the specificity question is the category that the conditions are necessary but *not sufficient* has virtually no research support. They did not find one direct study which supported this assertion. Conclusions were, at best, extrapolations of flawed logic. That is, the logic that supports Rogers' hypothesis is weak; hence, something more must be needed.

A substantial body of evidence attempting to establish differential effectiveness leads to the conclusion that the outcomes of different psychotherapies with clinical populations are equivalent (Bohart and Rosenbaum, 1995; Stiles et al., 1986). Even so, some authors contend that specific treatment that is 'tailor made' to clients with particular dysfunctions is an established fact. With a market advocacy, a task force of Division 12 of the American Psychological Association (1993) has identified 26 'well established treatments' for dysfunctions that meet the committee determinations of criteria for empirically validated treatments. These studies include those that have a minimum of two group designs and are demonstrated to be superior to pill or psychological placebo or another treatment as part of the criteria. It is noteworthy that they identify *only* 26 studies that meet their criteria and that none of these studies deal with therapist/client relationships or extratherapeutic variables as contributing factors. Most of the dysfunctions are very specific behavioral problems treated through behavioral modalities. The committee has virtually ignored the reviews of psychotherapy outcome research.

Reviews of the research literature on psychotherapy efficacy (Bozarth, 1991; Bozarth and Stubbs, 1990; Norcross, 1992; Patterson, 1984; Stubbs and Bozarth, 1994) have acknowledged that the greatest contributors to the effectiveness of psychotherapy are client and relationship variables. Behaviorists who accept these conclusions (Lazarus, 1993; and Norcross, 1993) continue the specificity paradigm by assuming that the therapist can create a particular role designated relationship for a particular client; hence, the expert therapist can predict and become the chameleon (Lazarus, 1993) that is needed by the client (as determined by the therapist's assessment).

Research reviews (e.g., Bohart, 1995; Bohart and Rosenbaum, 1995; Lambert et al., 1986) provide the soil for renewed consideration of Rogers' hypothesis. Historically, several colleagues and I (Mitchell et al., 1977) noted that the research studies supporting Rogers' hypothesis of the conditions being necessary and sufficient were not as strong as originally concluded. We indicated that 'our conclusion must be that the relationship between the interpersonal skills and client outcome has not been investigated and, consequently, nothing definitive can be said about the relative efficacy of high and low levels of empathy, warmth, and genuineness' (Mitchell et al., 1977: 488). Other research reviews reached similar conclusions. These included such statements as the following: 'more complex relationships exist among therapist, patients, and techniques' (Parloff et al., 1978: 503); and 'such relationship dimensions are rarely sufficient for patient change' (Gurman, 1977: 503). However, Mitchell et al. noted that it may be clinically important that the statistically significant findings in nearly all studies involve the comparisons of client improvements for those who are clients of high*er* level condition therapists rather than *high* level condition therapists. That is, therapists placed as high level therapists for purposes of comparing their client outcomes are seldom high as operationally defined on the rating instruments.

Later, I concluded that the research on *client-centered therapy in the USA* was sparse and severely confounded by a number of variables. I stated:

> Recent research findings are confounded by several factors. The studies are primarily comprised of non-client-centered therapists. Human relations training models may often be mistakenly considered to be applied by client-centered therapists. Critical factors of client-centered therapy (e.g. locus of control, lack of presuppositions of what the client will be like, experiencing) have not been considered.
>
> (Bozarth, 1983: 113)

It now becomes clearer that the research on the Rogerian hypothesis during the 1960s, 1970s and 1980s was generated from Rogers' integrative statement and not from his statement concerning client-centered therapy. Hence, there are few studies of client-centered therapy. The studies revolve around the core conditions of the therapist and these studies are flawed by the lack of high level condition therapists in the studies.

However, Duncan and Moynihan (1994) present an intriguing argument for what is, in essence, the Rogerian approach when they propose a model predicated on recent conclusions concerning the research on psychotherapy outcome. Reviews of outcome research (Lambert, 1992; Lambert et al., 1986) suggest that 30 per cent of the outcome variance is accounted for by client-therapist relationships, techniques account for 15 per cent of the variance, as does placebo effect, and 40 per cent of the variance is accounted for by extratherapeutic change variables (factors unique to the client and his/her environment). Duncan and Moynihan point out that the research suggests the utility of intentionally utilizing the client's frame of reference. Indeed, they resonate the Rogerian view:

> Empathy, then, is not an invariant, specific therapist behavior or attitude (e.g. reflection of feeling is inherently empathic), nor is it a means to gain a relationship so that the therapist may promote a particular orientation or personal value, nor a way of teaching clients what a relationship should be. Rather, empathy is therapist attitudes and behaviors that place the client's perceptions and experiences above theoretical content and personal values (Duncan, Solovey & Rusk, 1992); empathy is manifested by therapist attempts to work within the frame of reference of the client. When the therapist acts in a way that demonstrates consistency with the client's frame of reference, then empathy may be perceived, and common factor effects enhanced. Empathy, therefore, is a function of the client's unique perceptions and experience and requires that therapists respond flexibly to clients' needs, rather than from a particular theoretical frame of reference or behavioral set.
>
> (Duncan and Moynihan, 1994: 295)

Duncan and Moynihan, like many researchers, identify Rogerian empathy with specific behaviors rather than from the bedrock of the empathic attitude in the theory. As such, they apparently do not realize that they are actually proposing an operational concept that is representative of Rogers' view of empathy.

In summary, the research concerned with the person-centered stance in psychotherapy suggests that: (1) the specific core conditions posed by

Rogers have not been adequately studied as attitudinal qualities; (2) the client-centered/person-centered therapy has not truly been researched; (3) the current foundation of psychotherapy practice which focuses on the specificity question has little viable research support; and (4) the current research on psychotherapy outcome in general substantiates the vitality of Rogers' theory of therapy as well as the core qualities of therapies postulated in Rogers' integrative statement. Overall, much of the direction and nature of research in psychotherapy effectiveness 'has proved "significantly insufficient to help" and often obscures what is most significantly helpful' (Stubbs and Bozarth, 1994: 117). What is significantly helpful, however, are variables that are embedded in person-centered principles of relationship and to giving attention to the frame of reference of the client.

Implications of Rogers' theory of therapy

Rogers' theory of therapy is predicated upon the assumption that there is one motivational force that is natural and constructive for all human beings. This natural constructive force is propelled by the client's experience of certain attitudinal qualities. As such, the therapy is viable for all 'kinds' of clients. It involves one attitudinal treatment modality which is interpersonally and behaviorally different for each individual. From a clinical standpoint, each individual *is* the theory. Psychotherapy effectiveness is related to the relationship of the client and therapist and, in addition, to the therapist's attention to the client's perceptions of the extratherapeutic variables (internal and external) accessible to him/her. The research findings have finally ferreted out the most potent of the variables, that is, the client. The person-centered therapist focuses on both the attitudinal variables in relationship with the client and on the frame of reference of the client which ultimately identifies the extratherapeutic variables. The abiding trust of the therapist in the client as her/his own best expert about his/her life is integrally related to these two variables.

Research and clinical experiences have demonstrated the approach as viable as other approaches with all types of dysfunctions, ranging from those neurotic or depressed or psychotic (Bohart and Rosenbaum, 1995), in spite of the restricted representation of bona fide client-centered therapists. My own experience of relating to diagnosed institutionalized psychotics in mental hospitals solidifies my personal position of trusting the client and his/her inner resources and potentials.

Rogers' integration statement has hit the mark as an explanation of why all therapies work equally well. His contention that the various therapies and techniques 'are relatively unimportant except to the extent that they serve as channels for fulfilling one of the conditions' (Rogers, 1957: 233) is remarkably meaningful in consideration of the recent research conclusions and the claims of equality of effect among therapies. Neil Jacobson's (1995) sobering scientific critique of the therapies in addition to Masson's (1988) railing of the therapies puts forward a call to question the effectiveness of all therapies. Miller, Hubble and Duncan's (1995) similar conclusion must, in all reasonableness, 'make therapists squirm' (Jacobson, 1995: 46–7). Miller et al. state: 'thirty years of clinical outcome research have not found any one theory, model, method, or package of techniques to be reliably better than any other' (cited in O'Hara, 1995: 19). What has been found is that the relationship of the therapist and client (accounting for 30 per cent of the variance) and the extratherapeutic variables of the client (accounting for 40 per cent of the variance) account for the effectiveness. Techniques and particular approaches account for the same variance as placebo effect (i.e., 15 per cent). It is the therapists' attention to the clients' frames of reference and the therapists' offerings of a supportive and understanding relationship that are the overriding variables of effectiveness. The various therapies are not effective (regardless of whether client-centered, psychodynamic or behavioral) when the therapist is not immersed in these two factors. When they do immerse themselves in these ways with their clients, it doesn't matter so much what approach or techniques they use. The therapeutic system and particular approaches become, perhaps, 'the metaphoric system, the frames of reference, the meaning-laden narratives, through which experience can be understood' (O'Hara, 1995: 30). Rogers' clinical and research demonstrations are closely related to any common effectiveness among therapists. As O'Hara states:

> [Rogers] demonstrated through enormous amounts of research, admittedly by Jacobson's standards methodologically flawed, that therapy works best when:
>
> - clients are free to determine their own agenda for their life and for their therapy and to describe their own subjective experience in their own way;
> - they are accompanied by someone who has faith in them, listens empathically and accurately for the deeper meanings of their expressions, and who deals with them honestly without roles and manipulative games;
> - the relationship is as egalitarian as possible without the 'power-over' authoritarian posture so common to medical and educational settings of the 1940s.
> (O'Hara, 1995: 19)

O'Hara's words resonate with Whitaker and Malone (1981) in their view that all types of therapists do what they do to bring their humanity to their clients.

My particular aversions are not to therapies; rather, they are to therapists who tend to manipulate, attempt to control and think that they know what is best for any given individual. Although the predominant psychotherapeutic treatment model is predicated upon the fiction of the 'specificity question', I believe that it is more the therapist rather than the type of therapy that dictates the manipulative attitude. This seems to me to be in accord with Rogers' integrative statement which underlines the fact that Rogers was referring to attitudes of the therapist and not to a method of treatment. *It is not so much what therapists do as who they are in their attitudes towards their clients.* Their attitudes, of course, dictate how they relate to their clients. My aversion is best described as being aversive towards the situation in which the therapist assumes that he/she knows what is best for the client, what is wrong with the client or in what direction the client should go (Bozarth, 1992). As the research findings have ferreted out the most potent of the variables (i.e., the client), the implications of Rogers' theory become more viable. Person-centered theory focuses on those variables which account for the most variance in effectiveness; that is the attitudinal variables in relationship with the client and on the frame of reference of the client which ultimately identifies the extratherapeutic variables.

Where to from here?

An observation in the study of research of psychotherapy efficacy (Stubbs and Bozarth, 1994) that there are at least two views of humans and, as well, of research seems likely to remain a constant source of influence in the future. These two views of human beings are the reactive view and the proactive view. The particular view taken at any given time will determine, in part, whether or not relationship and attention to extratherapeutic variables or technique and approach is emphasized. The reactive view emphasizes the diagnostic, prescriptive, therapist-as-expert view and the proactive view emphasizes the client's self-determination and self-healing process.

The direction of mental health care is infused with these two competing views. Variables such as economics, attempts to maintain and expand professional turf, changes in health management, politics, dedication to scientificism and strivings for technical expertise seem likely to continue to influence the future of treatment modalities. Thus, a continuous reactive view is likely to be maintained. On the other hand, some directions from the medical profession may eventually promote a more proactive view. The emergence of a new era in psychotherapeutic treatment similar to the new era in medical treatment (Dossey, 1994) may begin to have an influence. For example, Dossey has identified three eras of medicine. These are: *Era I* – the mechanical or physical medicine era, which refers to any form of therapy focusing on things on the body; *Era II* – mind–body medicine, which refers to the effects of consciousness within a particular body; and *Era III* – transpersonal medicine, which refers to any therapy in which effects of consciousness bridge between different persons (Dossey, 1994: 40–1). Whereas *Era II* treatments are now on the scene in therapeutic contacts, *Era III* approaches in medicine or therapy are reluctantly received. *Era II* treatments include those of biofeedback, hypnosis, relaxation therapy, and psychoneuroimmunology. *Era III* approaches would include such forms as distant healing, diagnosis at a distance, telesomatic events and noncontact therapeutic touch. The implications are 'mind blowing' to most practicing psychotherapists and raise possibilities concerning the viability of right hemisphere function and reactions (Samples, 1976) as emerging models in therapy. Rogers refers to times when his therapy relationship 'transcends itself and becomes a part of something larger' (Rogers, 1980: 129). Thorne is convinced that Rogers' words must be taken seriously in order 'to ensure the vitality and the development of the client-centered tradition' (Thorne, 1991: 183). Such concepts are consistent with the realm of openness to inner resources of individuals that is a basic assumption of the person-centered approach.

Although there will be a tendency for the mental health profession to cling to the reactive view of the 'specificity model' and continue to perpetuate the myth of that model to the detriment of mental health care, there may also be more focus on the inner resources of the client and upon self-help, as well as more consideration of the client as his or her own best expert about her or himself. Although it is probable that the political system, logical positivists and the 'experts' will resist and re-direct any such developments, I personally believe that the people will ultimately 'help themselves'. Scientific evidence (Bohart and Rosenbaum, 1995) supports the clear message of the person-centered approach, which O'Hara aptly summarizes:

> It isn't the technique, it isn't the therapist, it isn't the level of training, it isn't the new wonder drug, it isn't the diagnosis. It is our clients' own inborn capacities for self-healing, and it is the meeting – the relationship in which two or more sovereign and sacred 'I's' meet as a 'we' to engage with significant questions of existence.
>
> (O'Hara, 1995: 19, 30–1)

One of the directions suggested by this message is summarized by Rogers (1980) from a personal paper first written in 1974. He states:

> . . . we are wiser than our intellects . . . that our organisms as a whole have a wisdom and purposiveness which goes well beyond our conscious thought. . . . I think men and women, individually and collectively are inwardly and organismically rejecting the view of one single culture-approved reality. I believe they are moving inevitably toward the acceptance of millions of separate, challenging exciting informative *individual* perceptions of reality. I regard it as possible that this view – like the sudden and separate discovery of the principles of quantum mechanics by scientists in different countries – may begin to come into effective existence in many parts of the world at once. If so, we would be living in a totally new universe, different from any in history. Is it conceivable that such a change can come about?
>
> (Rogers, 1980: 106–7)

Rogers' work will prove to be a major factor facilitating and tempering this direction and the potency of the person-centered stance will be increasingly realized.

References

American Psychological Association (1993, October) *Task Force on Promotion and Dissemination of Psychological Procedures: A Report by the Division 12 Board*. Washington, DC: Author.

Baldwin, M. (1987) Interview with Carl Rogers on the use of self in therapy. In M. Baldwin and V. Satir (eds), *The Use of the Self in Therapy* (pp. 45–52). Binghamton, NY: Hawarth Press, Inc.

Bohart, A.C. (1995) The person-centered therapies. In A.S. Gurman and S.B. Messer (eds), *Modern Psychotherapies*. New York: Guilford Press.

Bohart, A. and Rosenbaum, R. (1995) The dance of empathy: empathy, diversity, and technical eclecticism. *The Person-Centered Journal*, 2 (2), 5–29.

Bozarth, J.D. (1983) Current research on client-centered therapy in the USA. In M. Wolf-Rudiger and H. Wolfgang (eds), *Research on Psychotherapeutic Approaches: Proceedings of the 1st European Conference on Psychotherapy Research, Trier, 11* (pp. 105–15). Frankfurt: Verlag Peter Lang.

Bozarth, J.D. (1984) Beyond reflection: emergent modes of empathy. In R.F. Levant and J.M. Shlien (eds), *Client-Centered Therapy and the Person-Centered Approach: New Directions in Theory Research and Practice* (pp. 59–75). New York: Praeger.

Bozarth, J.D. (1985) Quantum theory and the person-centered approach. *Journal of Counseling and Development*, 64 (3), 179–82.

Bozarth, J.D. (1990) The essence of client-centered and person-centered therapy. In G. Lietaer, J. Rombauts and R. VanBalen (eds), *Client-Centered and Experiential Psychotherapy Towards the Nineties* (pp. 88–99). Leuven: Katholieke Universiteit to Leuven.

Bozarth, J.D. (1991) Rejoinder: perplexing perceptual ploys. *Journal of Counseling and Development*, 69 (5), 466–8.

Bozarth, J.D. (1992) Coterminous intermingling of doing and being in Person-Centered Therapy. *The Person-Centered Journal*, 1 (1), 33–9.

Bozarth, J.D. (1993) *A Reconceptualization of the Necessary and Sufficient Conditions for Therapeutic Personality Change*. Paper presented at the Fifth International Forum on The Person-Centered Approach, Terscheling, Holland, July 1993.

Bozarth, J.D. (1995) Person-centered therapy: a misunderstood paradigmatic difference? *The Person-Centered Journal*, 2 (2), 40–5.

Bozarth, J.D. (1996) A reconceptualization: a theoretical of the necessary and sufficient conditions for therapeutic personality change. *The Person-Centered Journal*, 3 (1), 44–51.

Bozarth, J.D. (in press) Empathy from the framework of the Person-Centered Approach. In A. Bohart and L. Greenberg (eds), *Empathy Reconsidered*. New York: American Psychological Association.

Bozarth, J.D. and Brodley, B.T. (1984) Client-centered/person-centered psychotherapy: a statement of understanding. *Person-Centered Review*, 1 (3), 262–5.

Bozarth, J.D. and Brodley, B.T. (1991) Actualization: a functional concept in client-centered therapy. *Journal of Social Behavior and Personality*, Special Issue, 6 (5), 45–59.

Bozarth, J.D. and Stubbs, J.P. (1990) *Research on Psychotherapy Efficacy Research*. Paper presented at the national conference of the American Psychological Association, Boston, MA, August 1990.

Brodley, B.T. (1988) *A Client-Centered Psychotherapy Practice*. Paper presented at the Third Annual Meeting of the Association for the development of the Person-Centered Approach. New York, May 1988.

Brodley, B.T. and Brody, A. (1994) *Can One Use Techniques and Still Be Client-Centered?* Paper presented at the International Conference on Client-Centered and Experiential Psychotherapy, Gmunden, Austria, September 1994.

Cain, D.J. (1993) The uncertain future of client-centered counseling. *Journal of Humanistic Education and Development*, 31, 133–9.

Dossey, L. (1994) *Healing Words*. San Francisco: Harper & Row.

Duncan, B.L. and Moynihan, D.W. (1994) Applying outcome research: intentional utilization of the clients frame of reference. *Psychotherapy*, 31, 294–301.

Duncan, B., Solovey, A. and Rusk, G. (1992) *Changing the Rules: A Client-Directed Approach to Therapy*. New York: Guilford Press.

Egan, G. (1994) *The Skilled Helper: A Problem-Management Approach to Helping*. (5th edn) Pacific Grove, CA: Brooks/Cole Publishing.

Fay, A. and Lazarus, A.A. (1992) *On Necessity and Sufficiency in Psychotherapy*. Paper presented at the 100th annual convention of the American Psychological Association, Washington, DC, August 1992.

Ford, G. (1994) Extending Rogers' thoughts on human destructiveness. *The Person-Centered Journal*, 1 (3), 52–63.

Gurman, A.S. (1977) The patient's perception of the therapeutic relationship. In S.L. Garfield and A.E. Bergin (eds), *Handbook of Psychotherapy and Behavior Change* (2nd edn, pp. 503–43). New York: John Wiley & Sons.

Jacobson, N.S. (1995) The overselling of psychotherapy. *Networker*, March/April, 41–7.

Kirschenbaum, H. (1979) *On Becoming Carl Rogers*. New York: Delta/Dell.

Lambert, M. (1992) Psychotherapy outcome research. In J.C. Norcross and M.R. Goldfried (eds), *Handbook of Psychotherapy Integration* (pp. 94–129). New York: Basic Books.

Lambert, M.J., Shapiro, D.A. and Bergin, A.E. (1986) The effectiveness of psychotherapy. In S.L. Garfield and A.E. Bergin (eds), *Handbook of Psychotherapy and Behavior Change* (3rd edn, pp. 157–212). New York: John Wiley & Sons.

Lazarus, A.A. (1993) Tailoring therapeutic relationship, or being an authentic chameleon. *Psychotherapy*, 30 (3), 404–7.

Masson, J.M. (1988) *Against Therapy*. New York: Atheneum.

Miller, S., Hubble, M. and Duncan, B. (1995) No more bells and whistles. *Family Therapy Networks*, 19, 52–63.

Mitchell, K.M., Bozarth, J.D. and Krauft, C.C. (1977) A reappraisal of the therapeutic effectiveness of accurate empathy, nonpossessive warmth, and genuineness. In A.S. Gurman and A.M. Razin (eds), *Effective Psychotherapy: A Handbook of Research* (pp. 482–502). New York: Pergamon Press.

Norcross, J.C. (1992) *Are There Necessary and Sufficient Conditions for Therapeutic Change?* Paper presented at the 100th annual convention of the American Psychological Association, Washington, DC, August 1992.

Norcross, J.C. (1993) Tailoring relationship stances to client needs: an introduction. *Psychotherapy*, 30 (3), 402–3.

O'Hara, M. (1995) Why is this man laughing? *AHP Perspective*, May/June, 19 and 30–31.

Parloff, M.B., Waskow, I.E. and Wolfe, B.E. (1979) Research on therapist variables in relation to process and outcome. In S.L. Garfield and A.E. Bergin (eds), *Handbook of Psychotherapy and Behavior Change* (2nd edn, pp. 233–82). New York: John Wiley & Sons.

Patterson, C.H. (1984) Empathy, warmth, and genuineness in psychotherapy. A review of reviews. *Psychotherapy*, 21, 431–8.

Paul, G.L. (1967) Strategy of outcome research in psychotherapy. *Journal of Consulting Psychology*, 31, 109–19.

Quinn, R. (1993) Confronting Carl Rogers: a developmental-interactional approach to person-centered therapy. *Journal of Humanistic Psychology*, 33 (1), 6–23.

Raskin, N. (1988) What do we mean by person-centered therapy? Paper presented at the meeting of the Association for the Development of the Person-Centered Approach, New York, May 1988.

Rogers, C.R. (1957) The necessary and sufficient conditions of therapeutic personality change. *Journal of Consulting Psychology*, 21, 95–103.

Rogers, C.R. (1959) A theory of therapy, personality, and interpersonal relationships as developed in the client-centered framework. In S. Koch (ed.), *Psychology: Vol. 3, A Study of Science. Formulation of the Person and the Social Context* (pp. 184–256). New York: McGraw-Hill.

Rogers, C.R. (1961) A therapist's view of the good life: the fully functioning person. In C.R. Rogers (ed.), *Becoming a Person* (pp. 183–96). Boston, MA: Houghton Mifflin.

Rogers, C.R. (1977) *Carl Rogers on Personal Power*. New York: Delacarte.

Rogers, C.R. (1980) *A Way of Being*. Boston, MA: Houghton Mifflin.

Rogers, C.R. (1986) Client-centered approach to therapy. In I.L. Kutash and A. Wolf (eds), *Psychotherapist's Casebook: Theory and Technique in Practice* (pp. 197–208). San Francisco: Jossey-Bass.

Samples, R. (1976) *The Metaphoric Mind: A Celebration of Creative Consciousness*. Reading, MA: Addison-Wesley.

Stiles, W.B., Shapiro, D.A. and Elliott, R. (1986) Are all psychotherapies equivalent? *American Psychologist*, 41, 165–80.

Stubbs, J.P. and Bozarth, J.D. (1994) The dodo bird revisited: a qualitative study of psychotherapy efficacy research. *Journal of Applied and Preventive Psychology*, 3 (2), 109–20.

Stubbs, J.P. and Bozarth, J.D. (1996) The integrative statement of Carl Rogers. In R. Hutterer, G. Pawlowsky, P.F. Schmid and R. Stipsits (eds), *Client-Centered and Experiential Psychotherapy: A Paradigm in Motion.* (pp. 25–33). New York: Peter Lang.

Teich, N. (1992) Rogerian empathy. In N. Teich (ed.), *Rogerian Perspectives: Collaborative Rhetoric for Oral and Written Communication* (pp. 249–56). Norwood, NJ: Ablex.

Thorne, B. (1991) *Person-Centered Counselling: Therapeutic & Spiritual Dimensions.* London: Whurr.

Van Belle, H.A. (1990) Rogers' later move toward mysticism: implications for client-centered therapy. In G. Lietaer, J. Rombauts and R. VanBalen (eds), *Client-Centered and Experiential Psychotherapy Towards the Nineties* (pp. 47–57). Leuven: Katholieke Universiteit te Leuven.

Whitaker, C.A. and Malone, T.P. (1981) *The Roots of Psychotherapy* (Rev. edn). New York: Brunner/Mazel.

3

Integrative Psychotherapy, Integrating Psychotherapies, or Psychotherapy After 'Schoolism'?

Petruska Clarkson

> Shallow ideas can be assimilated; ideas that require people to reorganize their picture of the world provoke hostility. A physicist at the Georgia Institute of Technology, Joseph Ford, started quoting Tolstoy: 'I know that most men, including those at ease with problems of the greatest complexity, can seldom accept even the simplest and most obvious truth if it be such as would oblige them to admit the falsity of conclusions which they have delighted in explaining to colleagues, which they have proudly taught to others, and which they have woven, thread by thread, into the fabric of their lives. (Gleick, 1988: 38)

As Hillman and Ventura (1992) pointed out by the title of their best-selling book: *We've Had a Hundred Years of Psychotherapy and the World's Getting Worse*. Of course we have also had a hundred years of other things and a conviction that the world is getting worse has been the opinion of parents at least since the time of Plato. Psychotherapeutic work of some kind has probably existed since the dawn of time. But we stand in the light of that dawn and draw from those roots today whether we are aware of it or not. A hundred years is certainly a good span of time for reflection. And the next millennium is already on the horizon.

At this point near the end of the century we also have to cope with the thought that, despite fundamentalist convictions of some of the different theoretical schools of counselling and psychotherapy, none of them has been found to be any better than any of the others on most measures in a growing body of research (Seligman, 1995). The very proliferation of approaches – some 450 at last count – suggests more a desperate search than the discovery of certainty.

Several trends are characteristic of our current psychotherapy scene (Clarkson, 1995): psychotherapeutic approaches have proliferated *ad libitum*; there are no consensually agreed discernible outcome differences attributable to theoretical orientation; there is integration within schools – a kind of virtuous contagion; there is integration between schools – not least as they begin to acknowledge that certain commonalities such as the centrality of the therapeutic relationship outweigh doctrinal disputes and there is an attempt to reach consensus on certain issues such as standards, training procedures and professional ethics and practice – even to the extent where the differences in core syllabi are disappearing and trainees from very different schools share essentially the same core of reading and practice expectations. Compare, for example, several samples of curricula of UKCP training organizations of so-called different orientations or flag statements. One of the profound disadvantages may be exactly that the distinctiveness, uniqueness and individuality of different voices may be lost in this scramble for respectability, accountability and commonly agreed recognized standards, bureaucratically defined standards of accreditation of component competencies, and auditing rules and regulations. Not that the latter are not honourable objectives, only that they too have a shadow. The solution to any one problem so often contains the seeds of the next problem like invisible succulent shoots of virulent weeds under the pristine surface of the newly ploughed field.

The approach I currently espouse is psychotherapy. I think it is psychotherapy because it concerns therapy of the psyche or the soul and I do 'attend' this process in the original root meaning of the word.

The relationship as common factor

I chose to do psychotherapy because I have always been interested in healing, growth and creativity. I have unremittingly spent most of my personal and professional life learning about this process as well as teaching, supervising and being in receipt of others practising psychotherapy or psychoanalysis in one of its many variants. I have founded several organizations and institutes in these fields and I am the senior or sole designer of a number of Postgraduate Diploma and academic courses, and I teach at several universities in the UK (as Honorary Reader, for example, on the Surrey University PhD Counselling and Psychotherapy programme) as well as abroad. At PHYSIS I am the founder supervisor of the Independent Centre for Qualitative Research, where I also lead a training programme (or a 'design for learning') where advanced psychotherapists, psychologists and supervisors learn about psychotherapy and supervision within the contexts of culture, organization and social justice. Qualitative research is the overarching methodological and educational paradigm. Quite a number of people on this programme are using it to formulate, support or complete PhD research studies in their respective disciplines at a number of different universities they have chosen. (This programme is called Dieratao, which means Learning by Inquiry – see Clarkson, in press)

I am an accredited psychotherapist and teaching member and/or supervisor of several different approaches (UKCP recognized) and several different disciplines in this field. The three cornerstones of my work are: (a) a questioning, systemic research orientation – whether qualitative or quantitative; (b) a philosophical and practical preoccupation also with the notion of *physis* (otherwise known as *élan vital* or the life force) in terms of healing, creativity and evolution; and (c) the origination and development of models and conceptual structures which can account for different levels of epistemological or experiential discourse (such as the Seven Level Model (Clarkson, 1993)), and for use as theoretical, clinical and supervisory frameworks such as the development of the five therapeutic relationship model (Clarkson, 1990, 1995).

In this chapter I shall focus *on the therapeutic relationship as the common factor* in all psychotherapies. From my earliest personal and professional experiences, it seemed to me that human relationship was the *sine qua non* of existence. Research showed that one of the most overriding and influential factors in the outcome of psychotherapy is the relationship between psychotherapist and client (Frank, 1979; Hynan, 1981).

The more I studied, the more I found evidence that an accumulating body of research evidence also showed the therapeutic relationship is more commonly associated with effectiveness of outcome in psychotherapy than choice of theoretical orientation (Norcross, 1986; Beutler and Consoli, 1992; Lambert, 1992). The overridingly most important factor, therefore, which contributes to success in psychotherapy – however defined – appears to be the therapeutic relationship. It also provides perspectives from different approaches and schools and can be used to reach across and between (or over) them as I have tried to show elsewhere (Clarkson, 1996a).

A wealth of studies (e.g. Bergin and Lambert, 1978; Luborsky et al., 1983; O'Malley et al., 1983) demonstrate that it is the relationship between the client and psychotherapist, more than any other factor, which determines the effectiveness of psychotherapy, in terms of success as defined by the client. That is, success in psychotherapy can best be predicted by the properties of the patient, psychotherapist and their particular relationship (Norcross and Goldfried, 1992). Yet comparatively few books (for example Kahn, 1991) actually deal directly with the therapeutic relationship. Most of those which do deal centrally with the therapeutic relationship *per se* tend to focus on the working alliance and the transference–countertransference relationship, or the working alliance to the exclusion of others.

A growing body of research also pays attention to the match between client and psychotherapist, considering the influence of such factors as compatibility in terms of background, class, education and values (Garfield and Bergin, 1986). For Goldfried (1980), too, the relationship is the cornerstone of all psychotherapies. More recently, in his paper 'The effectiveness of psychotherapy', which discusses the Consumer Report study, Seligman wrote that: 'Long-term treatment did considerably better than short-term treatment. . . . No specific modality of psychotherapy did better than any other for any disorder. . . . Patients whose length of therapy or choice of therapist was limited by insurance or managed care did worse' (Seligman, 1995: 965). In discussing what Barkham (1995) has described as 'the pinnacle of research efforts in researching psychotherapy', Elkin (1995) concludes that there appears to be no significant difference which can be particularly ascribed to specific differences in approach, and she is now focusing 'on the actual patient–therapist interactions in the videotaped treatment sessions' (Elkin, 1995: 183). The recent special issue of the journal *Changes* (Vol. 13, No. 3) on outcome in psychotherapy, is well worth reading. In it Russell (1995) considers the work of Smith and Glass (1977), Lipsey and Wilson (1993), and Strupp (1979), and finds that they all seem to point to the conclusion that 'positive change was generally attributable to the healing effects of a benign human relationship' (Russell, 1995: 215).

So, the evidence for the relationship as the common factor across different psychotherapeutic approaches therefore exists in: (a) the psychotherapy outcome research literature; (b) an extensive qualitative study of the literature, theory and practice of psychotherapy (Clarkson, 1995, 1996c, 1996d; the first of these above publications surveying almost 800 specific publications in psychoanalysis, psychology and psychotherapy; (c) anecdotal form: in informal research, when asking clients or colleagues what had been the most important factor in their psychotherapy, clients tend not to report the effectiveness of insightful interpretations or elegantly facilitated catharsis but they tend to report the significance of the relationship – that someone was there, that someone cared, that it mattered (Howe, 1993); (d) finally, of course, it has been well documented throughout history that the relationship – whether with God, an idea or another person – is the matrix for facilitating major and permanent life changes in crisis, education, religious/political conversion or falling in love (see Clarkson, 1989).

If the relationship is the most central common core to all psychotherapists or approaches to psychotherapy, it seems to me that that is what psychotherapy is about – being in a relationship which is therapeutic. Of course one's way of being there will be the end product at that moment of one's entire past as well as present contact and future fears or aspirations.

The five relationship framework for psychotherapy, training and supervision

So, the therapeutic relationship is consistently being shown in research investigations as more significant than theoretical orientation. Therefore, it made sense to me to investigate this factor which appears to be of such overarching importance in statistical comparisons of outcome studies, subjective reports and clinical evaluation approaches. It also 'feels' true.

> We are born of relationship, nurtured in relationship, and educated in relationship. We represent every biological and social relationship of our forebears, as we interact and exist in a consensual domain called 'society' (Cottone, 1988: 363).

If indeed the psychotherapeutic relationship is one of the most, if not the most, important factor in successful psychotherapy, one would expect much of the training in psychotherapy to be training in the *intentional* use of relationship. Some psychotherapies claim that psychotherapy requires use of only one kind of relationship, or at most two. Some specifically exclude

the use of certain kinds of relationship. For example, Goulding and Goulding (1979), transactional analysts, minimize the use of transference, whereas
Moiso (1985), also in transactional analysis, sees it as a central focal point
of classical Berneian psychotherapy. Gestaltists Polster and Polster (1973)
and the existentialist May (1969) focus on the existential nature of the therapeutic relationship. Some psychotherapeutic approaches pay hardly any
theoretical attention to the nature of the relationship and they may attempt
to be entirely free of content (for example, in some approaches to hypnotherapy or NLP, therapeutic changes are claimed to be made by the
patient without the practitioner necessarily knowing what these changes
may be). Whereas, of course, the denial of the role of the relationship in
theory in these approaches is not the same as the skilful intentional use of
relationship, without such a theoretical framework but with consummate
mastery, as one can see in analysing the work of Milton Erickson (1967) by
using a theoretical framework such as the Five Relationships. In most
approaches, of course, stated policy and actual practice often diverge. As we
shall see later, even the actions of Freud (speaking perhaps louder than his
words) often belied the assumed orthodoxy of psychoanalytic practice.

   Considering psychotherapy from the vantage point of the different kinds
of relationships focused on by exponents of different orientations, it was
thought that all approaches to psychotherapy would find their respective
voices within the universe of discourse encompassed by the notion of 'the
therapeutic relationship'. Therefore, depending on the scope and range of
the practitioner, a comprehensive relationship framework could be more
comprehensive, theoretically hospitable and practically compatible with
almost all known approaches to psychotherapy. From my research (Clarkson, 1990) I identified five kinds of therapeutic relationship – five universes
of discourse across all the major approaches to psychotherapy about the
therapeutic relationship. These five modalities emerged as: the *Working
Alliance* as that aspect of the client–psychotherapist relationship that
enables the client and therapist to work together even when the patient or
client experiences strong desires to the contrary; the *transferential/counter-
transferential* relationship as the experience of unconscious wishes and fears
transferred on to or into the therapeutic partnership; the *reparative/devel-
opmentally needed* relationship as intentional provision by the psychotherapist of a corrective, reparative, or replenishing relationship or action where
the original parenting (or previous experience) was deficient, abusive or
overprotective; the *person-to-person* relationship as the real relationship or
core relationship, as opposed to object relationship; and the *transpersonal*
relationship as the timeless facet of the psychotherapeutic relationship,
which is impossible to describe, but refers to the spiritual dimension of the
healing relationship. It is important to remember these are not stages but
states in psychotherapy or psychoanalysis, often subtly 'overlapping', in and
between which a client construes his or her unique experiences (Clarkson,
1990). This relationship framework has been used by myself, my students
and others to form the inspiration or the basis for integration between or

beyond approaches – or simply to develop, question or hone one's own independent approach.

Integration or integrating psychotherapy

Personally, I would not necessarily always call this an approach. I imagine it is possible to be a systemic integrative psychotherapist of the kind that I write about in *Integrative and Eclectic Psychotherapy: A Handbook* (Dryden, 1992) where I describe using the seven-level model as a tool for either technical, experiential, epistemological, clinical or theoretical integration. I think, in a certain sense, it is also quite possible to use these models knowing that they are organizing matrices which have little reality of their own. They are brought into existence by what the practitioner reads and lives into, from and around them.

Frances (1988), for example, points out that Freud was also an integrationist. It may not be truly possible *not* to be an integrationist in certain senses, or to avoid 'integrative' psychotherapy falling prey to new orthodoxies. However, I prefer to designate this kind of activity by the verb *integrating*, acknowledging that any responsible psychotherapist of any 'school' will hopefully incorporate into their own theory, research and practice information from other approaches, their own development and the cultural, scientific and sociological currents around them on a continuing basis.

The recent decade or so has seen great change in the landscape of counselling, counselling psychology, psychotherapy and psychoanalysis. On the one hand, there has been an increased preoccupation with professionalization, accountability, theoretical sophistication and research interests. On the other hand, there has been a growth at least in terms of a willingness to listen and learn from other approaches and other orientations.

According to Norcross and Goldfried (1992), eight interacting, mutually reinforcing factors have fostered the development of integration in the past two decades: proliferation of therapies; inadequacy of single theories; external socio-economic contingencies; ascendancy of short-term, problem-focused treatments; opportunities to observe and experiment with various treatments; paucity of differential effectiveness among therapies; recognition that therapeutic commonalities heavily contribute to outcome variance; and development of a professional network for integration (Norcross and Goldfried, 1992: 7). My own work on the therapeutic relationship, as represented in my book *The Therapeutic Relationship* (1995), is best described by Hauke as follows:

> ... timely and sits very well in the current *zeitgeist*. It is presented primarily, but not solely, as a teaching text – one that can be viewed from, and used from different angles. For instance, from one position it suggests a range of different approaches to psychological and emotional treatment in the psychotherapies; viewed another way, the book suggests how *all* these different approaches may be found in any *one* psychotherapy treatment. Or rather, all are present sometimes

and some are present every time; this is not an eclectic view – the 'best of' – but a truly pluralistic view – the 'inclusive of' approach. (Hauke, 1996: 405)

Integrative psychotherapy

Integrative psychotherapy in general is thus not best seen as a unitary discipline but as a combination of many approaches to integration, eclecticism, juxtaposition or combinations of approaches – for better or worse. It is often distinguished from eclecticism by an avowed aspiration to coherence and a systematic re-combination of technical, strategic, theoretical or philosophical elements. For a dicussion of the subject, the reader is referred to Dryden and Norcross (1990). Norcross and Greencavage define eclecticism in a way which parallels the dictionary meaning:

> 'Choosing what is best from diverse sources, styles, and systems'; 'using techniques and rationales based on more than one orientation to meet the needs of the individual case'; 'the systematic use of a variety of therapeutic interventions in the treatment of a single patient' and 'the pragmatics of selecting a variety of procedures and wider interventions for specific problems'. The common thread is that technical eclecticism is relatively atheoretical, pragmatic and empirical. (Norcross and Greencavage, 1990: 10)

Critical views of eclectic psychotherapy practice emphasize the way it tends to span a gamut from diffuse supermarket models, pandering largely to the clinician's comfort, past experience and current preoccupations and/or rather formulaic cook-book approaches which require practitioners to follow decision trees in terms of diagnosis, intervention and assessment. In practice, especially in the UK, the appellation 'integrative' is favoured above that of 'eclectic'. This may be due to the fact that, in spite of the excellent work of Lazarus (1981), the connotations of the term eclectic tend to be more negative. However, this does not necessarily accurately reflect the state of affairs in 'integrative psychotherapy'.

It should, of course, also be noted that there is not one kind of integrative psychotherapy – there are many. These range, for example, from simplistic juxtapositions of TA and Gestalt, on the one hand, to ultra-sophisticated multimodal packages for specific DSM categories on the other. And, as I have pointed out before, all competent and developing psychotherapists are probably always 'integrating'.

There are primarily two models of integrative psychotherapy training; I have designed and supervised examples of both kinds (Clarkson, 1992). The first one represents the polarity of integration from the beginning of psychotherapy training. The other polarity represents integration after a training in one or more 'pure' forms. Proponents of the first approach maintain that trainees are better able to learn academically and professionally because they develop the required skills of intellectual questioning and tolerance for other approaches at an early stage. Those who believe in the second approach maintain that integrative capacities develop from maturity and experience and will be stronger if based on the solid foundations of a singular approach which emotionally provides a sense of security early on and then later perhaps disillusionment and personal refinement as the limitations are discovered of any one particular approach (Norcross, 1986).

The argument for training in integration later (after a good solid grounding in one approach) usually embraces the notion that a good original training in one psychotherapeutic approach can be the beginning of *stimulating* students or practitioners of psychotherapy to want to know about comparisons and to understand that there is not only one way to think about human beings. It can create a hunger and curiosity for further growth and continuous learning for the rest of their professional lives. It provides them with a solid ground. When people actually have one theory on board, they can be encouraged to go back to the beginning with their increased experience, to see the fundamentals of their chosen approach with new eyes and to go back to original sources. So, integration can become a growing edge for psychotherapists' own developing expertise and competence and prevent them from stagnating in one system and believing that they have 'made it' and that their training has ended. It could give them the impetus to go on growing and developing personally and professionally.

It is desirable that most psychotherapists in the course of training, supervision, personal psychotherapy, through attendance at conferences and workshops and seeing colleagues at work, continue to accumulate valuable resources and revisions which are integrated into their psychotherapeutic work in an ongoing way. In this sense, every learning, developing, questing psychotherapist is probably an integrator. Reading the work of any major theoretician in this field as it unfolds over the period of their productive professional life bears out this observation. Klein's (1984), Ferenczi's (1980a, 1980b), and Rowan's (1988, 1993) collected papers are all clear examples of this integrating process at work, whether acknowledged or not.

We could also question who is doing the integrating

Might it be that no matter how carefully the psychotherapist separates out different schools and, for example, delivers them in measured doses in different sessions, it is the patient who will or will not take it, use it, discard it, ignore it and make it work – sometimes against all the odds. Rowe (personal communication, 1995) tells from her own clinical experience how sometimes clients would tell of the marvellous interventions she had made, the wonderfully enlightening interpretations she had given them, which changed their lives permanently for the better. In fact though, she had not given these pearls – they were self-created or manufactured. Any experienced clinician can add numerous similar examples of their own.

Classicism, fundamentalism even, has a certain purity of form even if it does act as some Procrustean bed upon which to slice or stretch all human phenomena. I believe that the ideas and ideals which have guided some 100 years in psychoanalysis, cognitive-behavioural therapy and humanistic/existential psychotherapy have each their own integrity, soundness and coherence within their respective ideological, epistemological and aesthetic universes of discourse. The problem with sure pure forms is when they acquire some hegemony of power, criteria-setting or reality definition – as if all the others are wrong. This of course, can also be true of 'integrative psychotherapy' or 'eclectic psychotherapy'.

There is some indication, from research that personal and anecdotal evidence supports, that the effectiveness of psychotherapy ultimately may not even depend on the psychotherapist, his or her training, experience or approach, but that it does depend on how the client uses it. My own informal research and that of others has borne out this rather obvious case. Clients most probably, notwithstanding our best or most mistaken assumptions, take, ignore, invent, pretend and create their healing or destructive journey in relationship with a variety of practitioners, approaches and settings.

The myth of the pure form in practice

Increasingly the realities of research, professional and personal experience are rapidly making a one-sided notion of integrating different approaches to psychotherapy redundant. Recent years have seen an enormous movement of cross-fertilization, if not straightforward integration, within and between schools. The very existence of what can conceivably be called 'pure forms' of any of these approaches can be doubted. This seems to me to be the current reality – however confusing or disconcerting it may be for seekers after certainty.

It is rare, and indeed (according to my investigations) unheard of, that any practitioner only and exclusively follows the practice prescriptions of his or her own exclusive and orthodox school and disregards all other information from outside his or her own training body or the particular 'bibles' of his or her own orientation. This is simply impractical. It is probably also dangerous, as if anyone can develop or grow as a psychotherapist or analyst without being influenced by other schools, other approaches and particularly new and unsettling ideas which impinge upon us from all kinds of other directions. I doubt that any 'school' can still formulate such a position. Even if this were possible, anecdotal research amply confirms that whatever the orthodox purist party line prescribes or proscribes, exceptions abound because the patients tell about it. Our profession is also old enough now that many of us also see patients who may have been in therapy or a previous analysis with friends, colleagues and even enemies. This is another way in which we hear not what is supposed to happen in the ideal pure forms, but what actually happens. Freud gossiped about other patients, Anna Freud and Eric Berne took phonecalls from patients during sessions, a most eminent Kleinian teaching analyst gave his patient his own handkerchief to wipe a teary eye and a runny nose, Gestalt therapists even 'interpret the transference', analytically trained group analysts allow patients to meet outside the sessions and so on and so forth. There are always exceptions and reasons for exceptions, and if these can't be found, in practice, they are often made.

Theoretical openness

It has been found (Heine, 1953) that it was not possible, from a description of therapist activity, to determine to which theoretical school psychotherapists belong. What differentiates between them is, in fact, the names and labels clients attach to the 'fundamental causes' of their troubles. Individual psychotherapists or psychoanalysts rarely fit into categories, particularly the more experienced they become. Fiedler (1950), for example, studied the differences between exponents of three different schools of psychotherapy – Freudian, Adlerian and Nondirective. He found that the differences in actual practice between experienced practitioners in different schools were considerably smaller than between beginners and their more senior colleagues in the same school. That is, it appears that the theory followed is much less important than experience of relationship. Fiedler's results are shown diagrammatically in Figure 3.1.

Research (Norcross, 1986; Beutler and Consoli, 1992; and Lambert, 1992) shows that theoretical differences between 'schools or approaches' is far less important in terms of successful outcome of counselling or psychotherapy, than the quality of the relationship between counsellor and client and certain client characteristics, including motivation for change and the willingness to take responsibility for their part in the process.

As I have shown, extensive research has found few, if any, differences in terms of effectiveness among different approaches to psychotherapy (Mahoney et al., 1989; Norcross and Newman, 1992; Lambert, 1992; Glass et al., 1993; Arnkoff et al., 1993). Of course it is also always possible to contest or question research results – and the justifications are infinite. They range from methodological criticisms on the one hand to a treasuring of the essentially ineffable mystery of the therapeutic encounter which intrinsically cannot (and, according to some views (for example, Plaut, 1996: 8), should not) be measured.

There are certainly some leaders in the field who are looking towards the possibilities of integration in terms of the commonalities between different schools of psychotherapy. Storr has prophesied that 'the labels of "Jungian", "Kleinian", "Freudian", will become less and less important as research discloses the common factors which lead to a successful outcome in psychotherapy, which is largely independent of the school to which the psychotherapist belongs' (Storr, 1979: viii).

The editor of the *British Journal of Psychotherapy*, Hinshelwood (1990)

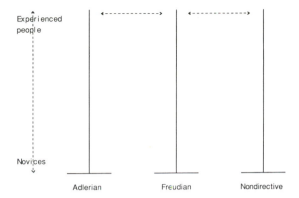

Figure 3.1   *Results of the Fiedler studies (1950), shown diagrammatically*

wrote about my original paper on the multiplicity of co-existing potential therapeutic relationships in any therapeutic encounter (Clarkson, 1990) that the five therapeutic relationship framework exists in all psychotherapies, even though different psychotherapies prioritize different levels. 'This offers a way of circumventing the inherent contradictions and incompatibilities that exist *between* different psychotherapies; instead of incompatibilities we have different priorities and emphasis. And this leaves a way open for the beginnings of a possible integration of psychotherapies' (Hinshelwood, 1990: 119). Gee (1995) displayed a similar willingness to integrate different theoretical and ideological positions in his research on supervision delivered at a recent 'Group for the Advancement of Therapy Supervision' Conference. He also emphasized that what unifies and makes integration possible is the centrality of the relationship in all approaches to psychotherapy and psychotherapy supervision. Jung, too, spoke of the importance of theory in this way: 'Learn your theories as well as you can, but put them aside when you touch the miracle of the living soul. Not theories but your own creative individuality alone must decide' (Jung, 1928: 361). I sincerely hope that there will continue to be a rich representation of both specialist and integrative approaches in the field, so that this endeavour of alleviating human distress and increasing human happiness can benefit from the uniqueness of classical exclusivity and purity, as well as from the complexity of synthesis or integration – or plurality. I also hope that, as a research orientation in psychotherapists emerges from the background of preconceived theories, psychotherapists may become indeed independent.

I do not think an approach to psychotherapy which utilizes the five different kinds of therapeutic relationship is particularly suited to certain clients or problems more than to others, because it stretches across that question to incorporate multiple narratives about the therapeutic endeavour. (Of course different clients at different times for different purposes may respond differentially to the different kinds of therapeutic relationship.) This way of thinking, practising and being can encompass perhaps all that is now known in psychotherapy and much that it yet to be discovered.

We will have to come to terms, as we stagger into the postmodern era, with the hard-to-avoid evidence that there are many different realities, and different ways of experiencing them, and that people seem to want to keep exploring them, and that there is only a limited amount any society can do to insure that its official reality is installed in the minds of most of its citizens most of the time. (Anderson, 1990: 152)

Unhelpful approaches

The only approaches I find particularly unhelpful, ineffective, misleading or dangerous are those where the practitioners err in terms of a carelessness on the one hand or a thoroughgoing fundamentalism on the other. As someone else (source unknown) said: 'There is nothing more dangerous than an idea – particularly one idea.' The importance and vitality of rigorously and frequently questioning all ideas and theories, including one's own, seem vital and productive to me.

Of course, I think that it is dangerous when an approach degenerates into theoretical or technical gibberish. It is not that I (or many others) actually believe that theory has much effect on the actual practice of psychotherapy – that is, what psychotherapists actually do. It seems very likely that much of theory is used post facto to explain, or 'talk about', the work that *had* been done. Again, from my own experience of participating in and leading masterclasses in psychotherapy and supervision, the *actions* of psychotherapists from vaunted different theoretical orientations appear to be very similar, but the *stories* (theories) they tell about their work are very different, and naturally correspond with their particular view of the world and the person of each one. Future research projects could be based around the rigorous analysis of some videotapes of master therapists at work with a discourse analysis of their subsequent reflections on such work. In my opinion, conflicts between universes of discourse are artifacts of a reductionist and simplistic reluctance to accept the co-existence of multiple levels of discourse and truth values. (For further discussion of these ideas, see Clarkson, 1993). But for the purposes of this chapter, at this stage in my life, I believe that the *mental discipline* of thinking about and being reflexive about all the assumptions and practices of this profession enhances the likelihood of responsible, ethical and effective psychotherapy. So it may not be so important *what* one thinks but *that* one thinks. It is perhaps even more important to subject all our theoretical and philosophical assumptions to continuing critical analysis and to ongoing research enquiry – not separately in the academy, but at the very heart of activity which characterizes as well as nourishes the consulting room.

I have shown the possibility of this approach by developing trainings and educational designs which centralize not an unquestioning adherence to any one theory, or even to one kind of integrative psychotherapy theory, but the ongoing clinical discipline of rigorous research, privileging what can be called 'learning by enquiry'.

This new project (dieratao) would draw, of the necessity of the time and my own situatedness, from a *postmodern qualitative research methodology, context and content which was grounded in a moral universe* where issues of values, ethics and the cultural/ecological situatedness of everyone constantly and inevitably accompany the investigation, instead of maintaining a pretence of objectivity, illusion of neutrality – or even authority. (Clarkson, in press)

Advice to potential clients seeking psychotherapy[1]

- Psychotherapy can be a good and effective way to help people reach their goals or ease their suffering, but it is not the only way.
- There are many alternatives to psychotherapy which may need to be explored first or at the same time, such as physical, medical, dietary, economic or social conditions.
- Psychotherapy comes in many different forms. There is short-term or brief psychotherapy as well as long-term psychotherapy and psychoanalysis. There is also couples therapy, family therapy, child therapy, and special therapy services designed for particular problems such as gambling, drug addiction, eating disorders, and so on.
- Research does not show that any one form of therapy is better than another, with two exceptions: drug therapy for acute psychosis, and cognitive behaviour therapy for some specific kinds of phobias (irrational fears) and depression-inducing obsessive thoughts.
- What appears most widely accepted on all sides is that the *quality of the relationship between client and psychotherapist is the most important factor in determining the success of psychotherapy, psychological counselling or psychoanalysis.*
- Notwithstanding all the libraries of books written about different theories and different approaches, it seems as if *theoretical orientation is not very important* in the effectiveness of psychotherapy. So the kind of 'approach' or 'school' should not necessarily determine your choice of practitioner.
- The relationship and your motivation for change are more important.
- Research has shown that very experienced clinicians in different approaches resemble each other more than beginners and inexperienced people resemble each other within any one approach. This means that the more experienced professionals in this field become, the more what they actually do in the consulting room becomes similar to each other rather than different.
- Thorough investigation reveals that the relationship is differently emphasized or given different terminology in the different approaches or schools. It appears to be always present in any therapeutic encounter.

1. This extract from P. Clarkson, *A Traveller's Companion: Everything You Wanted to Know About Therapy* ... (1995), London: PHYSIS, is presented in this format for ease of client access.

- The ancient physicians used to say: 'I administer the medicine, but it is Nature [or God or Physis] which cures' (see Clarkson, 1996b). Many modern doctors of the body or the soul would agree with them.
- Be cautious of any psychotherapist, analyst, psychologist or counsellor who will not explain the theoretical basis of his or her work. All theories carry values about what is good, normal, healthy, and so on. These *values* will affect the way you are treated. It is vital to get clarification on such issues before getting involved in long-term work. This is particularly important for anyone belonging to any minority or disadvantaged group in a culture.
- Group psychotherapy can be used instead of, or in addition to, individual therapy. It is a very powerful and effective form of psychotherapy and has many safeguards against abuse. This is partly because there are a number of other people in the group forming a laboratory of life where people can learn, experiment with and benefit from the experiences of the other group members in addition to the expertise of the group leader.
- Many people report benefit from group therapy. It is also usually cheaper than individual therapy. It may even be more effective, but this is not yet proven. Always ensure that your psychotherapist is appropriately qualified, supervised and open to questions of his or her conduct in the group.
- Shop around for a psychotherapist. Interview two or three and see how you feel about working with them. Do they make you feel too comfortable? Too cared for? Challenged enough? Take time to choose. Once you do, stick with it a while.
- It may be difficult to decide whether very positive or very negative feelings about your psychotherapist are beneficial or destructive. You must be able to discuss these with your psychotherapist. If such feelings persist, seek a second opinion from an independent psychologist, telling your psychotherapist that you will be doing so.
- Psychotherapists usually explain that they take their client work for supervision – and so they should. Why should clients not be able to take their part of the therapy for supervision or consultation?

The future

I don't know what the field will look like in 50 years' time. I hope that we will pay attention to our own experience as well as to the research of others if psychotherapy training is at all to be reflective of the current state of the art (science?) and to equip psychotherapists and their supervisors to deal effectively and authentically with the postmodern challenges facing these professions. Yet most, if not all, 'trainings' in psychotherapy are predicated on learning one of these theories and applying it to practice, or an 'integration' of theoretical approaches. Whether the 'integration' or the 'incorporation of the pure approach' has been successful usually determines whether the practitioner or supervisor will become 'accredited' or 'recognized'. This leaves vast tracts of moral responsibility and philosophical enquiry unexamined.

As Farrell (1979) pointed out, this also avoids serious consideration of the uncomfortable possibility that the participants or 'trainees' or workshop participants are considered to be 'cured' or 'trained' or 'analysed' or 'qualified' by a single, underlying criterion – they have adopted the WOT ('way of talking') of the leaders, governing bodies, examination boards and others of perceived status or power.

I hope that in 50 years' time the need for psychotherapy will have disappeared and that the healing capacity of our ordinary human relationships of friendship, colleagueship, community will have been restored to the extent that it is no longer necessary to pay a stranger to provide the relationship within which people can heal, support or develop themselves (see Smail, 1987). It may also be time to problematize *theory* itself, and the way it has led not only to 'schools' but also to 'schoolism'.

> The major problem with the notion of 'school' is its relative inflexibility in response to new ideas in psychotherapy. Schools have responded to varying degrees to psychotherapy innovation, but the value of schools has been to preserve good ideas. At this point in psychotherapy's history, these good ideas within schools have been preserved well enough. (Beitman, 1994: 210)

So, I also hope that we will be in a period 'After Schoolism' (Clarkson, 1996d) where 'schools' or 'orientations' or 'approaches' will be less important than relationship and a common commitment to the alleviation of suffering and the development of human potential will have replaced factionalism, rivalry and one-up one-down politics. Elsewhere I have explored the attendant destructiveness to creativity and innovation of such tendencies. I hope to see a time in which true intellectual and spiritual generosity extend beyond this need – particularly to the idiosyncratic, the unusual, the different, the non-conformist – since that is probably where our future lies. As the chaos and complexity researchers from the new sciences put it: creativity happens at far-from-equilibrium conditions (Gruber, 1988). Or in Rilke's words:

> Be patient toward all that is unsolved in your heart and to try to love the *questions themselves* like locked rooms and like books that are written in a very foreign tongue. Do not now seek the answers, which cannot be given you because you would not be able to live them. And the point is, to live everything. *Live* the questions now. Perhaps you will then gradually, without noticing it, live along some distant day into the answer. (Rilke, 1993: 35)

References

Anderson, W.T. (1990) *Reality Is Not What It Used To Be*. San Francisco: Harper & Row.

Arnkoff, D.B., Victor, B.J. and Glass, C.G. (1993) Empirical research on factors in psychotherapeutic change. In G. Stricker and J.R. Gold (eds), *Comprehensive Handbook of Psychotherapy Integration* (pp. 27–42). New York: Plenum.

Barkham, M. (1995) Editorial: why psychotherapy outcomes are important now. *Changes*, 13 (3), 161–3.

Beitman, B.D. (1994) Stop exploring! Start defining the principles of a psychotherapy integration: Call for a consensus conference. *Journal of Psychotherapy Integration*, 4 (3), 203–28.

Bergin, A.E. and Lambert, M.J. (1978) The evaluation of therapeutic outcomes. In S.L. Garfield and A.E.Bergin (eds), *Handbook of Psychotherapy and Behavior Change* (2nd edn) (pp. 139–89). New York: Wiley.

Beutler, L.E. and Consoli, A.J. (1992) Systemic eclectic psychotherapy. In J.C. Norcross and M.R. Goldfried (eds), *Handbook of Psychotherapy Integration* (pp. 264–99). New York: Basic Books.

Clarkson, P. (1989) Metanoia: a process of transformation. *Transactional Analysis Journal*, 19 (4), 224–34.

Clarkson, P. (1990) A multiplicity of psychotherapeutic relationships. *British Journal of Psychotherapy*, 7 (2), 148–63.

Clarkson, P. (1992) Systemic integrative psychotherapy training. In W. Dryden (ed.), *Integrative and Eclectic Therapy* (pp. 269–95). Buckingham: Open University Press.

Clarkson, P. (1993) *On Psychotherapy*. London: Whurr. ('The Seven Level Model' was first delivered as an Invitational Paper at University of Pretoria, November 1975.)

Clarkson, P. (1995) *The Therapeutic Relationship*. London: Whurr.

Clarkson, P. (1996a) The eclectic and integrative paradigm: between the scylla of confluence and the charybdis of confusion. In R. Woolfe and W. Dryden (eds), *Handbook of Counselling Psychology* (pp. 258–83). London: Sage.

Clarkson, P. (1996b) The archetype of physis: the soul of nature – our nature. *Harvest: Journal for Jungian Studies*, 42 (1), 70–93.

Clarkson, P. (1996c) Researching the 'therapeutic relationship' in psychoanalysis, counselling psychology and psychotherapy. *Counselling Psychology Quarterly*, 9 (2), 143–62.

Clarkson, P. (1996d) *After Schoolism*. Workshop given at 1st Congress of the World Council for Psychotherapy, Vienna, 2 July 1996.

Clarkson, P. (in press) Dieratao – learning by inquiry – concerning the education of psychologists, psychotherapists, supervisors and organisational consultants. In P. Clarkson (ed.), *Counselling Psychology: Integration of Theory, Research and Supervised Practice*. London: Routledge.

Cottone, R.R. (1988) Epistemological and ontological issues in counselling: implications of social systems theory. *Counselling Psychology Quarterly*, 1 (4), 357–65.

Dryden, W. (ed.) (1992) *Integrative and Eclectic Therapy: A Handbook*. Buckingham: Open University Press.

Dryden, W. and Norcross, J.C. (eds) (1990) *Eclecticism and Integration in Counselling and Psychotherapy*. Loughton: Gale Centre.

Elkin, I. (1995) The NIMH treatment of depression collaborative research program: major results and clinical implications. *Changes*, 13 (3), 178–85.

Erickson, M.H. (1967) *Advanced Techniques of Hypnosis and Therapy*. New York: Grune & Stratton.

Farrell, B.A. (1979) Work in small groups: some philosophical considerations. In B. Babington Smith and B.A. Farrell (eds), *Training in Small Groups: A Study of Five Groups* (pp. 103–15). Oxford: Pergamon.

Ferenczi, S. (1980a) *First Contributions to Psycho-analysis* (E. Jones, trans.). London: Maresfield Reprints.

Ferenczi, S. (1980b) *Final Contributions to the Problems and Methods of Psycho-analysis* (E. Mosbacher, trans.). London: Maresfield Reprints.

Fiedler, F.E. (1950) A comparison of therapeutic relationships in psychoanalytic nondirective and Adlerian therapy. *Journal of Consulting Psychology*, 14, 436–45.

Frances, A. (1988) *Sigmund Freud: The First Integrative Therapist*. Invited address to the fourth annual convention of the Society for the Exploration of Psychotherapy Integration, Boston, MA, May 1988.

Frank, J.D. (1979) The present status of outcome studies. *Journal of Consulting and Clinical Psychology*, 47, 310–16.

Garfield, S.L. and Bergin, A.E. (eds) (1986) *Handbook of Psychotherapy and Behavior Change* (3rd edn). New York: Wiley.

Gee, H. (1995) Supervision: relating and defining (the essence of supervision). Talk delivered at Spring Conference and Special General Meeting of Group for the Advancement of Therapy Supervision, London, 20 May 1995.

Glass, C.G., Victor, B.J. and Arnkoff, D.B. (1993) Empirical research on integrative and eclectic psychotherapies. In G. Stricker and J.R. Gold (eds), *Comprehensive Handbook of Psychotherapy Integration* (pp. 9–26). New York: Plenum.

Gleick, J. (1988) *Chaos: Making a New Science*. London: Heinemann.

Goldfried, M.R. (1980) Toward the delineation of the therapeutic change principle. *American Psychologist*, 35, 991–9.

Goulding, M.M. and Goulding, R.L. (1979) *Changing Lives Through Redecision Therapy*. New York: Grove Press.

Gruber, H. (1988) Inching our way up Mount Olympus: the evolving systems approach to creative thinking. In R.J. Sternberg (ed.), *The Nature of Creativity*. Cambridge: Cambridge University Press.

Hauke, C. (1996) Book review of *The Therapeutic Relationship* by Petruska Clarkson. *British Journal of Psychotherapy*, 12 (3), 405–7.

Heine, R.W. (1953) A comparison of patients' reports on psychotherapeutic experience with psychoanalytic, nondirective and Adlerian therapists. *American Journal of Psychotherapy*, 7, 16–23.

Hillman, J. and Ventura, M. (1992) *We've Had a Hundred Years of Psychotherapy and the World's Getting Worse*. San Francisco: HarperCollins.

Hinshelwood, R.D. (1990) Editorial. *British Journal of Psychotherapy*, 7 (2), 119–20.

Howe, D. (1993) *On Being a Client*. London: Sage.

Hynan, M.T. (1981) On the advantages of assuming that the techniques of psychotherapy are ineffective. *Psychotherapy: Theory, Research and Practice*, 18, 11–13.

Jung, C.G. (1928) Analytical psychology and education. In *Contributions to Analytical Psychology* (H.G. Baynes and F.C. Baynes, trans.) (pp. 313–82). London: Trench Trubner.

Kahn, M.D. (1991) *Between the Therapist and the Client: The New Relationship*. New York: W.H. Freeman.

Klein, M. (1984) *Envy and Gratitude and Other Works 1946–1963*. London: Hogarth Press and the Institute of Psycho-analysis.

Lambert, M.J. (1992) Psychotherapy outcome research: implications for integrative and eclectic therapists. In J.C. Norcross and M.R. Goldfried (eds), *Handbook of Psychotherapy Integration* (pp. 94–129). New York: Basic Books.

Lazarus, A.A. (1981) *The Practice of Multimodal Therapy*. New York: McGraw-Hill.

Lipsey, M.W. and Wilson, D.B. (1993) The efficacy of psychological, educational and behavioral treatment. *American Psychologist*, December, 1181–1209.

Luborsky, L., Crits-Christoph, R., Alexander, L., Margolis, M. and Cohen, M. (1983) Two helping alliance methods of predicting outcomes of psychotherapy. *Journal of Nervous and Mental Disease*, 171, 480–91.

Mahoney, M.J., Norcross, J.C., Prochaska, J.O. and Missar, C.D. (1989) Psychological development and optimal psychotherapy: converging perspectives among clinical psychologists. *Journal of Integrative and Eclectic Psychotherapy*, 8, 251–63.

May, R. (1969) *Love and Will*. London: Collins.

Moiso, C. (1985) Ego states and transference. *Transactional Analysis Journal*, 15 (3), 194–201.

Norcross, J.C. (ed.) (1986) *Handbook of Eclectic Psychotherapy*. New York: Brunner/Mazel.

Norcross, J.C. and Goldfried, M.R. (1992) *Handbook of Psychotherapy Integration*. New York: Basic Books.

Norcross, J.C. and Greencavage, L.M. (1990) Eclecticism and integration in counselling and psychotherapy: major themes and obstacles. In W. Dryden and J.C. Norcross (eds), *Eclecticism and Integration in Counselling and Psychotherapy* (pp. 1–33). Loughton: Gale Centre.

Norcross, J.C. and Newman, C.F. (1992) Psychotherapy integration: setting the context. In J.C.

Norcross and M.R. Goldfried (eds), *Handbook of Psychotherapy Integration* (pp. 3–45). New York: Basic Books.

O'Malley, S.S., Suh, C.S. and Strupp, H.H. (1983) The Vanderbilt psychotherapy process scale: a report on the scale development and a process outcome study. *Journal of Consulting and Clinical Psychology*, 51, 581–6.

Plaut, F. (1996) Why people still want analysis. *Harvest*, 42 (1), 7–26.

Polster, E. and Polster, M. (1973) *Gestalt Therapy Integrated: Contours of Theory and Practice*. New York: Random House.

Rilke, R.M. (1993) *Letters to a Young Poet* (M.D. Herter Norton, trans.; Rev. edn.). New York: W.W. Norton.

Rowan, J. (1988) *Ordinary Ecstasy: Humanistic Psychology in Action*. London: Routledge.

Rowan, J. (1993) *The Transpersonal: Psychotherapy and Counselling*. London: Routledge.

Russell, R. (1995) What works in psychotherapy when it does work? *Changes*, 13 (3), 213–18.

Seligman, M.E.P. (1995) The effectiveness of psychotherapy. *American Psychologist*, 50 (12), 965–74.

Smail, D. (1987) *Taking Care: An Alternative to Therapy*. London: J.M. Dent.

Smith, M.L. and Glass, G.V. (1977) Meta-analysis of psychotherapy outcome studies. *American Psychologist*, 32, 752–60.

Storr, A. (1979) *The Art of Psychotherapy*. London: Heinemann.

Strupp, H.H. (1979) Specific versus non-specific factors in psychotherapy. *Archives of General Psychiatry*, 36, 1125–36.

4

Rational Emotive Behavior Therapy

Albert R. Ellis

What were the factors leading you to choose, found, or adapt the approach, Rational Emotive Behavior Therapy (REBT), which you currently practise?

I found my first approach to therapy, eclectic active-directive therapy, fairly effective in the short run but rarely leading to deep and intensive personality change. So I was trained in psychoanalysis, practiced it from 1947 to 1953, and found that it deeply and intensively went into every irrelevancy under the sun but missed all the philosophical relevancies that led disturbed people to think, feel, and act self-defeatingly. I saw that it was less effective and more wasteful than most other therapies and, especially when it was classical, often did more harm than good.

I first found that my clients couldn't afford two or more sessions a week for several years, and I therefore was often forced to practice psychoanalytic-oriented psychotherapy instead of classical analysis. I saw them face to face (instead of their lying on a sofa) on a once-a-week or once-every-other-week basis. To my surprise, they often improved more quickly and more intensively than when I used classical analysis.

Thus, I once saw two 28-year-old sisters who were identical twins, Sara for classical analysis and Sandy (who had less money and couldn't afford analysis four times a week) on a once-a-week basis for psychoanalytic psychotherapy. Both suffered from extreme social anxiety and both went with 'safe' males who were below their intellectual level and bored them – because they were afraid to seek out, and likely get rejected by, 'unsafe' and more exciting partners.

Sara and Sandy had similar family backgrounds, both were equally intelligent, were competent and well-liked legal secretaries, and had a good relationship with me. I showed them that they were overly attached to their adoring father and afraid to risk going with an exciting man who might discover their weakness and reject them. They agreed with these analytic interpretations but Sandy used her therapeutic insights to help herself take more social risks and Sara did not. After a year of therapy, Sandy had an exciting lover and stayed with him even when he was critical of her and was far from adoring. Sara, however, after three years of classical analysis followed her same old pattern of refusing to let herself get close to any man, especially when he was in the least critical and unadoring. Moreover, she became overattached to me and wanted to go on – safely – in therapy forever. But Sandy felt so improved that she quit therapy 15 months after she had started, and afterwards lived a much more social and loving life than Sara.

I reluctantly saw that my psychoanalytically-oriented therapy with Sandy had been much more effective than my classical analytic therapy with her sister. Indeed, classical analysis, I found was generally less effective – and sometimes iatrogenic.

Spurred by my increasing success with several other clients with whom I used analytically-oriented therapy and by my poorer results with classical analysis, I experimented with more behavioral methods, especially activity homework assignments. I soon found that the less analytic and more actively behavioral I was, the better results I got with most of my clients. So in 1953 I stopped doing psychoanalysis, called myself a psychotherapist again instead of an analyst, and began developing Rational Therapy (RT) (Ellis, 1957, 1962; Ellis and Harper, 1961, 1975).

To formulate RT, I went back to philosophy, which had been my main hobby from the age of 16 onward, and took from a number of ancient and modern philosophers the crucial idea that people rarely *get* upset by their early and later environment but that they largely, both consciously and unconsciously, *make* themselves neurotic. They do this mainly by taking some of their strong desires for success, approval, and comfort – which are biologically based and also culturally learned – and grandiosely raising them to absolutistic shoulds, musts, and demands, which they then often deny having and refuse to change. When they construct and hang on to their irrational imperatives, they create a number of self-defeating and socially sabotaging thoughts, feelings, and behaviors, which interact and coalesce with each other. Most people, fortunately, also have the innate constructivist ability to work hard and persistently at changing their neurotic demands. In order to enable them to do so, Rational Emotive Behavior Therapy (REBT) makes them aware of and shows them how to effectively use a large number of cognitive, emotive, and behavioral methods. It has several distinct theories of human disturbances, which overlap with those of the other cognitive-behavior therapies that followed it in the 1960s, after I founded it in January 1955. Its methods are especially cognitive and philosophical, but it focuses on the individual problems and situations of each unique client and therefore uses an unusual number of multimodal and eclectic techniques designed to fit specific individuals (Ellis, 1962, 1985, 1988, 1994, 1995a, 1995b; Ellis and Dryden, 1997).

Even when I called REBT Rational Therapy (RT) in the 1950s, I vigorously and emotively, as well as cognitively and didactically, showed my clients how to discover and to forcefully dispute their irrational, self-defeating beliefs and to change them to more sensible and more useful philosophies. I also stressed and helped them get in touch with their disturbed *feelings* (e.g., severe anxiety, depression, and rage) and to change them, when they encountered losses and misfortunes, to healthy negative feelings (such as strong feelings of sorrow, grief, and frustration). So RT was always an emotional as well as a cognitive therapy. But partly because it was called rational therapy and was heavily philosophical, it was often wrongly criticized for ignoring and playing down feelings. To try to forestall some of this misleading impression of RT, I conferred with Robert A. Harper, who in 1956 was the first therapist to practice RT with me, and we devised the new name of rational-emotive therapy (RET), which it was known by, and became famous as, from 1961 to 1993.

I also, in the 1960s, added a number of highly emotional, evocative, and dramatic techniques to RET, some of which I adopted or adapted from experiential therapy and from the encounter therapy movement and several of which – like my famous shame attacking exercises – I invented. So RET became highly emotive, as well as intensely cognitive. In this respect, it went far beyond the other cognitive-behavior therapies, such as those of Aaron Beck (1976), Donald Meichenbaum (1977), and Richard Lazarus (Lazarus and Folkman, 1984). Still, however, a number of critics wrongly saw it as being rigidly 'rational' (Guidano, 1991; Mahoney, 1991). They ignored the fact that it has always been more constructivist than the great majority of other therapies (Ellis, 1990, 1994). Some of RET's critics also still identified me as a logical positivist, when I gave up that philosophy in 1976 and am now somewhat allied to postmodernism, though still strongly in the scientific camp (Ellis, 1994, 1995a, 1995b).

To make matters even more confused, a number of commentators tended to forget RET's powerful behavioral aspects – especially its use of *in vivo* desensitization and exposure (Ellis, 1962). So in the 1980s Raymond Corsini began urging me to change its name to Rational Emotive Behavior Therapy (REBT). I knew that Ray was correct but I at first was loath to go along with him because RET was widely known – in fact, famous – under that name and was prominently mentioned in hundreds of articles and books, as well as in scores of scientific studies. I finally agreed with Ray in 1993, and now its official name is, and will most probably remain, REBT (Ellis, 1993, 1995c).

Although Arnold Lazarus (1989) invented the name Multimodal Therapy (MMT) in the 1970s, RET was clearly promoting a multiplicity of cognitive, emotive, and behavioral techniques in the 1960s and began to be pioneeringly multimodal in its individual and group therapy, in its rational encounter marathons, in its workshops for the profession and the public, in its rational emotive education for children, in its applications to organizational and business problems and in its other ventures (Bernard and Joyce, 1984; Ellis, 1960, 1963, 1969, 1972a, 1973, 1985, 1988, 1994; Ellis and Abrahms, 1978; Ellis and Dryden, 1987; Knaus, 1974; Vernon, 1989).

Instead of rigorously (and sometimes rigidly) covering Lazarus' (1989) BASIC I.D. modalities (Behavior, Affect, Sensation, Imagery, Cognition, Interpersonal Relations, and Drugs and Biology), REBT always uses a number of cognitive, emotive, and behavioral methods, explores and helps enhance interpersonal relationships, does practical problem-solving and skill training, and investigates biological tendencies toward clients' disturbances and the possible use of psychotropic medication. With most clients, it employs all the main aspects of Lazarus' Multimodal Therapy, but not *equally*. It especially emphasizes cognition more than Lazarus and his followers do – including imagery, which is a form of cognition – and it tries to teach most clients how to make a profound philosophical change, which Multimodal Therapy often plays down or ignores. In many respects, then, REBT is similar to Multimodal Therapy, but it includes humanistic, existential, and deep philosophical methods that most multimodal therapists tend to omit. One could say that REBT closely resembles MMT but adds to it major anti-musturbatory existential-humanistic techniques. It particularly emphasizes effective psychotherapy *plus* self-actualization and social cooperation, which MMT may or may not encompass (Ellis, 1991, 1994).

Arnold Lazarus would probably disagree with what I have just said and hold that REBT is *too* cognitive and that it doesn't address *all* the modalities in disturbance. He would be correct in that REBT does not *insist* that all these modalities be implosively (and long-windedly) assessed and dealt with, but mainly deals with them when they are quite relevant to the individual client's problems. It often, for example, uses imagery methods – and very often uses its particular techniques of rational emotive imagery (Ellis, 1993; Maultsby, 1971). But REBT practitioners would hardly *always* include imagery techniques. It usually explores biological and drug potentialities, especially in the case of individuals with severe personality disorders. But not necessarily with all clients who are afraid of driving on thruways or anxious about public speaking. All told, REBT practitioners tend to use as many as 20 cognitive, 20 emotive, and 20 behavioral methods but, like most multimodal therapists, they use them selectively, depending on what kind of disturbances each individual client has. They are generally multimodal – much more than Arnold Lazarus usually acknowledges – but rarely would include *all* the diagnostic and therapeutic modalities that some of Lazarus' followers sometimes compulsively follow. They can therefore often get to some clients' *core* philosophic, emotional, and behavioral disturbances quicker – and, I wager, more thoroughly – than many multimodal therapists do. But, once again, of all the scores of major therapies that now exist, REBT overlaps most with the other general cognitive-behavior therapies, especially with Multimodal Therapy.

REBT is not only multimodal in its techniques, but also largely endorses Lazarus' (1989) technical eclecticism. When clients have a particular kind of problem – such as panic about riding in elevators or constant fighting with their mate – and when they come to therapy only to overcome that problem and not to become generally less disturbable, its practitioners may employ one or a few specialized techniques instead of the more comprehensive use of REBT. And when clients will only use 'unscientific' or 'irrational' methods – such as pollyannaish or devoutly religious ones – it may unideally use them. Whatever works may be seen as 'rational'!

Moreover, where Multimodal Therapy uses social learning theory – which includes some good psychological ideas – REBT largely goes along with this theory but adds to it a number of specific therapeutic hypotheses and ties its practices to these assumptions. For example:

1 Emotional disturbances include dysfunctional thoughts, feelings, and actions, and have cognitive, emotive, and behavioral aspects, all of which importantly interact. Therefore, changing these disturbances usually requires employing a number of thinking, feeling, and action techniques.

2 All people are both biologically predisposed and also are often socially influenced to be neurotic or self-defeating. They therefore had better be active-directively and forcefully taught how to make themselves less disturbed. Passive methods of therapy won't usually work very well.

3 Almost all people – and therapists! – assume that unfortunate Activating Events or Adversities (As) directly cause them to have disturbed feelings and behaviors (Consequences or Cs), when actually their strong Beliefs (Bs) *about* these As importantly contribute to their disruptive Cs.

4 When people strongly hold Beliefs (Bs) about Adversities (As), that lead to their neurotic Consequences (Cs), their Bs are usually irrational – meaning, unrealistic, illogical, and self-sabotaging. They may have many irrational Beliefs (iBs) but their core iBs are usually absolutistic shoulds, oughts, musts, and commands on themselves, on others, and on world conditions.

5 People may learn their self-defeating musts from their family and their culture but they frequently take their desires and preferences – which are largely socially learned – and *construct* them into grandiose demands, and thereby neuroticize themselves. They have powerful innate tendencies to musturbate.

6 Clients are largely unconscious or unaware of how they make themselves neurotic, but their underlying dysfunctional thoughts, feelings, and actions are rarely deeply hidden or repressed but can fairly easily be brought to awareness by a competent therapist, who can show clients how to understand and change them.

7 People who behave neurotically are often strongly habituated to think, feel, and act self-defeatingly and usually have to work hard and persistently to change and stay healthy. Therefore, they had better be encouraged and shown how to use a number of forceful and dramatic cognitive, emotive, and behavioral methods to help themselves change (Ellis, 1976, 1985, 1988, 1994, 1995a, 1995b).

These and several other REBT theories are in themselves multimodal, in that they cover several different aspects of psychotherapy. They also include assumptions that obviously encourage REBT practitioners to use a number of multifaceted techniques.

Do you consider REBT to be one among many others and equally valid, or more effective, elegant or more comprehensive?

Naturally, I consider it to be a special kind of therapy. My firm – though hardly dogmatic – belief is that its theory of disturbance and change is more valid and its techniques are more effective than any of the other psychotherapies. It is also more elegant and more comprehensive – that is, deeper and more intensive – than the other popular therapies in that its main purpose is not only to help people make themselves significantly less disturbed but, after therapy has ended, distinctly less disturb*able*. To this end, it encourages them to make deep emotional and behavioral changes but especially to make a profound philosophical change (Ellis, 1979b, 1985, 1988, 1994, 1995a). It is one of the rare therapies that, as I pointed out in 1972, tries to help people *get* better and not, as most therapies mainly try to do, help them *feel* better. Yes, feel better during their therapy sessions, and generally for a short period of time after therapy ends (Ellis, 1962, 1972b, 1994, 1995a).

On the contrary, REBT aims to help people, during therapy *and* long after it has ended, to be much less *demanding* and much more *preferring*. When clients *feel* better in therapy they usually retain their arrogant demands for success, approval, and comfort and convince themselves that these will somehow be achieved. When they use REBT to *get* better, they train themselves to be distinctly less upsettable *whether or not* they achieve their important goals. Quite a difference!

Again, REBT shows people how to live and in some ways enjoy themselves even when beset with great troubles, problems, handicaps, and adversities. How? By acknowledging their main absolutistic *musts* and demands – 'I *must* perform well and be lovable!', 'Other people *have to* treat me kindly and fairly' and 'My life conditions always *must* be comfortable and enjoyable!' – and changing these dogmatic *demands* into realistic and flexible *preferences*.

Besides any subjective preference for Rational Emotive Behavior Therapy, is there any objective (research or other) evidence or rationale which you consider compelling in its favour?

Yes, a large amount of clinical evidence favoring it exists. However, this is not to be taken too seriously, because it largely consists of successful case histories, which, like most case histories, may possibly be fictitious or exaggerated. Much more convincing are the hundreds of controlled studies that have been published that tend to substantiate its main theories. These studies show first, that people who persistently hold irrational or self-defeating beliefs are more disturbed than those who hold them less often and less forcefully. This favors one of the main REBT hypotheses (Baisden, 1980; DiGiuseppe et al., 1979; Ellis, 1979a; Hollon and Beck, 1994; Woods,

1992). Secondly, several hundred additional controlled studies have reported that when REBT and similar cognitive-behavior therapies (such as those of Aaron Beck, David Barlow, and Donald Meichenbaum) show clients how to become aware of and change their dysfunctional to functional beliefs, their neurotic symptoms significantly improve (Haaga and Davison, 1989; Hajzler and Bernard, 1991; Hollon and Beck, 1994; Lyons and Woods, 1991; McGovern and Silverman, 1984; Silverman et al., 1992; Smith and Glass, 1977). Thirdly, scores of neurological and biochemical studies show, as REBT hypothesizes, that many – perhaps most – people have strong biological tendencies to become disturbed and to seriously upset themselves when unfortunate conditions occur in their lives; and that a combination of REBT and other cognitive-behavior therapies, together with appropriate psychotropic medications, is most effective in helping them to be less disturbed (Berridge and Robinson, 1995; Cloninger et al., 1993; Greist, 1993; Hauser, 1992; Kramer, 1993; Linehan, 1993; Meehl, 1962; Olevitch, 1995; Steketee, 1993; Stone, 1990).

Do you think that REBT is particularly suited to certain clients or client problems than to others?

Yes, as is also true with most therapies, people using REBT do better when they are YAVIS-type individuals – Young, Active, Verbal, Intelligent, and Successful. But REBT has also been shown to work well with a large variety of clients, including children, adolescents, older people, less educated individuals, phobics, panicked individuals, depressives, and severe personality disordered and psychotic individuals. It is especially effective with people who will forego magical and pollyannaish attempts to solve their emotional problems and will work hard to implement the cognitive, emotive, and behavioral techniques that REBT practitioners teach. REBT and cognitive-behavioral therapy have also been found very helpful when presented in self-help materials, such as books and audio and video cassettes (Dryden, 1995; Ellis, 1994; Yankura and Dryden, 1994).

Which criticisms of your approach by other therapists do you believe have some validity?

Several criticisms: (1) It has to be modified and simplified with clients who have limited intelligence and education. (2) It had better be modified, and often supplemented, with psychotropic medication for clients with severe personality disorders and with psychotic states. (3) It is less effective than usual with clients who have severe low frustration tolerance and who refuse to work at changing themselves. (4) It sometimes doesn't work too well with clients who have been babied for a long time by their previous therapists and who now insist that their REBT practitioner baby them as well.

What about the criticism of REBT, by psychoanalysts, existential and experiential therapists, that it encourages people to make superficial changes and to suppress their real, deep feelings and conflicts? It would take me many pages to answer these charges adequately, and I have already included much of this material in Chapter 14 of the revised and updated edition of *Reason and Emotion in Psychotherapy* (Ellis, 1994). Let me briefly answer them here.

First, REBT includes many emotive-evocative methods (such as rational emotive imagery, shame-attacking and secret-revealing exercises) which focus on clients' intense, deep, and often suppressed feelings, and bring them out. It also defines many negative feelings – such as intense grief over loss of a loved one and fear of drunken drivers – as healthy feelings, distinguishes them from emotional disturbances, and encourages people to feel and express them. It often encourages rape and post-traumatic stress disorder victims to re-experience their violent feelings, in order to work through them and benefit from experiential exposure.

Secondly, REBT does not merely encourage clients to make superficial changes, as when they scream and yell in primal therapy or have a strong positive transference in psychoanalysis. Instead, it gets to the clients' basic dysfunctional core philosophies with which they block themselves from strong positive feelings (like love and adventure) and that lead them to create powerful unhealthy feelings (like panic and despair). By ceaselessly looking for people's underlying, and often unconscious, dysfunctional attitudes, and by helping them to change these for self-actualizing ones, REBT encourages people to make a profound philosophical, and preferably lasting change that psychoanalysis and other 'deep' therapies rarely seem to achieve (Ellis, 1991, 1994, 1995a).

More specifically, REBT teaches people to believe that they always *can* accept themselves and others as fallible humans, that they *can* stand 'awful' adversities and handicaps, and that they *are* able to enjoy and fulfill themselves even under execrable life conditions. It shows them how to make *enduring* personality changes to live happier and *more* self-fulfilling lives. It tries to deal with the fundamental human disturbances and the basic potential pleasures of human existence, which many 'deep' therapies often ignore (Ellis, 1985, 1991, 1994, 1995a; Ellis and Abrams, 1994).

Which other psychotherapeutic approaches beside REBT command your respect or strike you as especially effective or promising?

Several of the other cognitive-behavioral therapies, some of which directly stem from REBT – including Aaron Beck's Cognitive Therapy, David Barlow's Anxiety Reduction Therapy, Maxie Maultsby's Rational Behavior Therapy, Donald Meichenbaum's Self-Instructional Training, and Arnold Lazarus's Multimodal Therapy. The main differences between REBT and these somewhat related therapies include the following.

1 REBT specifically looks for people's basic or core irrational beliefs and not mainly for their automatic thoughts and inferences which, it assumes, largely *stem from* their basic unrealistic, illogical, and dysfunctional assumptions or core philosophies.

2 REBT specifically seeks for and ferrets out the absolutistic shoulds, musts, oughts, demands, and commands that people consciously and unconsciously, overtly and tacitly, hold. It theorizes that these *musts* usually underlie and lead to their more superficial automatic thoughts and cognitive distortions. Thus, the irrational belief, 'Now that I have failed several times at this important task, I will *always* fail and *never* succeed', tends to be a derivative of the underlying musturbatory belief, 'When I attempt an important task, I *absolutely must* always succeed and *absolutely must* never fail. When I don't succeed as I *must*, that proves that I will *always* fail'. And the core belief, 'I am a *worthless person* who doesn't *deserve* good things in life!' tends to stem from the super-core belief, 'Because I *absolutely must* do well and be lovable, and because I am not doing as well and proving as lovable as I *absolutely must*, therefore I am a *worthless person* who doesn't *deserve* good things in life!' Where the other cognitive-behavior and multimodal therapies usually get to *some* of people's dysfunctional cognitions, they often fail to get to their *basic* musts and therefore offer them relatively superficial, and often unlasting, help.

3 REBT teaches clients (and non-clients who read and listen to its teachings) how to be their *own* therapists, how to think better and less musturbatorily *for themselves*, and how to prophylactically and curatively carry its teachings with them, preferably for the rest of their lives. They thereby can make themselves less disturbed and less disturb*able* (Ellis, 1994, 1995a, 1995b).

4 As noted above, REBT strives to help people *feel* better and *get* better – by their making effective and important emotional and behavioral changes, but also by their making some *profound philosophical* changes that may even, though hardly always, result in some fundamental personality changes. Where supposedly 'deep' therapies, such as psychoanalysis, give people a 'deep' understanding of how they historically got the way they now are and give them 'deep' insight into the therapist's interpretations of their psychodynamics, REBT tries to give them a 'deep' understanding of how they, themselves, *created* most of their neuroses and how they can now (and in the future) *un*create them and *re*create their own healthy thoughts, feelings, and actions.

Some of the newer narrative psychotherapies 'deeply' show people how to invent a new and 'better' narrative for their lives, but often do so in a pollyannaish and unrealistic way. REBT, however, tries to help them see how they created a misleading and false old narrative, and how they can stay with their personal and social *desires* and *wishes*, instead of their arrogant demands to create goals and values for the present and future.

Many therapists, especially today, show clients that in order to help themselves they *need* to depend on a 'Higher Power' or on magical and transpersonal 'spiritual' forces. REBT, however, shows them how they can tap into their *own chosen* vital absorbing goals and interests and build their *own* life purposes to which (if they wish) they can dedicate themselves *without* any babyish reliance on hypothetical (and most probably non-existent) gods, spirits, and miracles.

5 REBT is quite humanistic, in that it encourages people to accept their own and others' human fallibility and never to damn themselves nor other humans and thereby create mythical hells for them to fear. It also humanistically endorses social as well as individual interest and encourages people to help themselves *and* the communities in which they choose to live (Ellis, 1965, 1994). But it largely stays with secular humanism rather than religious, spiritual, or transpersonal humanism and doesn't – ironically! – invent 'cosmic' or superhuman reasons why humans have to be devoutly 'humanistic'. It pragmatically recommends a secular humanistic philosophy because it can be shown to *work* for individuals and social groups, and not because some supernatural forces command it to be followed.

6 REBT doesn't overemphasize early childhood and other environmental influences as some cognitive-behavioral therapies – such as those of Mahoney (1991) and Guidano (1991) do. It equally emphasizes the important biological factors that impel people to *both* constructively think, feel *and* act against their own interests. It realistically accepts the apparent facts of humans having strong innate, biological tendencies to foolishly escalate their strong desires (which they often learn) to grandiose demands and thereby to needlessly upset themselves (Ellis, 1976; Piatelli-Palmarini, 1994). Because of its realistic acceptance of biological influences as well as environmental learning, rational emotive behavior therapists realize that it is often *very* hard – though not impossible – for people to help themselves become less disturbed and less distur*bable*. So it deliberately uses a large number of cognitive, emotive, and behavioral techniques to help them *forcefully* and *persistently* do this; and it often recommends that pharmacological intervention be combined with psychotherapy.

7 Although, like most other cognitive-behavioral therapies, REBT recommends therapist–client *collaboration*, it realistically acknowledges that many clients, because of their innate and acquired limitations, tend to be poor collaborators and to self-defeatingly *resist* changing themselves for the better. Therefore – somewhat like 'pure' Behavior Therapy (BT) – REBT is often honestly and forcefully active-directive. It is an unusually *teaching* and *persuasive* therapy and often does not hesitate to *encourage* and *push* clients to get off their butts and *persist* at self-change. It honestly acknowledges that therapists had better know *more* than their clients; preferably be health*ier* than are most counselees, and consequently be effective *instructors* of improved mental health.

8 Although, as noted above, REBT practitioners unconditionally *accept* clients and thoroughly *respect* their constructive ability to change themselves, and although they are active-directive *teachers*, they usually go out of their way to avoid encouraging their clients to *need* them and to become

dependent on them. They therefore avoid giving their clients *conditional* acceptance and helping them to feel that they are 'good' or 'successful' *because* their therapists approve of them. They unusually stress their clients' working to be their *own* person, and soon encourage freeing themselves of *needing* the support and approval of their therapeutic teachers.

9 As noted elsewhere in this chapter, REBT is practically the only cognitive-behavior therapy that keeps stressing and teaching clients how to achieve unconditional self-acceptance (USA) in two main ways: first, accepting and liking themselves *whether or not* they succeed at important projects and *whether or not* anyone – yes, including their therapist! – loves them. Secondly, *only* rating or evaluating their thoughts, feelings, and actions according to how these help them achieve their basic goals and purposes, and practically *never* globally rating their *selves*, their *being*, their *essence*, or their 'soul'.

However, all the cognitive-behavior therapies that I mentioned I respect in the first paragraph of this section use some of the main aspects of REBT – especially its theory that people mainly *neurotize themselves* instead of just *get upset* by other people and events. These therapies therefore use several of the main REBT cognitive, emotive, and behavioral methods and teach their clients how to minimize their self-upsetting tendencies. They also, as REBT does, show clients how to cope with serious Adversities – such as injustice, abuse, disease, and handicaps – that are foisted on them, and how to stop mainly complaining and whining about them, and thereby aggravating their bad effects.

So most of the other cognitive-behavior therapies follow many of the pioneering theories and practices that REBT started in the 1950s; and, with or without giving credit to REBT, they significantly overlap with it. In my obviously prejudiced opinion, they are largely toned-down and less effective versions of REBT. But they still often work! – as many outcome studies have shown (Beck, 1991; Elkin, 1994; Hollon and Beck, 1994).

Which approaches do you find particularly unhelpful, unappealing, ineffective, misleading, or dangerous? Why?

1 Religious, mystical, transpersonal, and spiritual therapies that encourage people to believe that there is some Higher Power or Spiritual Force that will help them, instead of their using their own constructive tendencies to work hard at helping themselves. These include Alcoholics Anonymous, Transcendental Meditation, A Course in Miracles, shamanism, channeling, exorcism, Christian Science, Swedenborgism, and almost innumerable other forms of religious, transpersonal, mystical, and supernatural-oriented therapies (Ellis, 1972c; Ellis and Yeager, 1989; Kaminer, 1993; Kurtz, 1986).

2 Passive and non-directive therapies – such as classical psychoanalysis and person-centered therapy – that refuse to show clients what they are specifically doing to needlessly upset themselves and that refrain from teaching them concrete methods of reducing their disturbances.

3 One-sided therapies – such as primal therapy and Reichian therapy – that use only one main technique and refrain from employing, with a number of clients, different and special methods that might be at times particularly helpful to them.

4 Therapies – such as psychoanalysis, person-centered, and transpersonal therapy – that reinforce clients' dependency needs, and help them believe that they must have their therapist's or some guru's, or some leader's approval. These therapies tend to reinforce clients' dependency and discourage them from taking their power to change themselves into their own hands, and from unconditionally accepting themselves *whether or not* they are loved and helped by others (Ellis, 1962, 1994; Ellis and Yeager, 1989).

5 Therapies that help clients *feel* better but not make a profound philosophical change that will help them *get* better. Virtually all today's popular therapies – except, of course, REBT – emphasize and strive for clients' feeling relaxed, self-efficacious, and socially accepted instead of helping them to make themselves philosophically unupsettable even when faced with adversities, failure, and social rejection. Thus, Jay Haley (1990), Spivak, Platt and Shure (1976) and other therapists help people to solve problems without helping them to carry on effectively when their life problems are still unresolved. Virginia Satir (1978) showed clients how to communicate better but not to accept themselves when their communication with others is still ineffective. Albert Bandura teaches people how to be more self-efficacious but not to be unconditionally self-accepting when they are not self-efficient. Neil Jacobson (1992) and many family therapists help couples and families to change the family system in which they live but not to basically change the core self-defeating philosophies of each of the individuals in the family system (Ellis, 1993; Huber and Baruth, 1989).

How do you account for research which suggests that no one approach seems more effective than any other?

Practically all published research, especially the newer process research, uses as the criterion for 'effectiveness' how well clients *feel* during and after therapy. But this is a dubious criterion because even in the most inefficient therapies – such as psychoanalysis and person-centered therapy – clients feel better because they are accepted and carefully listened to by their therapist and *not* because they are shown more effective ways of thinking, feeling, and behaving. Even when, at the end of therapy, they are awfulizing, whining, and demanding as much as or more than before therapy, they *feel* that they have been significantly helped and that they have made 'great' progress. Philosophically and behaviorally many or most of these 'improved' clients are probably as sick as or sicker than they were before therapy.

Moreover, as Jerome Frank (1985) has shown, practically all the major therapies include common goals, directions, and values – such as a close, confiding relationship with a helping therapist who is definitely on the client's side; a healing setting that gives safety and privacy; giving clients a rationale, explanation, or even a believable myth that they will accept as a plausible explanation for their disturbed symptoms; and a procedure, series of tasks or rituals that clients believe will restore their functioning.

My own prejudiced view says that almost all therapists, whatever the theory they ostensibly practice, really sense pretty well that their clients have unrealistic, illogical, and ineffective ideas and philosophies. These therapists see or sense that their clients have irrational beliefs, such as that they *absolutely have to* do well, and that it is *awful* (more than bad) and that they are *inadequate persons* when they don't succeed as well as they *must*. When therapists, whatever their orientation, see or sense these major human irrationalities, I think that, in one way or another, they try to talk their clients out of their self-defeating ideas and the feelings and actions to which they lead. In this way, I hypothesize, most therapists do some amount of REBT, whether or not they realize that they do. They don't do REBT systematically or well. But also they do not merely follow the non-directive principles of their therapies that they say they follow. Instead, to some extent they directly and indirectly try to persuade their clients to be more rational and less self-defeating – as REBT and CBT more honestly try to do. When they succeed in doing this, their clients significantly improve.

In other words, even when they have poor or palliative therapy, many clients *feel* better and misleadingly tell therapy researchers that they *are* better. And many other clients actually *get* somewhat better because their therapists have – unwittingly and inefficiently – helped them to become more rational. This, of course, is only my theory, and I am going to have one hell of a time finding evidence to substantiate it!

How do you account historically for the vast number of differing approaches and for their continuing proliferation?

First, a sucker is born every minute, and most clients, particularly when they are in emotional pain, will strongly believe in almost *any* form of therapy that loudly, dramatically, and persistently promises them miracles.

Secondly, clients rarely ask for or check studies of the effectiveness of therapy and therefore never learn that many therapies – such as person-centered and Gestalt Therapy – have very few studies demonstrating their effectiveness, and that many other therapies – such as primal therapy and dramatic experiential therapy – have often been shown to be harmful.

Thirdly, many clients select a charismatic therapist, leader, or guru who has no professional qualifications but looks and sounds great in workshops or on TV. Whether or not his or her system of therapy actually *works* is one of their *least* considerations.

Fourthly, because many therapies rarely are effective and because clients themselves often fail to make the effort required by some effective therapies, many clients keep seeking a new and different kind of therapy just *because* it differs from those they have previously 'tried'.

How would you advise distressed people seeking therapy to choose a therapist and therapeutic orientation?

Try several things: (1) Normally, only choose a therapist with confirmed professional qualifications and a license to practice. (2) Read a good deal of the therapeutic literature, including outcome studies and accounts of harmful and wasteful therapies. Read, for example, the reviews of Strupp and Hadley (1977), Lambert and Hill (1994), and Zilbergeld (1983), who showed that therapists often do more harm than good and of Yalom (1995), who showed that group therapy of a highly expressive nature often leads to anti-therapeutic results. (3) Have a few experimental sessions with someone they think is okay but don't commit themselves to a large number of continuing sessions. (4) Talk to some present or previous clients of the therapist they consider choosing. (5) Distrust and be skeptical about any therapist who is very charming, loving, tactful, or needy of his or her clients' approval and love.

What are your views on eclecticism and integration?

I would say to therapists: Don't integrate your theory of disturbance and therapy with opposing or conflicting theories. While staying (unrigidly!) with your own theory, eclectically use a number of techniques, especially with clients who don't seem to use or benefit from your main techniques. Preferably, formulate a comprehensive theory – such as that of Rational Emotive Behavior Therapy – that is integrative in that it encourages the use of a good many cognitive, emotive, and behavioral methods. The current trend, sparked by therapists like Paul Wachtel (1994), Marvin Goldfried (Goldfried and Davison, 1994), John Norcross (Norcross and Goldfried, 1992), is definitely on the right track in that it encourages therapists with a poor theory (such as psychoanalysis and person-centered therapy) to use a number of techniques that they normally would never use. This is fine! But much more research had better be done to credit effective and discredit ineffective theories of psychotherapy. In the final analysis, a good theory *plus* a wide range of eclectic practices will presumably prevail. Naturally, of all the existing therapies, I think that REBT best fills this bill. Let us see if scientific research bears me out!

Can you hazard a guess as to what the field will look like in, say, 50 years' time? Which approaches will thrive and which will prosper?

My strong guess is that most of the one-sided therapies – such as classical psychoanalysis, person-centered, Reichian, and primal therapy – will rarely be used, although some elements of them may be incorporated in cognitive-behavioral and multimodal therapies, which will ultimately be shown to be more efficient for most clients most of the time. Because humans, including human therapists, are often born and reared to think and act irrationally and unscientifically, ineffective and harmful therapies and self-help groups will still attract many clients and devotees. But, hopefully, sensible and scientifically tested therapies will prevail.

References

Baisden, H.E. (1980) *Irrational Beliefs: A Construct Validation Study*. Unpublished doctoral dissertation. University of Minnesota, Minneapolis.

Beck, A.T. (1976) *Cognitive Therapy and the Emotional Disorders*. New York: International Universities Press.

Beck, A.T. (1991) Cognitive therapy: a 30-year retrospective. *American Psychologist*, 46, 383–9.

Bernard, M.E. and Joyce, M.R. (1984) *Rational-Emotive Therapy with Children and Adolescents* (2nd edn). New York: Wiley.

Berridge, K.C. and Robinson, T.E. (1995) The mind of an addicted brain: neural sensitization of wanting versus liking. *Current Directions in Psychological Science*, 4, 71–6.

Cloninger, C.R., Svrakic, D.M. and Przybek, T.R. (1993) A psychobiological model of temperament and character. *Archives of General Psychiatry*, 50, 975–90.

DiGiuseppe, R.A., Miller, N.J. and Trexler, L.D. (1979) A review of rational-emotive psychotherapy outcome studies. In A. Ellis and J.M. Whiteley (eds), *Theoretical and Empirical Foundations of Rational-Emotive Therapy* (pp. 218–35). Monterey, CA: Brooks/Cole.

Dryden, W. (1995) *Brief Rational Emotive Behaviour Therapy*. Chichester: Wiley.

D'Zurilla, T.J. (1990) Problem-solving training for effective stress management and prevention. *Journal of Cognitive Psychotherapy*, 4, 327–54.

Elkin, I. (1994) The NIMH treatment of depression collaborative research program: where we began and where we are. In A.E. Bergin and S.L. Garfield (eds), *Handbook of Psychotherapy and Behavior Change* (pp. 114–39). New York: Wiley.

Ellis, A. (1957) *How To Live with a Neurotic: At Home and At Work*. New York: Crown. Rev. edn, Hollywood, CA: Wilshire Books, 1975.

Ellis, A. (1960) *The Art and Science of Love*. New York: Lyle Stuart & Bantam.

Ellis, A. (1962) *Reason and Emotion in Psychotherapy*. Secaucus, NJ: Citadel.

Ellis, A. (1963) *The Intelligent Woman's guide to Manhunting*. New York: Dell Publishing. Rev. edn, *The Intelligent Woman's Guide To Dating and Mating*. Secaucus, NJ: Lyle Stuart, 1979.

Ellis, A. (1965) *Suppressed: Seven Key Essays Publishers Dared Not Print*. Chicago: New Classics House.

Ellis, A. (1969) A weekend of rational encounter. *Rational Living*, 4 (2), 1–8. Reprinted in A. Ellis and W. Dryden, *The Practice of Rational-Emotive Therapy* (pp. 180–91). New York: Springer, 1997.

Ellis, A. (1972a) *Executive Leadership: The Rational-Emotive Approach*. New York: Institute for Rational-Emotive Therapy.

Ellis, A. (1972b) Helping people get better rather than merely feel better. *Rational Living*, 7 (2), 2–9.

Ellis, A. (1972c) What does transpersonal psychology have to offer the art and science of psychotherapy? *Voices*, 8 (1), 20–8.

Ellis, A. (1973) *Humanistic Psychotherapy: The Rational-Emotive Approach*. New York: McGraw-Hill.

Ellis, A. (1976) The biological basis of human irrationality. *Journal of Individual Psychology*, 32, 145–68. Reprinted: New York: Institute for Rational-Emotive Therapy.

Ellis, A. (1979a) Rational-emotive therapy: research data that support the clinical and personality hypotheses of RET and other modes of cognitive-behavior therapy. In A. Ellis and J.M. Whiteley (eds), *Theoretical and Empirical Foundations of Rational-Emotive Therapy* (pp. 101–73). Monterey, CA: Brooks/Cole.

Ellis, A. (1979b) Rejoinder: elegant and inelegant RET. In A. Ellis and J.M. Whiteley (eds), *Theoretical and Empirical Foundations of Rational-Emotive Therapy* (pp. 240–67). Monterey, CA: Brooks/Cole.

Ellis, A. (1985) *Overcoming Resistance*. New York: Springer.

Ellis, A. (1988) *How To Stubbornly Refuse To Make Yourself Miserable About Anything – Yes, Anything!* Secaucus, NJ: Lyle Stuart.

Ellis, A. (1990) Is rational-emotive therapy (RET) 'rationalist' or 'constructivist'? In A. Ellis and W. Dryden, *The Essential Albert Ellis* (pp. 114–41). New York: Springer.

Ellis, A. (1991) Achieving self-actualization. *Journal of Social Behavior and Personality*, 6 (5), 1–18. Reprinted: New York: Institute for Rational-Emotive Therapy.

Ellis, A. (1993) The rational emotive therapy approach to marriage and family therapy. *Family Journal*, 1, 292–307.

Ellis, A. (1994) *Reason and Emotion in Psychotherapy* (Revised and updated). New York: Birch Lane Press.

Ellis, A. (1995a) *Better, Deeper and More Enduring Brief Therapy*. New York: Brunner/Mazel.

Ellis, A. (1995b) Rational emotive behavior therapy. In R. Corsini and D. Wedding (eds), *Current Psychotherapies* (pp. 162–96). Itasca, IL: Peacock.

Ellis, A. (1995c) The creation of rational emotive behavior therapy (REBT). *Voices*, 31, 78–81.

Ellis, A. and Abrahms, E. (1978) *Brief Psychotherapy in Medical and Health Practice*. New York: Springer.

Ellis, A. and Abrams, M. (1994) *How To Cope with a Fatal Illness*. New York: Barricade Books.

Ellis, A. and Dryden, W. (1997) *The Practice of Rational-Emotive Therapy*. New York: Springer.

Ellis, A. and Harper, R.A. (1961) *A Guide To Successful Marriage*. North Hollywood, CA: Wilshire Books.

Ellis, A. and Harper, R.A. (1975) *A New Guide to Rational Living* (Revised and updated, 1997). North Hollywood, CA: Wilshire Books.

Ellis, A. and Yeager, R. (1989) *Why Some Therapies Don't Work: The Dangers of Transpersonal Psychology*. Buffalo, NY: Prometheus.

Frank, J. (1985) Therapeutic components shared by all psychotherapies. In M. Mahoney and A. Freeman (eds), *Cognition and Psychotherapy* (pp. 49–79). New York: Plenum.

Goldfried, M.R. and Davison, G.C. (1994) *Clinical Behavior Therapy* (Expanded edn). New York: Wiley.

Greist, J.H. (1993) *Obsessive Compulsive Disorder*. Madison, WI: Dean Foundation for Health and Education.

Guidano, V.F. (1991) *The Self in Process*. New York: Guilford Press.

Haaga, D.A. and Davison, G.C. (1989) Outcome studies of rational-emotive therapy. In M.E. Bernard and R. DiGiuseppe (eds), *Inside Rational-Emotive Therapy* (pp. 155–97). San Diego, CA: Academic Press.

Hajzler, D. and Bernard, M.E. (1991) A review of rational-emotive outcome studies. *School Psychology Quarterly*, 6 (1), 27–49.

Haley, J. (1990) *Problem Solving Therapy*. San Francisco: Jossey-Bass.

Hauser, P. (1992) *Brain Imaging and the Pathology of Affective Disorders: Hope Deferred*. Washington, DC: American Psychiatric Press.

Hollon, S.D. and Beck, A.T. (1994) Cognitive and cognitive-behavioral therapies. In A.E. Bergin and S.L. Garfield (eds), *Handbook of Psychotherapy and Behavior Change* (pp. 428–66). New York: Wiley.

Huber, C.H. and Baruth, L.G. (1989) *Rational-Emotive and Systems Family Therapy*. New York: Springer.

Jacobson, N. (1992) Behavioral therapy: a new beginning. *Behavior Therapy*, 23, 491–506.

Kaminer, W. (1993) *I'm Dysfunctional, You're Dysfunctional*. New York: Vintage.

Knaus, W. (1974) *Rational-Emotive Education*. New York: Institute for Rational-Emotive Therapy.

Korzybski, A. (1933) *Science and Sanity*. San Francisco: International Society of General Semantics.

Kramer, P.D. (1993) *Listening To Prozac*. New York: Penguin.

Kurtz, P. (1986) *The Transcendental Temptation*. Buffalo, NY: Prometheus,

Lambert, M.J. and Hill, C.E. (1994) Assessing psychotherapy outcomes and processes. In A.E. Bergin and S.L. Garfield (eds), *Handbook of Psychotherapy and Behavior Change* (4th edn, pp. 72–113). New York: Wiley.

Lazarus, A.A. (1989) *The Practice of Multimodal Therapy*. Baltimore, MD: Johns Hopkins University Press.

Lazarus, R.S. and Folkman, S. (1984) *Stress, Appraisal and Coping*. New York: Springer.

Linehan, M.M. (1993) *Cognitive-Behavioral Treatment of Borderline Personality Disorders*. New York: Guilford Press.

Lyons, L.C. and Woods, P.J. (1991) The efficacy of rational-emotive therapy: a quantitative review of the outcome research. *Clinical Psychology Review*, 11, 357–69.

Mahoney, M.J. (1991) *Human Change Processes*. New York: Basic Books.

Maultsby, M.C., Jr. (1971) Rational emotive imagery. *Rational Living*, 6 (1), 24–7.

McGovern, T.E. and Silverman, M.S. (1984) A review of outcome studies of rational-emotive therapy from 1977 to 1982. *Journal of Rational-Emotive Therapy*, 2 (1), 7–18.

Meehl, P.E. (1962) Schizotaxia, schizotypy, schizophrenia. *American Psychologist*, 17, 827–38.

Meichenbaum, D. (1977) *Cognitive-Behavior Modification*. New York: Plenum.

Norcross, J.C. and Goldfried, M.P. (1992) *Psychotherapy Integration*. New York: Basic Books.

Olevitch, B.A. (1995) *Cognitive Approaches to the Seriously Mentally Ill*. Westport, CT: Praeger.

Piatelli-Palmarini, M. (1994) *Inevitable Illusions: How Mistakes of Reason Rule Our Minds*. New York: Wiley.

Satir, V. (1978) *People Making*. Palo Alto, CA: Science & Behavior Books.

Silverman, M.S., McCarthy, M. and McGovern, T. (1992) A review of outcome studies of rational-emotive therapy from 1982–1989. *Journal of Rational-Emotive and Cognitive-Behavior Therapy*, 10 (3), 111–86.

Smith, M.L. and Glass, G.V. (1977) Meta-analysis of psychotherapy outcome studies. *American Psychologist*, 32, 752–60.

Spivack, G., Platt, J. and Shure, M. (1976) *The Problem-Solving Approach to Adjustment*. San Francisco: Jossey-Bass.

Steketee, G.S. (1993) *Treatment of Obsessive Compulsive Disorder*. New York: Guilford Press.

Stone, M.H. (1990) *The Fate of Borderline Patients: Successful Outcome and Psychiatric Practice*. New York: Guilford Press.

Strupp, H.H. and Hadley, S.W. (1977) A tripartite model of mental health and therapeutic outcomes: with special reference to negative effects in psychotherapy. *American Psychologist*, 32, 187–96.

Vernon, A. (1989) *Thinking, Feeling, Behaving: An Emotional Education Curriculum for Children*. Champaign, IL: Research Press.

Wachtel, P.L. (1994) From eclectism to synthesis: toward a more seamless psychotherapeutic integration. *Journal of Psychotherapeutic Integration*, 1, 43–54.

Woods, P.J. (1992) A study of belief and non-belief items from the Jones' irrational beliefs test with implications for the theory of RET. *Journal of Rational-Emotive and Cognitive-Behavior Therapy*, 10, 41–52.

Yalom, I.D. (1995) *The Theory and Practice of Group Psychotherapy* (4th edn). New York: Basic Books.

Yankura, J. and Dryden, W. (1994) *Albert Ellis*. London: Sage.

Zilbergeld, B. (1983) *The Shrinking of America*. Boston: Little, Brown & Co.

5

Existential Psychotherapy

John M. Heaton

One of the main attractions of existential therapy to me is that it is not a psychological school of therapy founded by a charismatic leader who claims to have discovered some *truth* with profound therapeutic implications to humanity. Inevitably, disciples form around him/her, books are written, a special journal is started, and an institute and training course are founded. Most of these psychological schools depend on a simplified model of what it is to be human, distorting or ignoring vast areas of human experience. Insularity, exclusivity, and wild speculations characterize them.

Existential therapy, on the other hand, is rooted in philosophical thinking, that is, a way of thinking that has a long history and so experience of the complexity and depth of human experience. So there is no possibility that any one person or school could hope to comprehend it. Existential therapy makes no claim to any specific theory or technique derived from it that could heal the pains and sorrows that are our human lot. Most theories throw some light on the human condition and most therapeutic techniques have a place. There are particular circumstances in which they may be efficacious, but none can occupy *the place* as a cure for all.

The immeasurable quality of human life cannot be represented by theories, general rules, and techniques, nor can it be comprehended by following some charismatic therapist, for these all too easily become a substitute for exerting patience, discrimination and impartiality. The source of therapy for an existential therapist comes from a life vivid and intense enough to have created a wide fellow-feeling with all that is human and from hard-earned experience in helping people in mental pain and confusion.

History

History is of great importance to philosophy and so to existential therapists and this differentiates them from most therapists in this century. Freud, for example, had little interest in or knowledge of the history of psychotherapy. This was because he understood neurosis as a given, as illness, and his problem was to cure it; he thought that he had found the theory and method to do so, that is psychoanalysis. Seeing things this way makes history unimportant; it becomes only a story of failed efforts to find a solution to the problem of neurosis, obviously of little interest to someone who thought he had found a solution or at any rate found the definitive way to it.

But there is another way of understanding history and its relevance to psychotherapy. The emphasis here is not so much on solving the problems of neurosis and psychosis as on gaining a deeper understanding of what the problems are, why they arise, what gives them their force, why they grip us or fail to grip us. For neurosis and psychosis as defined by Freud and psychiatrists in the nineteenth and twentieth centuries have not always been with us. Human unhappiness and despair, mental conflict and confusion, the influence of mind on body, have been understood in many different ways in human history and by different cultures. The construction and development of psychopathology is by no means the only way to understand despair. Much psychiatric and therapeutic thought occurs in a historical vacuum and so it fails to understand itself.

Psychotherapy is an enterprise in which the meaningfulness of its terms and the correctness of its procedures is always an issue. Psychotherapists have been concerned with driving out demons, curing false beliefs, assuaging the wrath of the ancestors, and much else in the course of history. Each requires different beliefs, concepts and techniques and so creates different meanings. In the modern world of psychotherapy confusion reigns. Some experienced people say the whole enterprise is a complete waste of time and often harmful. Among practising therapists there are hundreds of schools of therapy, each with its own cluster of theories, techniques, special languages and heroes and each clamouring to be the best, some using rhetoric to persuade, others perhaps more cleverly using the levers of institutional and political power to get their way. Of course there is no objective and widely agreed procedure to assess which is the most effective. Furthermore, there never will be because there can be no general agreement on the meaningfulness of the terms of each individual therapy. One cannot make what is subjective objective. Meaning is not an object and to turn it into one leads to falsification.

Psychotherapy is in some ways like art. There is no objective procedure to show that Bach is a greater musician than The Beatles. If someone thrills to the music of The Beatles and is bored by Bach, no objective procedure can make him enjoy Bach or show that the Bach lover is intrinsically superior to someone who finds The Beatles more meaningful.

Human suffering is similar. It sets off a process of meaning-making. The sufferer, his or her family and the therapist are all involved in making sense and coming to terms with what is happening. Suffering, like art, is dialogical. It is multiply constituted in ways that are often conflicting. It unfolds in time, joining memory and anticipation like a symphony or a novel. It involves many perspectives which themselves emerge in a time fraught with anxiety and hope. To objectify it in the terms of a supposedly neutral scientific observer is to falsify it, misunderstand the nature of science, and reproduce a particular power structure (Good, 1994).

Mark Twain observed that giving up smoking was easy, he had done it a

hundred times; the same might be said for psychotherapy's attempts to repu-
diate its history and establish itself on a new and scientific footing. Certainty
and the power that goes with it is tempting and very persuasive but there is
no evidence that the problems of the human condition can be solved this
way.

The motive for being aware of the history of psychotherapy in existential
therapy is that it can lead to some self-understanding in the practice of the
craft. For psychotherapy often requires one to be aware of the fundamental
presuppositions of human knowledge and activity. We sometimes see people
who do not know if they are alive or dead, who feel they have committed
the unforgivable sin, who feel they are damned for eternity, who think they
are Judas Iscariot and so on. An activity which seeks to make some sense of
these foundational disorders must inevitably be concerned with its own
fundamental presuppositions; and once these are at stake this will play an
essential role in the practice of therapy. For to question them is to question
all the conclusions, dogmas and techniques that we may have reached or
practised.

Existential therapy is concerned with self-knowledge and so its questioning is directed, in the first instance, not against the ignorance of others but
against one's own confusions. What one hopes to gain is not, primarily, positive doctrine, but rather a clearer mind and a deeper insight into one's position in the world. This enables one to act more truthfully towards those
people who seek one's help.

The Enlightenment and utilitarianism

Psychotherapy in this century has been, with few exceptions, a product of
the Enlightenment. This great tradition of thought stretches from the
Renaissance to the present-day, when it is under very heavy attack. There
are certain beliefs common to Enlightenment thought. Briefly, they are that
nature is a single whole, subject to a single set of laws that are discoverable
by man. The laws that govern inanimate matter are essentially the same as
those that govern living creatures and the mind of man. Man is capable of
improvement as there are certain objectively recognizable goals which all
reasonable men recognize, namely happiness, mental health, liberty. Human
misery and vice are due to ignorance of these goals because of insufficient
knowledge of the laws of nature. Human nature is fundamentally the same
at all times and places although some people are more primitive or less
developed than others. Those holding the beliefs of the Enlightenment are
nearer the goal of humanity than the rest.

The Enlightenment rests on three strong pillars. The first is faith in reason,
that is a logically connected structure of laws and generalizations susceptible to demonstration and verification. The second is the identity of human
nature and so the possibility of universal human goals. The third is the belief
that we can attain these universal goals by means of reason, which is capable

of analysing everything into its ultimate constituents and of discovering their interrelations and the laws which they obey.

But what are these goals which reason will enable us to attain? For psychotherapists, roughly speaking, the goal is mental health, ordinary human happiness, absence of neurosis and perversion, growth and change, making the unconscious conscious, self-understanding, modification of mal-adaptive behaviour and so on. It is very significant that different therapists have different goals. This is the reason why a general theory must precede any particular truths that we come across as a result of the application of the theory. For we need the theory to enable us to judge on what grounds particular judgements must be made. The theory tells us whether our judge-ments are adequate from the standpoint of reason. We cannot proceed rationally without first knowing the theory that determines what is to count as a rational way of proceeding. For example, if we believe that the aim of therapy is to make the unconscious conscious, we need to know what this means, that is the theory behind this belief, to decide whether our interpre-tations have done this or not. If we think that psychological growth is the aim, then we need to know just what this is to see if our activities produce growth.

In short, most psychotherapies in this century are utilitarian in inspira-tion. They are activities aimed at some end – growth, getting rid of depres-sion, solving emotional problems, etc. – and their techniques take their whole character and colour from the end to which they are subservient. Freud, the great founder of psychotherapy in this century was an admirer of J.S. Mill (1863) the Victorian exponent of utilitarianism. He translated some of his essays in his youth. Utilitarian beliefs are everywhere in Freud. Thus he assumed that humankind is governed at root by pain and pleasure. He thought that the psychoanalytic method was 'an impartial instrument, like the infinitesimal calculus' and so was the one and only rational method for man to conquer the irrational. He assumed that human nature was essen-tially the same at all times and places. This enabled him to judge that women, neurotics, and 'primitive' people are inferior, less developed and less rational than scientifically educated males and that psychoanalysts are the most rational and superior of all.

Of course not all schools of psychotherapy have Freud's beliefs. But the essential pattern of utilitarian thought is there in most. There is some desir-able end which is clothed in a theory and there are one or more techniques developed to attain that end. And as psychotherapy purports to deal with some of the most significant features of human life, then heavy weight is put on the value of the theory of the therapy itself. So the 'best' patients become therapists themselves for the therapy seems to have absolute value. And therapists consider themselves qualified to pronounce on most aspects of human life, Freud leading the way with lofty pronouncements on the past and future of civilization, the illusions of religion, the foundations of moral-ity, how we should bring up our children and so on.

Existentialists have, on the whole, been bitter opponents of nearly all the ideals and beliefs of the Enlightenment. Isaiah Berlin (1994) shows that modern existential thought derives not from Kierkegaard but from J.G. Hamann, who was greatly admired by Kierkegaard. Hamann was a Prussian philosopher who lived in the eighteenth century, he was a friend of Kant. As Berlin puts it: 'The most passionate, consistent, extreme and implacable enemy of the Enlightenment and, in particular, of all forms of rationalism of his time was Johann Georg Hamann' (Berlin, 1994: 1).

I will give a few quotations from Hamann, as translated by Berlin, as they give something of the flavour of existential thought; although I would add that not all existentialists would agree with everything written by Hamann. Existentialism is more a movement than a uniform and policed school of thought. Even its name is in question; Heidegger did not like being called an existentialist which is a term made popular by Sartre.

> Passion alone gives to abstractions and hypotheses hands, feet, wings; images it endows with spirit, life, language. Where are swifter arguments to be found? Where the rolling thunder of eloquence, and its companion, the monosyllabic brevity of lightening? (Berlin, 1994: 61)

> The *pudenda* of our organisms are so closely united to the secret depths of our *heart* and *brain* that a total rupture of this natural union is impossible. (1994: 62)

> ... language is the first and last organ and criterion of reason ... (1994: 76)

> ... nature is our old grandmother ... and to commit incest with this grandmother is the most important commandment of the Koran of the arts, and it is not obeyed. (1994: 99)

> ... nothing but the descent to hell of self-knowledge builds the path to becoming divine. (1994: 116).

Hamann was a great admirer of the sceptic and empiricist Hume who sought to purge ordinary life and thought of false philosophy and considered that 'reason is, and ought only to be the slave of the passions' (Hume, 1978: 415). We must learn to see the limits of reason rather than glorifying it as the basis of human life. To displace desire, passion and faith to the second rate is a self-mutilation which leads to a distortion of truth. Hamann thought that ideals like reason, progress, liberty and equality were vast balloon-like constructions of unrealistic minds. They lead to a distortion of the many sidedness of human life which is misrepresented, narrowed, done injustice to, by being squeezed into the framework of some a priori pseudo-scientific schema conceived by some fanatical manager of facts.

The existentialist critique of reason must not be construed as a rejection of reason altogether. It is rather an attempt to bring reason – especially in its modern techno-scientific form – before the tribunal of reason itself. It is thinking or enquiring into reason. This type of enquiry is rarely done by psychotherapists, although they treat people who are said to be 'unreasonable' or 'irrational'. What precisely is this 'reason' they are supposed to lack? What evidence is there that psychotherapists possess 'reason'? The proliferation of psychotherapy schools would suggest that there are many versions of 'reason' at play. Some order in the field will only be obtained when therapists are prepared to seek clarity on the nature and origins of reason and then they might be able to assess the effectiveness of different therapies.

In order to understand the origins of reason we must not make an unconditioned use of what we seek to account for – namely reason; if we did then thought would merely go round in a circle. Neither can the origins be determined as the mere opposite of reason, the irrational, for this is determined in terms of reason, that is as its opposite. The origins of reason must be expatiated upon in a way of their own. They must lie in things which most intimately belong to reason as well as those things which reason can never possess; something exterior to reason but also that without which reason could not be what it is. Pioneering efforts in this direction have been made by Wittgenstein in *On Certainty* (1969) and Derrida in *Of Grammatology* (1976).

Theory

Hamann argued that many human problems are not generated by mistakes in logic and observation so much as by fanatical belief in the universal and eternal validity of theories as such. It is this addiction to theory that breeds imaginary entities which are confounded with reality and leads to mental confusion and spiritual torment. Existential thinkers from Kierkegaard to Heidegger to Wittgenstein have argued that theory in philosophy blinds, and therapists influenced by them have said the same for psychotherapy. It should be said in parenthesis here that we are not criticizing theory in the natural sciences where, of course, it has an essential role. But a human being is not, for an existential therapist, a scientific object. It is attention and thoughtfulness that are important in understanding the despairs and conflicts that bring people to therapy. Or, to put the point more technically, existential therapy is concerned with the uniqueness of persons and the clarification and creation of concepts rather than making and applying theories.

It is perhaps useful to remind ourselves of what a great philosopher who was very far from being an existentialist wrote about theory: 'As one with a long experience of the difficulties of logic and of the deceptiveness of theories which seem irrefutable, I find myself unable to be sure of the rightness of a theory, merely on the ground that I cannot see any point on which it is wrong' (Russell, 1961: xxii).

So let us take a brief look at how most therapists in this century have used theory. It is significant that generally therapies are named after either the founding hero – Freud, Jung, etc. – or after the theory on which the therapy is based – object relations, Gestalt, cognitive therapy, etc. It is either a charismatic person or a theory that directs the therapy. Why is this so? Must it be so?

Unfortunately, the place of theory in psychotherapy and human action is not so simple as therapists assume and I will briefly consider some of the difficulties. First of all, it should provoke some unease that there are so many theories claiming to be basic. This is in marked contrast to the natural sciences where the place of theory is well understood; there may be arguments in physics as to whether string theory should replace quantum electrodynamics but there are not hundreds of basic theories jostling for position, as in psychotherapy. Also, there is no evidence that the application of any one theory in psychotherapy cures more people than another.

Freud's theoretical position led him to believe that observation was the way to confirming his theories about human nature and its disorders of neurosis and psychosis. Freud here was guided by his positivist epistemology which is still widespread in many psychotherapy schools. Psychological knowledge in this paradigm is constituted through its depiction of empirical reality; it is obtained by describing what it supposed to be going on in the mind, the family, between mother and baby, between therapist and patient. It is assumed that reports on observations simply mirror nature and the task is to depict in language what has been observed. Language in this paradigm is understood as being a pliant instrument of rationality which, when used rationally, correctly represents what has been observed. So meaning is constituted through the referential linking of the elements of language and those in the natural world; the meaning of a proposition is almost wholly dependent on how the world is as a matter of empirical fact. In short, our system of knowledge reflects the natural order and so our categories are natural and descriptive rather than cultural and classificatory.

Now this way of understanding knowledge and language and their relationship to theory has been extensively criticized in this century; in the existential tradition Heidegger (1962) was a pioneer and in the analytic tradition, Wittgenstein (1953). There is now a huge literature in philosophy, linguistics, anthropology and sociology, which backs up and elaborates on these critiques. I will only mention a few points from psychotherapy.

The case history

The case history is fundamental to theoretical work in nearly all schools of therapy. But is it objective? Is it a true report of what 'really' happened? Does it capture the actual meaning to every participant of what was said? Who decides on what is true and by what right? Foucault (1972) argues that investigation of how discourses produce, rather than passively and 'objectively' represent, their objects must begin with the questions: 'Who is speaking? Who, among the totality of speaking individuals, is accorded the right to use this sort of language? Who is qualified to do so? Who derives from it his own special quality, his prestige, and from whom, in return, does he receive if not the assurance, at least the presumption that what he says is true?' (Foucault, 1972: 50). I have often asked patients who have left an analyst or therapist what went wrong. Usually they have told me their version but on enquiring as to whether they told their therapist this, they have said no as they did not feel empowered to speak in a critical way. So what was 'really' happening in the therapy session? I have known patients who have read their 'case' in books and have said that the author's account was remote from what they felt was happening. Is the author's account true just because the patient was neurotic?

Most case histories are not merely a completely one-sided account of what happened, but they so lack detail and nuance that they prevent the reader from drawing his or her own conclusions from the evidence. Anecdotal remarks simply highlight the clinical observations that conform to the clinician's expectations. As has been pointed out (Spence, 1994), Freud was a master at taking associations, dreams and memories and weaving them into a compelling and persuasive narrative. Therapists of all persuasions, including behaviour and cognitive therapists who create 'scientific' stories, have weaved their material into a persuasive story that promises therapeutic success. A well-constructed story possesses a truth that is real and immediate, but is this sort of truth really amenable for inferring an objective structure of the mind. Novelists write gripping stories which may show great insight into the human mind and behaviour but they do not go on to infer that these stories reflect objective structures in the mind. Is this a deficit on their part or does it show greater understanding of the place of language in human understanding and interaction? Does theorizing about the structure of the mind actually create structure? Do we not create the structure of our minds through what we do, through our capacity to describe actions in different ways? (Sharpe, 1990)

Furthermore, it has been shown (Wittgenstein, 1953) that first-person psychological utterances, such as 'I want . . .', have a very different logic and use from third-person ones, such as 'He wants . . .'. This leads to a penumbra of indeterminacy about understanding others' motives, desires, and so on. It completely undermines any psychological theory that claims certainty about human desire and that asserts it can plot out an objective structure to the mind or the 'inner' world simply from studying psychological experiences such as desiring, hoping, thinking.

Therapists often create mythical characters and activities, like novelists. Thus such terms as mental process, internal object, superego, personal construct, instinct, do not refer to any object or process that is in the mind or anywhere else. They cannot be pointed to and verified as we do with empirical reality. They only have meaning in the context of a dense semiotic network. They are part of a language game. To understand them is like understanding a character in a novel. We have to participate in the practice through which they are enacted and reproduced, and they require attention to the complex array of conceptual systems in which they make sense.

Narrative replaces meaning for a straightforward copy of the events recounted. It creates a coherence to events and so enables or provokes the listener to enter into and sympathize with the world of experience painted by the narrator. In the case of narratives about illness and suffering, they give a shape to the experience in a way which is heavily dependent on the

culture of the people involved in the suffering and its alleviation. It depends
on their beliefs about the nature of the world and the causes and cure for
human suffering: spirits, demons, unconscious forces, witches, the shades,
insulted or neglected ancestors, and so on. In one form or other it is always
an attempt to give shape to the unknown, especially in the case of 'psychological' illness. So the narrative cannot be separated from its cultural
context; and as culture is always changing, so do illness narratives (Good,
1994).

The grand narratives created by Freud in his case histories no longer carry
the conviction they once had. Narratives bringing in computerability, black
holes and chaos theory are more convincing to us. But the point is that these
narratives are no more scientific than the older ones. For the natural sciences are not based on the logic of narrative but on the logic of inference,
of models of the world with strict correspondence rules linking the model
with what is observed.

But this is not relevant to the practice of psychotherapy. For psychotherapy is a *practice* rather than the application of a theory. It is closer to
the practices of the arts than the sciences. For a cultural practice is creative
and obedient to its own more 'human' logic; it is not the sign of other realities and does not represent or attempt to picture and explain 'reality' as do
the natural sciences.

Contrast an anatomical drawing of the human body with a drawing by a
great artist. The former is representational whereas the latter is expressive,
it moves us and we judge its effectiveness and appreciate it in a very different way from the anatomical drawing. Now the logic of this 'movement' of
the soul is similar to the therapeutic movement that occurs in good psychotherapy. This 'movement' has a logic that is very different from the logic of
motion that is studied in the natural sciences. For example, in motion a
moving thing goes from one place to another, which is not so in the 'movement' of the soul. A different understanding of time is required to comprehend these two notions. A great deal of the latter part of Heidegger's *Being
and Time* (1962) is devoted to this question.

Narratives not only report experiences but they depict the unfolding of
desire. They open certain possibilities and close others. They project us
towards imagined ends or forms of experience which we feel we must fulfil.
They direct the way the therapy must go. A Freudian narrative does not end
up with an archetypal experience whereas a Jungian might. This is why existentialists are suspicious of narrative. From Kierkegaard to Beckett they
have emphasized the performative effects of language; it does not merely
report but does things to people in various ways. Attention to language use
reveals the often agonistic desires in the speakers. For we use language to
persuade or soothe ourselves as well as others. Our desire for a unitary and
totalizing truth is wrapped up in the way we use language. Attention to the
dialogical essence of language helps to undermine this and enables us to
question desire rather than simply reproduce one person's desire as is done
in so many case histories.

Another problem of case histories that is rarely addressed by therapists is the problem of putting things into words. How do we put our experience into words? The names for our experiences are not lying around to be picked up and matched with experience like counters. And when we have, usually tentatively, put our experience into words, how does the listener know he or she has correctly understood them? Many experiences are too fleeting to be captured. Does this mean they are unimportant? Speech, especially about intimate matters, is full of private connotations, habits of stress, of elision or periphrase. Their weight and semantic field always have individual variations. It may take a fine ear to pick them up. But this requires listening and a cultivated ear rather than the observant eye of a scientist who wants to record the observed facts of the case on which to build and confirm his theory of the mind.

Ordinary talk

Psychotherapy is mostly conducted through talk; it is the 'talking cure'. Contrary to scientific writing, the directly informative content of natural speech is small. Information about experience does not come naked; it is only computer languages that require bare information. Ordinary talk, which is what most patients engage in, is full of lies or partial truths, counter-factual propositions, images, shapes of will and evasion with which we charge our mental being and by which we build the changing and largely fictive milieu of our existence. The 'messiness' of ordinary talk, its critical difference from the ordered, closed systematization of formal logic, the polysemy of individual words, are not a defect to be ironed out by creating a theory of the mind with nicely ordered functions to which we can apply some therapeutic technique when it is dysfunctional. Rather, the 'looseness' of natural speech, the way it can conceal more than it confides, blurs more than defines, distances more than connects, is essential to being human.

This is why attempts to sanitize therapeutic language, as is attempted by communicative psychoanalysts, is a misguided undertaking. For language is not only for communication, but is essential for thought and so for therapy. Thus naming is essential to language for it brings things to appearance. Just watch a child learning to speak. When it names things it is able to attend to them and think about them. It may do this in babbling in its cot when nobody is around as far as it knows so there is no question of communication here. The use of metaphor and metonymy, finding the appropriate word for an experience, dreaming, are immensely important parts of therapy but these are not to be understood in solely communicative terms – one dreams alone for example. When one says things, one is often showing or hiding things from oneself as much as communicating.

Dreams and narratives are not encoded meanings as is believed by communicative therapists. Decoding a message implies that the decoder and the person who sent the message both have a language in common. Unscrambling a message is not the same as interpreting it. Even in sophisticated decoding keys are required, an encryption key and a decryption one. And the decoding is best done by computers. None of this is applicable to dreams and other unconscious activities. These are activities in which new concepts are being forged and old ones extended; they are creative and so require interpretation, which is more of an art than a computation.

The judgements made in the course of psychotherapy are not made on the basis of clear information as in the natural sciences as they are based on attending to the indefiniteness of ordinary speech. This point is well summarized by Wittgenstein:

> Is there such a thing as 'expert judgement' about the genuineness of expressions of feeling? – Even here, there are those whose judgement is 'better' and those whose judgement is 'worse'. Correcter prognoses will generally issue from the judgements of those with better knowledge of mankind.
>
> Can one learn this knowledge? Yes; some can. Not, however, by taking a course in it, but through *experience*. – Can someone else be a man's teacher in this? Certainly. From time to time he gives him the right *tip*. – This is what 'learning' and 'teaching' are like here. – What one acquires here is not a technique; one learns correct judgements. There are also rules, but they do not form a system, and only experienced people can apply them right. Unlike calculating rules.
>
> What is most difficult here is to put this indefiniteness, correctly and unfalsified, into words. (Wittgenstein, 1953: 22).

Most theoreticians in psychotherapy pass this problem by, led by Freud. They avoid the 'indefiniteness' or put a name in its place – the unconscious, the transpersonal, etc. – thinking that by giving 'it' a name they understand so they can master 'it'. They then develop techniques on the basis of the theory and collect students who are taught to apply these techniques. No longer are people treated justly, but are subjected to the latest psychological theory. Thoughtfulness and attention to the uniqueness of what is happening, which can lead to correct judgement, are ignored.

A genuine response to persons is different from a prescribed or mechanical one. It is not regulated by the principle of reason or burdened by a theoretical apparatus that has to be applied. For how can one answer the call to respond responsibly and responsively if in advance all responses have been pre-narrated and anticipated? People require to be treated with justice rather than by applied theories, and justice always addresses itself to singularity, to the singularity of the other person, and so exceeds everything that could have been anticipated as a response.

One of the most sensitive students of conversation was Harvey Sacks whose *Lectures on Conversation* (1992) should be required reading for therapists. He studied extremely short snatches of conversation such as: 'The baby cried. The Mommy picked it up'. Or a telephone conversation:

A: Hello
B: Hello
A: What are you doing?
B: Nothing

He analyses the different meanings they have and most importantly what the words said are doing, how they indicate what is permitted to the speakers, what logics they suggested, what possibilities they entail and the many different ways of taking them. He shows how subtle is the meaning of even simple snatches of conversation.

A famous story among anthropologists is about when Fortune came back with his manuscript on the Dobu. His professor, who had a theory of poss-ible conditions under which a society could exist that turned on issues of the amount of hostility that was around, conflicts, etc., saw the manuscript and said: 'It's impossible. No such society could exist.' He checked it out further, found that they unfortunately did exist, and said: 'They don't *deserve* to exist.' Many therapists have the same attitude. If the patient does not fit their theory, then they are regarded as unanalysable or untreatable and rude words are attached to them such as 'borderline' or suffering from congenital envy. And if they are treated successfully by a therapist of another school, then they have not 'really' been treated – it was merely suggestion, seduction, good luck, or whatever. I have never met a patient who is unanalysable, although I have certainly met patients who did not want to see me any more – probably very wisely!

It was pointed out by Wittgenstein (1993) that it is a characteristic of our culture to seek explanations and that this is part of our mythology. It is not generally realized that explanation seeking leads to only one way of looking at the data and often distorts it. Thus in psychotherapy it is not merely the case that if we have a problem we can then set out to construct an expla-nation. Rather, it is assumed that only those facts are possible for which there is an explanation. Therefore something that actually has occurred can be treated as not so, by virtue of the fact that there is not an explanation for it.

This is a very powerful weapon in the hands of psychoanalysts. Thus a patient turns up late for a session and says truthfully that he overslept. This is a happening that occurs at times to us all. But not so to the analyst. The patient cannot have something just happen; a fact without an explanation is not possible according to the analyst's beliefs, who, like a paranoid person, does not understand the concept of chance – to him there must be a cause. So an interpretation is given – the patient unconsciously did not want to come or whatever. And so the unwary patient is trapped into believ-ing some form or other of psychoanalytic mythology pursuing an ever elusive goal – making the unconscious conscious.

Wittgenstein wrote: 'Superstition is nothing but belief in the causal nexus' (1961: 5.1361). Much of psychoanalysis and other psychotherapies are based on this superstition.

Rational Emotive Behaviour Therapy

This raises the question of the nature and place of belief in psychotherapy. Ellis, who founded Rational Emotive Behaviour Therapy (REBT), argues that we can increase our emotional well-being by adopting a policy of long-range hedonism; of course this belief is part of the utilitarian programme and is subject to all the criticisms of it. He also thinks that our beliefs greatly determine emotional health and that dogmatic or 'musturbatory' beliefs are especially harmful and should be replaced by non-dogmatic preferences. People, he thinks, need to understand that emotional and behavioural disturbance stem largely from irrational absolutist beliefs. They must learn to discriminate irrational beliefs from rational ones and dispute the irrational beliefs by means of scientific reasoning. Ellis encourages people to 'work, work, work' at changing their irrational beliefs. They must continue this process for the rest of their lives. Like psychoanalysis, REBT never lets go. Once caught, we are embroiled in its beliefs for the rest of our lives!

Ellis recognizes that much of his thought derives from the Stoics. The Stoics were one of the main Hellenic schools of philosophy and therapy, along with the Sceptics and Epicureans (Nussbaum, 1994). Philosophers and physicians from these schools practised psychotherapy among the Greeks and Romans from about the late fourth century BC to the fourth century AD. The most important critics of the Stoics were the Sceptics. Both influenced each other; many of the terms used by the Sceptics were created by the Stoics and many insights and arguments used by the Stoics had to be changed under Sceptical criticism. Existential thought has always been influenced by Scepticism. As I said earlier, Hume heavily influenced Hamann; Kierkegaard in many places discusses the Greek Sceptics, his *Philosophical Fragments* being a notable example; Husserl, the founder of phenomenology which is fundamental to existential therapy, took the epoche to be central to his thought as it was to the Sceptics and so on.

There is no room here to give much of an account of Sceptical therapy (see Hankinson, 1995; Heaton, 1997). The basic position was proposed by Pyrrho around 250BC. He is reported to have stated that we must not say of reality that it is, that it is not, that it is and is not, nor can we say that it neither is nor is not. There is a vast literature both ancient and modern, Eastern and Western, which tries to untangle this gnomic utterance, known as the quadrilemma. For our purposes it contains a radical critique of Stoicism and REBT. It implies that any belief about reality is false. The Sceptics would agree that any dogmatic or musturbatory belief leads to psychological disturbance. But they argued that if this is taken as a true statement, then it too becomes an absolutist one and so a dogmatic belief. It leads to intense pursuit of a goal – the goal of freedom from irrational beliefs – and that intense pursuit or avoidance of any generalized goal in life is the root of all unhappiness. As Ellis says, we have to 'work, work, work' to uproot our irrational beliefs. He assumes we all believe in the Protestant work ethic, an assumption which would have little pull in Hellenic Greece or in many other cultures and which is an irrational belief.

The Sceptics had many different types of argument against dogmatic beliefs (Annas and Barnes, 1985). Their aim was to lead to a suspension of judgement about the nature of reality and so to peace of mind. They argued that mental pain is produced when we become chained to a system of belief, for it leads to perpetual straining to reach an impossible goal. Also, they argued that to believe that scientific reasoning is the only form of rationality is dogmatic. Rationality takes many forms, there are reasonable and unreasonable ways of conducting love affairs, being a mother, and so on, and these vary from one person to another and from one culture to another. There is no evidence that scientists are better at these activities than ordinary people or in the Enlightenment belief that reason is monolithic and possessed especially by European white culture.

The Sceptics taught that there is no expertise in living so there is no teaching of it either, for there is nothing to teach or to learn. This insight into the human condition of issuelessness resembles that depicted in Kafka's fiction and Beckett's fiction and plays, works which contend that there is no escape from what we do inasmuch as every movement we make is a movement on the path *we* make. So Sceptical therapy is not a technique to obtain a goal in life, that is it does not have a goal which requires a length of time to reach it. It is rather a way of getting clear about the network of activities – desiring to reach a goal in life, having theories about it, etc. – that get in the way of enjoying living which is essentially issueless.

Above all, as the ancient Sceptic wrote and as is quoted by Wittgenstein in the *Tractatus*: 'We must throw away the ladder after we have climbed it' (Wittgenstein, 1961: 6–54). We must be sceptical even about reason and scepticism and not carry them around with us as systems of belief. For there is nothing ultimately 'special' about any therapy. Chemotherapy may be invaluable at times but that does not mean we should always be taking it. It is the same with psychotherapy – its beliefs pervert ordinary living.

Rhetoric

An important part of the therapist's armory is rhetoric which is usually used by modern therapists to persuade themselves and others that their therapy is the best. Rhetoric was originally the study of the resources of speech which can lead to truth without using proofs. It was distinguished from sophistry. The sophist aims at an external end – his own success or the success or pleasure of someone else – whereas the honest rhetorician follows the powers of his art, excellence of speech, which lead to truth (Garver, 1994).

Freud was a master at using rhetoric as a masquerade for evidence of his theories (Spence, 1994). He wanted to appear scientific, for posing as a scientist would most likely lead to his theories being believed and so to fame for their author. But he only had a few detailed case histories, some choice specimens and favourite examples, and anecdotal evidence from his own self-analysis. From this meagre resource he wanted to produce theories about the minds of the whole human race, past, present and to come! So he gave up seeking inductive proof for his theories and resorted to sophistical rhetoric. His example has been followed with variations by many therapists who wanted to set up their own school of therapy.

A study of all the rhetorical devices used by therapists in this century would take many books. I will look briefly at a few. It is important for a therapist creating a new theory to appear special for from this he or she can derive his or her authority and so the authority of the theory and techniques deriving from it. One easy way of appearing special is to make a secret of the source of one's specialness. Exotic experiences are helpful here; for example, studying, usually for a brief period, with some shaman from some obscure tribe or culture and then claiming one has special knowledge and healing powers. It is important that the experiences and teaching be remote for then neither other therapists, let alone ordinary people, can check up on the teaching or experience. However, this ploy is not too persuasive for those susceptible to scientific rhetoric so let us look briefly at the legend of Freud's self-analysis which quite rightly has been seen as the foundation of psychoanalysis.

Around 1897 he started analysing his dreams and found that they were a sort of time machine which enabled him to travel to his early life if he used free associations. As is shown in detail by Spence (1994) the evidence for this assertion is scanty in the extreme. Roughly because Freud believed in the universality of causation, he had to believe that dreams had a cause and so 'to our surprise, *we find the child and the child's impulses still living on in the dream*' (Freud, 1954: 191; italics in the original). His beliefs guided his free associations. Unknown to himself, he was subject to a standard rhetorical figure known as metalepsis which is defined as attributing a present effect to a remote cause.

This belief in universal causation and the effect of remote causes was aided by one of Freud's favourite foundational metaphors, that of archaeology. He was fascinated by archaeology and part of its fascination was that its discoveries lay there in remarkable preservation. It is as if time had stopped. Freud thought that the same happened in mental life. 'In mental life,' he wrote, 'nothing which has once been formed can perish ... everything is somehow preserved and ... in suitable circumstances it can once more be brought to light' (Freud, 1930: 69). In fact, he thought the psychoanalyst's material is more certain than the archaeologist's as it is indestructible. Its facts are transparent, there is no room for interpretation, psychoanalytic method enables one to contact the actual past so psychoanalysis is the only truly scientific psychology, all the rest is mere suggestion.

The evidence for these wild assertions is really only Freud's own analysis, whose content is not open to public inspection other than a few scattered allusions to it in letters and in his work. So as we have no access to the primary data, Freud's 'findings' are not open to questioning. His status as the supremely qualified investigator provides all-round protection for his 'discoveries'. This is very attractive to many as it promises certainty – if all memories are but skulls and mummies, then we have reached psychic bedrock at last. The Oedipus complex, the importance of infantile sexuality, concepts of transference and resistance are all derived from it.

Freud's self-analysis had to be turned into a heroic feat to produce real conviction. This myth was started by Ernest Jones and continued by modern historians who speak of his descent into the underworld of the unconscious, his extraordinary suffering, and so on. The historian Peter Gay writes of 'this act of patient heroism, to be admired and palely imitated but never repeated, . . . the founding act of psychoanalysis' (Gay, 1988: 96). Very little is actually known of Freud's analysis. Wisely, he did not write much about it, except of its 'discoveries' which we would call inventions. Secrecy is an important part of a hero myth.

Many people in the course of history have sought to know themselves. One thinks of Augustine's *Confessions*, Pascal's *Pensées*, Montaigne's *Essays*, and many others. Usually these acts of self-discovery have led to a transformation in the person, a conversion, a soul-shaking and humbling experience. This was not so with Freud. His self-analysis was a continuation of his Enlightenment project of the march of reason over unreason. There is no evidence that Freud's self-discoveries are true descriptions in the sense that *this* is the way things happen in the mind. What he did do was to couch his 'findings' in a form that would be persuasive to his contemporaries, blinding them with his rhetoric, and in this he has been enormously successful.

Sexuality

Problems over sexual activity are common. Existential therapists, especially those influenced by Foucault, such as Laing, have a rather different approach to them from most other therapists. An important part of the discourse of modernity is that sexuality is at the core of human identity and that it is a stubborn drive, constantly at war with repressive powers. Furthermore, the family is unified in the individual by placing the incest desire at the centre of the individual's life. Sexuality is the index of one's subjectivity, of one's true self. The kinship of subjectivity–truth–sexuality is the linchpin of Freudian thought. Part of the rhetoric of psychoanalysis and many other therapies is that it can help to free us from the repressions of sexuality. Freud boasted that he called a spade a spade in sexual matters and that this would help to free us from repressions. He thought that children should be given the facts of sexual life without question; knowledge would prevent or cure sexual difficulties (Freud, 1959).

Like so many Enlightenment projects, things do not seem to have turned out quite as Freud expected. Perhaps more people can masturbate with less guilt than in the nineteenth century, and children and adults are given more information about sex probably than at any other time. But even in places where psychoanalysts and therapists swarm, there are huge problems with sexuality. There is no evidence that there is less impotence and frigidity in these centres. Marital problems, problems of loneliness and despair caused by the break up of families, often by people searching for sexual liberation, are probably more common in these centres than in places that are less 'liberated'. Forms of liberation inspired by the Enlightenment probably create more unhappiness than they cure. There is no evidence that giving information about sex enables people to enjoy it more.

Even Freud's avoidance of sexual euphemisms and his belief that sexuality is just a matter of giving people facts about sex has been shown to have nothing to do with being comfortable with sexuality. The Cuna Indians, a South American tribe, have been studied and it has been shown that their language is full of euphemisms about sexuality. Conception becomes 'to buy a child', pregnancy 'a worm entered', and so on. Sexuality is never discussed publicly by them. The anthropologist remarked that there is an unremitting effort to keep children ignorant of everything concerning sex (Taussig, 1993). But these people seem to be more at ease about sexual matters than 'liberated' Europeans. It seems that the Cuna Indians, like many other supposedly primitive people according to Enlightenment thinking, are aware of the importance of the mystery of sexuality, of awe at our origins; they do not superstitiously believe in the causal nexus, they are aware of the dangers of knowledge, and they understand that sexuality is not just a matter of knowing facts. Their customs may enhance the pleasures of sex without spelling havoc on the whole social structure.

Foucault argues that our eagerness to talk of sex in terms of repression and to claim that one or other form of therapy has the power to liberate us from this repression is part of a technology of power, a further inroad of the Enlightenment on our lives (Foucault, 1978). It is very gratifying to the speaker to hold forth about something that is repressed. It gives him the appearance of upsetting established power, of anticipating the coming freedom, perhaps of being 'liberated' himself. Some of the ancient functions of prophecy are activated; tomorrow sex will be good again. Such a discourse gives the speaker power.

The Enlightenment has replaced the ancient *ars erotica* with a *scientia sexualis*. In the former truth is derived from pleasure itself. Pleasure and joy are considered in relation to themselves, to the logic appropriate to them instead of some external criterion of utility, of what is or is not permitted according to some theory or other, backed up by a jargon of growth, maturity, adjustment and security. Our civilization is perhaps the only one to practise a *scientia sexualis*. It probably developed from the confession and has become one of the West's most highly developed techniques for producing truth. One must tell all, with the greatest precision, whatever is the most difficult to tell. This is supposed to set one free.

But the transformation of sex into discourse makes the speaking subject become subjected to the statement. The truth of sex becomes caught up in this discursive form. A form far removed from the one governing the *ars erotica*. The agency of domination becomes not the one who speaks, for it is he or she that is constrained, but the one who listens, who receives the confession and scientifically validates it. It thus becomes integrated into scientific discourse and so susceptible to pathological classifications calling for normalizing interventions. Instead of a dialogue which is attentive to the logic of pleasure and joy and so empowers the participants, there is a movement of power towards the one who listens, the 'rational' expert, the one who knows.

Conclusion

Laing, perhaps the most influential existential psychiatrist in the English-speaking world in this half-century, wrote: 'Psychotherapy must remain *an obstinate attempt of two people to recover the wholeness of being human through the relationship between them*' (Laing, 1967: 45). It is 'obstinate' because it is difficult. Some complain of the difficulty of existential writing and there is no doubt that some of it is difficult, although the novels of Sartre, Camus, and the plays of Beckett have reached and appealed to a large audience, as have the writings of Laing. The point is that existential writing, like most philosophy, requires endless interpretation. It has not a univocal meaning which can be passively read and assimilated as is most scientific and psychotherapeutic writing. New insights into and interpretations of Plato are still appearing although he wrote over two thousand years ago. This is because philosophy is concerned with thought and it is only persons who think. Neither persons nor thought can be summed up in a theory or created by a technique. They are not subsumable under a discursive formation because they cannot be understood by means of a simple linking of propositions which are defined by their reference. Existential therapy is concerned with experience, modes of existence, and possibilities of life which cannot be represented by propositions alone. Scientific notions are defined by propositions whereas concepts which move one are the concern of philosophy and existential therapy (Deleuze and Guattari, 1994).

Persons are not minds plus bodies which are somehow welded together. Existential thought and practice has always been concerned to overcome dualistic thinking, the separation of mind from body, of thought from nature. Once again these are very difficult questions which are slurred over by most psychotherapy schools. For example, self-knowledge is not knowledge of an inner world, of a self which is to be found after a long search; both inner world and self are projections of the therapist's own desires and cravings.

Existential therapy is opposed to any instrumental approach to the knowledge of persons, for such an approach splits him or her into parts whereas persons are wholes. Methods are always determined, they have their source in the region to which they apply, as in the sciences. Methods appropriate to quantum mechanics are not appropriate to organic chemistry. The method is an instrument for representing a given field, and is applied to that field from the outside. But when two persons meet and respect one another, one is not outside the other, applying a technique to the other as a person. One might apply a technique to another person's body as in surgery, but a body is not a person any more than a mind is one.

Existential therapy is one that follows the intrinsic and spontaneous movement of truth. It is a thoughtful questioning which does not rush to its goal, the reply. What counts is the manner of questioning which does not hurry to seize and exhibit some object which will count as the cause or reason for the phenomenon in question. Rather, we must allow ourselves to be disturbed by the question, staying with it, in a meditative response to it, without neutralizing its power of disquiet by some explanation. What is vital is not the cleverness of therapist or patient, but the ungraspable and undeniable 'presence' of something which is other than mind and which 'from time to time', occurs.

References

Annas, J. and Barnes, J. (1985) *The Modes of Scepticism.* Cambridge: Cambridge University Press.

Berlin, Isaiah (1994) *The Magus of the North* (Ed. H. Hardy). London: Fontana Press.

Deleuze, G. and Guattari, F. (1994) *What is Philosophy?* (H. Tomlinson and G. Burchill, trans.). London: Verso.

Derrida, J. (1976) *Of Grammatology* (G. Spivak, trans.). Baltimore, MD: Johns Hopkins University Press.

Foucault, M. (1972) *The Archaeology of Knowledge* (A.M. Sheridan Smith, trans.). London: Tavistock.

Foucault, M. (1978). *The History of Sexuality* (R. Hurley, trans.). London: Penguin.

Freud, S. (1930) *Civilization and its Discontents* (S.E. 21) London: Hogarth Press.

Freud, S. (1954) *The Interpretation of Dreams* (J. Strachey, trans.). London: Allen & Unwin.

Freud, S. (1959) *The Sexual Enlightenment of Children* (S.E. 9) London: Hogarth Press.

Garver, E. (1994) *Aristotle's Rhetoric: An Art of Character.* Chicago: University of Chicago Press.

Gay, P. (1988) *Freud: A Life for Our Time.* New York: W.W. Norton.

Good, B.J. (1994) *Medicine, Rationality, and Experience.* Cambridge: Cambridge University Press.

Hankinson, R.J. (1995) *The Sceptics.* London: Routledge.

Heaton, J.M. (1997) Pyrrhonian scepticism: a therapeutic phenomenology. *Journal of the British Society of Phenomenology*, 28, 70.

Heidegger, M. (1962) *Being and Time* (J. MacQuarrie and E. Robinson, trans.). London: SCM Press.

Hume, D. (1978) *A Treatise of Human Nature* (2nd edn). Oxford: Clarendon Press.

Kierkegaard, S. (1985) *Philosophical Fragments.* (H.V. Hong and F. Hong, eds and trans.). Princeton, NJ. Princeton University Press.

Laing, R.D. (1967) The psychotherapeutic experience. In R.D. Laing, *The Politics of Experience.* London: Penguin.

Mill, J.S. (1863) Utilitarianism. In A. Ryan (ed.) (1987), *Utilitarianism and Other Essays.* London: Penguin.

Nussbaum, M.C. (1994) *The Therapy of Desire.* Princeton, NJ: Princeton University Press.

Russell, B. (1961) Introduction. In L. Wittgenstein, *Tractatus Logico-Philosophicus* (D.F. Pears and B.F. McGuiness, trans.). London: Routledge & Kegan Paul.

Sacks, H. (1992) *Lectures on Conversation* (Vols 1 and 2). (G. Jefferson, ed.). Oxford: Blackwell.

Sharpe, R.A. (1990) *Making the Human Mind*. London: Routledge.

Spence, D.P. (1994) *The Rhetorical Voice of Psychoanalysis*. Cambridge, MA: Harvard University Press.

Taussig, M. (1993) *Mimesis and Alterity*. New York: Routledge.

Wittgenstein, L. (1953) *Philosophical Investigations* (G.E.M. Anscombe, trans.). Oxford: Blackwell.

Wittgenstein, L. (1961) *Tractatus Logico-Philosophicus* (D.F. Pears and B.F. McGuiness, trans.). London: Routledge & Kegan Paul.

Wittgenstein, L. (1969) *On Certainty* (D. Paul and G.E.M. Anscombe, trans.). Oxford: Blackwell.

Wittgenstein, L. (1993) Remark's on Frazer's *Golden Bough*. In J.C. Klagge and A. Nordmann (eds), *Philosophical Occasions*. Indianapolis: Hackett Publishing Company.

6

The Communicative Approach

Robert Langs

The communicative approach to psychoanalysis and psychotherapy (I will use the two terms interchangeably) is a modern-day revisionistic version of psychoanalytic theory in which *adaptation* is the primary conceptual organizer; interaction and communication major focal points; and a hierarchical theory a prime feature. The basic precepts of the approach are Langs (1982, 1988, 1992a, 1993a) and Smith (1991):

1 Human beings are biological adaptive organisms.
2 Humans adapt to emotionally charged stimuli or impingements both consciously and unconsciously.
3 Unconscious efforts at adaptation are critical to the vicissitudes of emotional life, including emotional health and dysfunctions, and the process of psychotherapy designed to alleviate those dysfunctions from which a given person – a patient – suffers.
4 In the clinical situation, listening, organizing, formulating and giving meaning to the material from patients is developed on two levels: first, in terms of its manifest, direct meanings and their implications; and secondly, in terms of encoded or disguised meanings which are contained in the same material, especially when it is narrative in form. The surface level reflects conscious adaptations to known environmental events (stimuli or triggers), while the encoded level constitutes adaptations to repressed triggers or to the repressed meanings of known triggers.
5 The fundamental entity of adaptation in the emotional domain is *the emotion-processing mind*, a cognitive mental module comprised of two systems – *the conscious system* and *the deep unconscious system.*
6 A complete and commanding theory of psychoanalysis must be configured as a hierarchical theory of the emotionally relevant adaptations of the total human organism. No single perspective is capable of defining the full scope of the field, including the nature of emotional dysfunctions and of the transactions of psychotherapy.

With this as our orientation, I will present some features of the communicative approach and its developmental and evolutionary history.

Choosing the communicative approach

The communicative approach was my own invention. It emerged partly from personal efforts to complete my training analysis through self-analysis and partly from the clinical observations that I was making within my own practice and in my extensive teaching and supervising commitments. In the course of these efforts, various uncertainties arose which led me to take a fresh look at the treatment process. As I did so, I began to realize that phenomena that I had been taught to think of as patients' free floating, intrapsychically based projections and transferences actually were stimulated by *evocative triggers – adaptive contexts*, as I called them at the time – to which they were an adaptive response.

As the work I will describe testifies, this insight – essentially, that material from patients primarily is activated by and responsive to external events or stimuli – gave birth to the *communicative approach*, which initially was called *the adaptational–interactional approach*, and set it off on its long evolutionary trajectory. With this as its beginning, it took several additional years to realize that events outside of therapy seldom evoked the disguised – *encoded or unconscious* – communicated responses from patients and that their key adaptive contexts on this level virtually always were the interventions of their therapists. Thus, while a patient's conscious thinking wanders about and moves in and out of therapy, his or her unconscious thinking is concentrated on the therapist and the conditions and transactions of the therapeutic interaction.

By way of background, I had worked at New York University with George Klein and Robert Holt, psychoanalytically orientated psychologists who taught me to adopt a healthy skepticism regarding psychoanalytic theory and stressed the need to make one's own observations with as little bias and as much openness as possible. Even though a therapist needs a theory in order to organize his or her clinical observations, he or she also needs to be especially sensitive to observations and data that seem to run counter to the invested theory – both knowledge and ignorance, relatively fixed ideas and openness to revision are essential. These guiding principles helped to render the communicative approach a relatively strong observation-based theory and set of clinical precepts.

In time, the communicative approach was formalized into a set of basic principles for listening to and defining the meanings, conscious and unconscious, of the material from patients. This method, now called *trigger decoding*, became the observational and organizational base for communicative theory and practice. The main precepts of the approach's listening and formulating process (Langs, 1978) were, and still are:

1 The patient's free associations (and behaviors) are constituted as conscious and unconscious responses or adaptations to the immediate triggers or adaptation-evoking stimuli that arise within the therapeutic interaction. His or her *unconscious reactions* center on the interventions

of the therapist – silences, active comments of all kinds, including interpretations (however defined), and managements of the ground rules and setting of the therapy.

2   There are two essential components to listening and formulating:
   (a)   *The patient's material,* which, when in storied or narrative form, contains both manifest and latent (encoded, unconscious) meanings.
   (b)   *The therapist's interventions,* whose manifest and implied meanings evoke the patient's narrative imagery and its encoded themes and meanings. Should the therapist communicate his or her own narrative and images, the patient will also respond to the encoded messages so contained.

3   The listening process culminates in two ways:
   (a)   In an adaptational interpretation of the patient's unconscious experience of the therapist's efforts. This is done by linking the narrative themes to the trigger event – whatever the therapist said or did to evoke the encoded response in the first place. Communicative interpretations are presented as the patient's decoded unconscious *experiences* of the specific meanings of the therapist's efforts, and not as manifest or implied isolated, conscious or unconscious *fantasies.*
   (b)   In the therapist's handling of a ground rule of the therapy carried out in accordance with the patient's encoded, unconscious directives. These frame management efforts always involve establishing or sustaining a secured frame or securing an errant one (see below).

4   For a therapist's intervention to be considered correct and valid, and therefore potentially helpful to the patient, the responsive encoded narrative material from the patient must confirm the effort in one or both of two ways:
   (a)   The emergence of stories with positively toned images – tales of clever, helpful, insightful or otherwise constructive figures. This is called *unconscious interpersonal validation,* and it reflects the patient's unconscious perceptions of the well-functioning therapist's sound interpretive or frame management efforts.
   (b)   The emergence of narratives and themes that encode fresh perceptions of the therapist's intervention in ways that, when further interpreted, add new insights to those rendered by the intervention to which the patient is responding. This is called *cognitive validation* in that it adds previously unknown meaning to the therapist's prior interpretation or frame management response.

This methodology took many years to hone, but all along, whenever my own interventions and those of my supervisees followed these guidelines, both encoded validation and a diminution of symptoms transpired. It was the evident effectiveness of the approach, and the remarkable ways in which patients unconsciously validated efforts based on communicative precepts, that kept me fully invested in its doctrines.

The elegance and uniqueness of the approach

The communicative approach has travelled a lonely, singular path among psychoanalytic theories and techniques. Without exception, its basic precepts distinguish the approach from all other forms of treatment, nonanalytic and analytic. It has taken many years to be rather clear about what sets the approach apart and why it is that, given the validity of its principles and its strong array of supportive evidence, other forms of therapy and other versions of psychoanalytic theory have shunned its postulates and clinical precepts.

What sets the communicative approach apart from the rest of psychotherapy is its basic method of listening and formulating. The communicative approach alone uses a *two-tiered or two system, fundamentally strong adaptational approach* to organizing the material from patients. Where other approaches adopt either a weak adaptational position (the idea that patients do, of course, try to cope somewhere and somehow) or none at all, the communicative approach sees the patient attempting to cope at all times. Even more critically, the approach has been able to identify the design of the mental module that serves as the organ of adaptation in the emotional realm – *the emotion-processing mind* – and to carefully characterize in depth the essential nature of emotionally related adaptation (Langs, 1995a).

Through its use clinically of encoded, unconscious validation, the approach has discovered two vital features of these incessant adaptive efforts: first, that they operate on two levels, one linked to awareness and the other entirely outside of awareness; and secondly, that these two levels of coping are very different in that *conscious* adaptive efforts tend to wander about temporally into the past, present and future, and spatially into situations within and outside of therapy, while *unconscious* adaptation is entirely concentrated on the here and now situation – the conditions of therapy, and the therapist's handling of the ground rules and his or her other interventions, whatever they may be in words, affects and actions.

The first level of adaptation begins with conscious perceptions and involves *conscious processing*, along with some superficially unconscious or preconscious or intuitive processing as well. These efforts pertain to events, impressions, and meanings that are either within awareness or easily able to enter it. This mode of adaptation reflects the workings of *the conscious system* of the emotion-processing mind, and it is reflected in the manifest contents of the patient's material and the implications of these surface contents.

The second level of adaptation begins with subliminal or unconscious perceptions and involves *unconscious processing*. The workings of this *deep unconscious system* of the emotion-processing mind and its *wisdom subsystem* are reflected primarily in narrative material which encodes unconscious responses to specific adaptation-evoking stimuli or triggers – as noted, for therapy patients, these events are the therapist's interventions. To access this level of meaning, the therapist must identify the specific intervention to which the patient is reacting unconsciously and then decode the narrative imagery as valid perceptions of the meanings and implications of the therapist's effort. These unconscious perceptions are personally selected for response and expression in terms of the patient's own unconscious issues and needs, but they are quite veridical and not distorted. *Trigger decoding* alone accesses the adaptive processing of the second system of the emotion-processing mind – the deep unconscious system.

Noncommunicative forms of therapy address only the patient's manifest contents and their conscious and unconscious implications. They do not engage in specific efforts at trigger decoding. Those forms of therapy that operate cognitively simply explore the surface meanings of a patient's material and respond accordingly, while those forms of therapy that are psychoanalytically oriented propose a variety of supposed unconscious meanings which are implied in this surface material. In general, these therapists work with supposed links between the patient's conscious communications and past experiences and figures – so-called transferences – arguing that the patient misperceives the therapist's efforts and the present therapy situation because of the unconscious distorting influence of past events and their intrapsychic residues.

In contrast, the communicative approach argues that while patients may *consciously* distort their views of their therapists (largely, however, to protect both their therapists and themselves from painful and threatening conscious realizations of the meanings of hurtful interventions), *unconsciously*, they selectively but accurately perceive and work over the true nature of what a therapist says and does.

Where other approaches see meaning either in the surface of a patient's free associations or in postulated distortions projected into the situation by the patient and implied in his or her material, and on no other level, the communicative approach sees conscious meaning as distinctive from unconscious meaning – and has found that both are contained in the same storied free associations of the patient. These critical unconscious meanings *always are encoded* and they always are the result of a process that begins with unconscious perception and moves through unconscious processing to the generation of encoded narratives. Defining this sequence of unconscious psychological processes distinguishes the communicative approach from all other forms of therapy.

To cite a very brief illustration, Ms Reddy, a single woman in her late twenties, begins one of her sessions by telling her male therapist, Dr Lake, of an incident that occurred the previous night with her boyfriend, Doug. Ms Reddy had been feeling that Doug was acting strangely of late, and on the previous afternoon, one of her girlfriends had called her to tell her that she had seen Doug at a restaurant with another woman. That night, Ms Reddy confronted Doug with this information and he confessed that for the past two months he'd been seeing another woman. Ms Reddy was furious and nearly attacked him physically; she felt terribly betrayed. Despite Doug's protests and his pointing out that she had provoked him by breaking several recent engagements with him, she impulsively blurted out that she could never trust him again and would never see him again. She was furious with herself because she keeps picking men who hurt her like that.

There are countless possible ways to formulate and deal with this material. They range from proposing dating exercises and cognitive reframing, to training the patient as to how to meet suitable men and recognize men who are likely to be hurtful, to all manner of seeming interpretations of the unconscious implications of this segment of associations. The latter could range from interpretations of the patient's evident unconscious masochism to proposing the existence of a brother or father transference, or of unconscious seductive wishes towards the therapist which were being acted out with the boyfriend. Also possible are interpretations of relational dysfunctions, failures of mirroring and self-image, ego dysfunctions, and much more.

These interpretations all stem from weak adaptive positions. Those that deal with the betrayal of the boyfriend *per se* would be addressing the patient's adaptive responses to a conscious, manifest issue or trigger. There is, of course, validity to doing so, but the unconscious aspects of such interpretations are highly speculative and intellectualized, and they also are self-evident and trivial as far as the therapy and the process of cure are concerned – psychotherapy desperately needs a trivia meter. Further, interpretations that would attempt to deal with the patient's so-called transference reactions would imply that she is adapting to her relationship with her therapist, but would formulate the response entirely in terms of supposedly evident maladaptations stemming from the patient's unconscious fantasies, wishes, and projections on to the therapist – there would be no sense that the patient is adapting deeply unconsciously to aspects of her therapist's recent interventions.

The communicative approach alone would propose that the essential and most influential meanings of this material cannot be interpreted without knowing the unmentioned or repressed trigger event – the adaptation-evoking experience – to which the patient is responding unconsciously and which accounts for the critical *encoded meanings* of this story. The premise here, amply validated through past clinical work, is as noted, that these *unconscious* adaptive responses and their representations touch on the most significant level of effect in the emotional domain. This is not, then, a refutation of other levels of meaning – manifest, implied, isolated symbolic, etc. – but an argument that *the most compelling* processes, motives, and communications in the emotional domain occur outside of awareness and that their expression reaches awareness only in disguised, encoded form.

The communicative approach, then, would recognize this narrative as a reflection of an encoded perception of either a recent repressed intervention made by Dr Lake, or alternatively, the repressed meanings of an intervention that did register consciously in the patient – along with the responsive unconscious processing of, and reactions to, the meanings of this trigger event. There are no recognizable deep unconscious meanings to a patient's material until the unspoken trigger event or trigger-related meanings are identified and linked to the themes at hand.

In this instance, the missing trigger was a recent intervention made by Dr Lake – he had accepted the referral of Ms Reddy's cousin, Helene, into therapy with him. *Consciously and manifestly*, Ms Reddy had not only made the referral, but she was very pleased when Dr Lake was able to see her cousin in therapy.

However, when we link this trigger to the themes in the story about Doug, and thereby decode the imagery in light of the trigger event, we come upon a response to the trigger by Ms Reddy that is very different from her conscious reaction. Although disguised, the story is readily decoded to reveal that she had experienced this frame deviation, which modified the privacy and confidentiality of Ms Reddy's therapy, as an act of infidelity and disloyalty on Dr Lake's part – he was experienced as being unfaithful sexually to Ms Reddy, the patient whom he saw first. Indeed, without exception, frame deviations are experienced unconsciously as instinctualized, sexually and aggressively, and as damaging to all concerned. While Ms Reddy consciously was pleased with herself and her therapist, unconsciously she saw herself as having selected another hurtful man whom she should stop seeing – even though she did not do so.

We see then that the identification of the repressed implications of a trigger event that a patient perceives and processes unconsciously casts a distinctive light on the meanings of a patient's material and his or her behaviors – the picture is very different from the one that is visible directly or by extracting implications from surface imagery. Where the direct picture is positive, the encoded picture is very negative. But a fair assessment would indicate that the unconscious picture is more accurate and adaptively wiser than the conscious one – yet the patient's adaptive response to the trigger event follows the conscious view. This observation, repeated many times over, poses an unsolved puzzle (Kuhn, 1962) for the communicative approach – one that has not been recognized through any other means of listening and formulating.

As you can see, the communicative approach has adopted a strong adaptive position and has placed adaptation, the single most characteristic feature of biological organisms (Plotkin, 1994), center stage in understanding human behavior and both psychopathology and the therapeutic process. The central theorem of the approach sees the patient as coping with specific triggers and their meanings, consciously and unconsciously, and doing so in distinctive fashion in each system as well. The communicative approach is the only form of therapy that has defined unconscious experience in adaptive terms and with such precision.

In respect to intervening, the approach endeavors to capture the essence of a patient's unconscious experiences and adaptations within psychotherapy, interprets these experiences interactionally, works over the patient's unconscious perceptions of the therapist's correct and erroneous interventions, including his or her frame-securing and frame-altering efforts, and proceeds therapeutically from there. The result is a unique form of therapy that embraces the deep truths of the therapist's impact on the patient, whichever way the situation happens to fall out in a given session.

There are, in addition, several notable features that also distinguish the communicative approach from other modes of therapy (see also below). They include a concentration on the therapist's establishment and management of the ground rules and setting because it has been found empirically that the *unconsciously communicated, encoded narratives* from patients virtually always reflect responses to interventions in this area – the deep unconscious system is a frame-concentrated system. In addition, the communicative approach has designed a new form of psychotherapy, called empowered or self-processing (the communicative form of self-analysis) psychotherapy (Langs, 1993a), in which dreams and narratives are maximized, as is the search for adaptation-evoking triggers. It also has generated fresh approaches to supervision (Langs, 1994a), dream exploration (Langs, 1994b) and work with daydreams (Langs, 1995c).

All in all, because of its fundamentals – conscious and unconscious perception and adapting, the definition of encoded material, and the process of trigger decoding – the communicative approach stands alone but strong among the many forms of psychotherapy.

Support for the approach

In addition to considerable evidence for the curative value of the approach (a claim made by all forms of therapy, however), there are three major and unique ways in which the communicative approach has obtained confirmation and support: first, through the encoded or unconscious validation of interventions based on communicative principles and the nonvalidation of all other types of efforts by therapists; secondly, through extensive supportive findings from a series of mathematically based research investigations of the communicative exchanges between patients and therapists; and thirdly, through the unusual and rich evolutionary history of the communicative approach which has become the only truly hierarchical theory of not only psychoanalysis but of the emotional realm – a trajectory and richness of concepts that is possible only with a valid theory. I will discuss each of these types of supportive evidence.

Encoded validation

The communicative position has found strong clinical support for the thesis that only unconsciously validated interventions can lead to insightful deep psychological change and cure, and has found that only trigger decoded interventions obtain this type of confirmation. There is a large body of clinical observations that support this technical precept which actually has guided the communicative approach almost since its inception (Langs, 1978, 1992a, 1993a; Smith, 1991). The repeated unconscious validation of adaptationally crafted interventions, interpretive and frame-securing, provides considerable evidence for the wisdom and value of the approach.

Formal science

The communicative approach is the only version of psychoanalytic theory that has been able to create a quantitative, mathematically based, formal science for the field, replete with deep regularities and laws of a kind that are exceedingly rare in biological sciences (Langs, 1992c, 1993b; Langs and Badalamenti, 1992a, 1992b, 1994a, 1994b, in press). In brief, the science is based on weighted measures of *communicative vehicle* – the means by which patients and therapists express themselves. The five quantified variables we used essentially measured the extent to which a patient or therapist was expressing himself or herself via narrative imagery or via intellectualizations. This dimension of human communication proved to be an ever-present, relatively simple, quantifiable aspect of the language outputs of the human mind – we were dealing with qualities of a kind that usually speak for basic processes.

This research yielded two very different forms of support for the communicative approach. The first is simply put: the very success of this pursuit, which was based on communicative principles related to the importance of narrative and nonnarrative forms of expression, provided unusual evidence for the validity of the communicative approach.

In addition, however, the results of the pilot studies themselves lent considerable strength to the communicative position. These initial studies were carried out using ten consultations conducted by well-known psychoanalysts with five different patients who were in stalemated psychotherapies. The main analyses of data were carried out with the sessions from two women patients, each of whom saw three different analysts. The mathematician in the study was blind to the identity of both the patients and the analysts, and he assessed the results from each model in terms of the extent to which they spoke favorably or unfavorably for the work done by the analyst in the consultation session. The sample of therapists included psychoanalysts who worked according to principles derived from object relations theory, relational concepts, self-psychology and the communicative approach. To our surprise, over the course of a dozen or so models used to analyse the data, without exception, the work of the communicative analyst produced the most favorable comparative results.

These supportive findings came from many diverse models. The first involved measures of speaker duration (who spoke for how long, in sequence) which revealed that the communicative consultation showed the greatest amount of deep systemic stability. A statistical model used cross correlations to measure the extent of deep influence between the patient and therapist in respect to the five scored dimensions, and here the results showed that the communicative therapist had five times more effect than any of the other therapists in the study.

The research also unearthed a series of universal laws related to the progress of the scores for the five quantified dimensions as these sessions unfolded over time. One mathematical model measured the cumulative complexity of the patients' and therapists' use of communicative vehicles. The patient interviewed by the communicative therapist showed the most complexity and the therapist the least – a finding that suggested greater freedom and creativity in the patient's communicative expressions and greater control of expression by the communicative analyst.

It was possible to define a *communicative particle* in the form of a five-point vector (one for each measured dimension) that represented the vicissitudes of each patient's and therapist's communicative vehicles. This enabled us to garner evidence for the operation of a *communicative force field* that imparted work and energy for communicative expression to both the patient and therapist. Measures of work and force showed that the patient seen in communicative consultation had the most work done on her communicative particle, indicating a maximum opportunity to express herself. Further, the communicative patient took away the most energy from the communicative force field, energy that was postulated to be available for psychic change. All in all, the results we obtained from our formal science models spoke extremely well for the communicative approach and raised serious issues for the work of all but one of the other therapists studied (see Langs, 1992c).

The hierarchical theory

The communicative approach has created a multidimensional theory for psychoanalysis (Langs, 1996). It is widely agreed that biological entities are hierarchically structured and that a comprehensive biological theory therefore must be hierarchically structured as well (Dawkins, 1976a; Eldredge, 1995; Eldredge and Salthe, 1984; Grene, 1987; Plotkin, 1994; Salthe, 1985). As a subscience of the science of biology, psychoanalysis has long been remiss in this respect, clinging almost exclusively to the levels of psychodynamics and personal genetics and development for virtually all of its formulations and theoretical ideas (Wilson and Gedo, 1993). Relatively recently, some effort has been made to introduce both systems and evolutionary sub-theories into the field (see below), but these dimensions have not as yet been incorporated into the mainstream of analytic thinking.

The evolution of the communicative approach was driven by unexplained clinical phenomena – unsolved puzzles or anomalies (Kuhn, 1962). Most of the theories of psychotherapy, including psychoanalysis, are both unverifiable scientifically and so loosely constructed as to be able to explain virtually every phenomenon with which they are confronted. Indeed, the very existence of specific unsolved puzzles in the communicative approach speaks for its vitality and validity.

As for the nature of these anomalies, they center on the clinical finding that patients consistently unconsciously validate secured frames – adherence to the ideal basic ground rules of therapy, such as a set time, place and frequency of sessions; total privacy and confidentiality; the relative anonymity of the therapist; the almost exclusive use of adaptationally shaped, trigger-decoded interventions of the type that are likely to obtain encoded validation; and securing of the ground rules and setting at the behest of the patient's encoded material.

However, once the ground rules of therapy are secured in response to the patient's unconscious directives, a biphasic response sets in. On the one hand, the responsive encoded material from the patient consistently validates the frame-securing intervention. But on the other hand, the patient also will generate disturbing images of entrapment and danger of annihilation which, at bottom, reflect intense secured-frame anxieties largely connected with unresolved death anxieties – the secured frame of life comes with the inescapable, existential rule that it must be followed by death (Langs, 1996).

These *secured-frame anxieties* unconsciously cause the conscious system unwittingly to dread and oppose the very conditions for therapy that are optimally curative – secured frames inherently are supportive, ego enhancing, safe and constructive. As a result, some patients who unconsciously validate a therapist's secured-frame interventions experience so much unconsciously driven secured-frame anxiety that they rather quickly abandon the very treatment situation that they themselves have unconsciously and wisely asked for and have supported unconsciously, but now refute consciously and flee.

The need to understand this seemingly paradoxical and clearly self-defeating situation has pushed the communicative approach from one level of hierarchical understanding to another in the search for answers to this dilemma. The result is that the communicative approach is now a hierarchical theory which has a basic *nested* form (one entity set within another of greater power) with *control* features (one entity receiving information and commands from another of great authority). With the most basic subtheory listed first, the following are the ten current dimensions of the communicative version of psychoanalysis:

1 *A formal science of psychoanalysis.*   This level involves the search for deep laws, regularities, and rules of the mind – and of emotionally charged human communication and interactions (Langs, 1992c; Langs and Badalamenti, 1992a, 1992b, 1994a, 1994b, 1996). As science, this dimension, which is based on the use of mathematical models as applied to quantitative findings, is the most fundamental level of this hierarchy. Despite many nay-sayers, this kind of scientific research is essential to psychoanalysis as a biological science. As mentioned above, the communicative approach has forged such a science for communicative exchanges within the therapeutic interaction and for couples (dialogues) and individuals (monologues) who are working over and adapting to emotionally charged issues. The most basic propositions of psychoanalysis should pertain to this fundamental level of scientifically discovered laws and regularities.

2 *A psychoanalytic science based on stochastic and statistical mathematical models.* This level is characterized by the quest for deep regularities and patterns of communication and adaptation, although this subscience cannot, because of the limitations in its methods, establish deep laws (Shulman, 1990; see also Langs and Badalamenti, 1992b). The efforts by psychoanalysts to develop models within this science and to derive significant findings that could influence and reshape psychoanalytic theory have met with very little success – no major breakthrough has materialized. Still, studies carried out with the methods of this level of the hierarchy lend some independent clinical and laboratory support for selected psychoanalytic ideas, even as they also raise questions about some of the more cherished concepts held by practitioners in the field.

The research program of the communicative approach included stochastic studies of speaker duration and a statistical study, using a ten-minute window, of the patient's and therapist's deep influence on each other in respect to the five quantified measures of communicative vehicle we used. This subscience, as is true of the previous one, is still in its infancy. Yet if psychoanalysis and psychotherapy are ever to have sound clinical methods and practices, these first two subsciences must flourish and generate results and theoretical constructs that afford a solid foundation for the clinical theory of psychoanalysis and for the individually crafted work of each individual psychotherapist.

3 *Evolutionary psychoanalysis.* This level brings to psychoanalysis a relatively new subscience, a version of the science of evolution, which is in turn the most basic subscience of biology (Dennett, 1995; Plotkin, 1994). Evolutionary psychoanalysis involves two efforts: first, the classical Darwinian search for evolutionary histories and trajectories, and secondly, the investigation of current modes of adaptation.

As for the pursuit of evolutionary histories, the quest in evolutionary psychoanalysis is to determine how the principles, causes, regularities, and rules of evolution apply to psychoanalytic entities. The goal is to define and understand the evolution of psychic structures and processes through the development of what are termed explanatory *adaptationist programs* (Dennett, 1995; Gould and Lewontin, 1979; Mayr, 1983; Tooby and Cosmides, 1990a, 1990b), through which the specific evolutionary histories of these mental entities are detailed and fathomed.

Initial efforts of this kind also have had mixed results. They tend to be highly speculative; overly invested in the selfish gene theory (Dawkins, 1976b) and in nonhuman observations, especially as they pertain to current adaptations; inclined to overlook the emergent properties of our species, *homo sapiens sapiens*; and lacking in both well-defined, specific entities for study and specific evolutionary scenarios for their historical unfolding (see Badcock, 1986, 1990a, 1990b, 1994; Glantz and Pearce, 1989; Lloyd, 1990; Nesse, 1990a, 1990b; Nesse and Lloyd, 1992; Slavin and Kriegman, 1992; see also Langs 1995b).

The communicative approach has been able to identify a basic adaptive mental module for the experience and processing of emotionally charged environmental impingements – the emotion-processing mind. This has facilitated the development of an extensive adaptationist program for this entity over the six-million-year history of hominid existence (Langs, 1996). This effort served to greatly clarify many puzzling features of this mental model, much of it centering around the discovery of intense conscious system defenses against the direct registration of highly traumatic emotionally charged triggering events.

The main cognitive development that fueled the evolution of this adaptive mental structure appears to have been the emergence of human language (Bickerton, 1990; Corballis, 1991; Liberman, 1991; Pinker, 1994; Pinker and Bloom, 1990), which provided the means by which the emotion-processing mind could process and adapt to incoming information and meaning with great intelligence and rapidity. As for *selection pressures*, the most important factor seems to have been the ever-increasing complexity and intensity of hominid emotional life which caused such a degree of conscious system overload that it necessitated selection for a two-system mind lest the conscious system become dysfunctional and hominids, such as our own species, *homo sapiens sapiens*, become extinct. The finding that natural selection has had merely (in evolutionary time terms) some 150,000 years to forge an effective emotion-processing mind also clarifies why the conscious system has been fashioned in such a defensive manner – other options evidently were too costly or would take hundreds of thousands of years to develop.

The second type of evolutionary pursuit involves the investigation of our current mental adaptive resources through the development of *adaptiveness programs* (Tooby and Cosmides, 1990b) fashioned to explain the nature of immediate adaptations. The communicative approach has developed many insights on this level of this subscience by investigating the adaptive resources of the emotion-processing mind – the means by which humans cope with emotionally charged information and meaning (Langs, 1995a). It was through these efforts that the two systems of this mental module were discovered and explored (see below).

Specific to these communicative efforts is the attempt to apply evolutionary principles to the operations – the capabilities and adaptive efforts – of the emotion-processing mind. Using a term coined by Plotkin (1994), this pursuit involves determining if the emotion-processing mind is a *Darwin machine* – if it obeys the rules of universal Darwinism (Dawkins, 1983).

This very new line of study, which introduces the subject of *mental Darwinism* (see Edelman, 1987, 1992, re: neural Darwinism; and Langs, 1996) is best defined through the distinction between Darwinian and Lamarckian principles, which essentially revolves around the difference between *selectionism* and *instructionism* (Gazzaniga, 1992; Plotkin, 1994). The former theory, which holds for the basic modes of human adaptation (e.g., the brain, immune system and cognitive functions) proposes that the environment – comprehensively defined to include biological organisms, physical settings, and impacting events – *selects* from an organism's innate capabilities those responses that are best suited as adaptive responses to a given external impingement.

The latter – instructionism – views the organism as operating with limited inner resources and proposes that it is instructed by the environment as to how to respond to a given adaptation-evoking impingement. This theory leaves the organism without the ability to do anything other than what the environment directs it to do – there is no room for inner creativity and self-organization.

Initial studies along these lines suggest that the emotion-processing mind as a whole and its deep unconscious system operate entirely according to selection principles. On the other hand, the conscious system is open to a measure of instructionism, but more deeply, is guided by selection principles as well. That is, this system can be directed and retrained, but all the while, the basic architecture of this system of the mind is untouched by these directives and can be modified only through the therapeutic application of selectionistic principles – a key challenge yet to be met.

Given that we are inclined to take instructionism for granted, it is well to realize that the thesis that the emotion-processing mind is a Darwinian machine implies that dysfunctions of this mental module cannot be constructively modified by instructionistic intervention by therapists, even though they constitute today's mode of intervening across all forms of therapy. As you can see, this way of looking at these clinical issues – the perspectives we get from the evolutionary level of the science of psychoanalysis – raises new issues about the nature of emotional dysfunctions and their cure. The exploration of how to use selectionistic principles therapeutically is a current area of clinical research for the communicative approach (see also below).

4 *The systems theory of psychoanalysis.* This level of psychoanalytic conceptualizing, observing, formulating, and doing research was proposed initially by Peterfreund (1971) and Rosenblatt and Thickstun (1977). However, there was some intention by these authors to have this level replace rather than supplement the cherished levels of psychodynamics and personal genetics, and there has been little acceptance within the field of the ideas they have generated.

The communicative efforts in this direction were proposed as another level of theory that would supplement ideas derived from other levels in this hierarchy (Langs, 1992c), although these precepts also have not as yet been integrated into the main body of analytic thinking or clinical work. The communicative view sees the patient and therapist as a P/T system operating within a therapeutic space or bipersonal field defined through the physical setting and ground rules of therapy which establish both physical and psychological boundaries – or in some situations, their absence.

Another systemic concept is the proposition that all disturbances and improvements in the patient (and therapist) are the result of the system's events and behaviors – that is that all effects in psychotherapy are bipersonal and the consequence of the systemic transactions of the P/T system. There is as well the concept that every system has a finite capacity to deal with incoming information and meaning, beyond which *system overload* occurs and the system will malfunction, usually with disturbances within both patient and therapist.

One of the most important contributions of this level of the hierarchy is that it directs the investigation of both advances and regressions in the patient (and therapist) to considerations of contributions from both parties to therapy – every aspect of psychotherapy is dialectical, adaptive and interactional.

5 The science of psychoanatomy or model-making. There have been a small number of attempts to model and define the architecture of the emotion-processing mind – again, with little general success (Goleman, 1985). Freud (1895) set the tone for these efforts, which he later undermined, when he proposed a first model that was a mixture of mental and physical or brain features, and then shifted to an entirely mental model in 1900, with his landmark book, *The Interpretation of Dreams*. This latter model actually was adaptive and interactive in nature, but confused in many ways – it failed to include unconscious perception as one of the mind's intake mechanisms; was content rather than system orientated; confused representational processes, like disguise and condensation, with adaptive processes that deal with meaning and intention; missed the contact with reality made by the unconscious system; and was overly focused on internal conflict at the expense of appreciating the role played by external impingements on the mental apparatus.

Freud abandoned this model in 1923 when he introduced the tripartite structural model of ego, id and superego. This proved to be a model with little configurational subtlety or complexity, and with very limited potential for fresh insight – much of the understanding generated by the model has nothing to do with model-making. As a result, studies of psychoanatomy were all but abandoned by psychoanalytic thinkers.

The communicative approach has spent almost ten years creating and revising a model of the emotion-processing mind, the organ of emotional adaptation (Langs, 1986, 1987a, 1987b, 1988, 1992b, 1992c, 1995a). The essential architecture, as it is now understood, posits a cognitive mental module with two discontinuous systems – *the conscious system and the deep unconscious system* – each with its own range and focus of vision; values, needs and motives; processing methods; frame preferences; contact with emotionally charged reality; and ego, id and superego. These two parallel processing systems are seen as operating in tandem, and they process rather different meanings of emotionally charged impingements – and often deal with very different events as well.

The conscious system functions to orchestrate immediate adaptations to manifest, direct stimuli that pertain to long- and short-term survival and reproductive success. The system is, however, easily overloaded with the enormously excessive load of emotionally charged impingements experienced by humans. As a consequence, natural selection has provided it with a vast array of psychological defenses through which triggers and their meanings by-pass the system and do not register consciously – *knowledge reduction* is nature's main way of insuring smooth and effective conscious adaptive efforts.

These protective mechanisms include an evolved capacity for unconscious perception which by-passes conscious registration; ample use of repression and denial in responding consciously to emotionally charged trigger events and their recall; and the automatic use of displacement so that repressed and denied emotionally charged events are reacted to in situations and interactions other than their primary source – much of human emotional life, including experiences in psychotherapy, is lived out in the wrong place and with the wrong person. Finally, as support for these primary defenses, there are resistances unconsciously directed against the expression of unconscious meaning through narratives, and against linking encoded images to their trigger events to yield conscious realizations of unconscious experiences.

Conscious system overload appears to have been the main factor in the evolution of unconscious perception and deep unconscious processing and adaptation which serve as the basic means of reducing potentially disturbing impingements on the conscious mind. This means that the deep unconscious system processes a great deal of information and meaning that is highly charged emotionally and fraught with disturbing ramifications.

There is, on the perceptual level, an automatic shunting to unconscious perception, processing and adaptation of many potentially disturbing perceptions and meanings. However, the results of these adaptive processes are conveyed solely through the disguised or encoded meanings in narrative communications. To comprehend the meanings so contained, it is necessary to trigger decode these stories in light of their evocative stimuli. Failing that, these gifted processing efforts go unappreciated and *do not affect conscious adaptations* – they are unknown to the conscious mind. We pay an enormous price for the defense mechanisms that have evolved to protect the adaptive capacities of the conscious system.

The conscious system is frame insensitive and leans towards frame deviations, largely as a defense against entrapping, death-related secured-frame anxieties. In contrast, the deep unconscious system is exceedingly frame sensitive (rules, frames and boundaries are critical factors in the operations and survival of all biological organisms) and unswervingly inclined towards frame-securing efforts. Narratives evoked by frame impingements consistently lead to encoded images and themes that speak for the need to secure and maintain the unconsciously appreciated and validated ideal ground rules and settings of psychotherapy.

There is then a deep unconscious wisdom subsystem, with an adaptive intelligence in the emotional realm that far exceeds our conscious adaptive intelligence. Strangely, the system does not affect conscious adaptations despite its invaluable insights, but the conscious mind is unwittingly affected by a second subsystem of the deep unconscious system, *the fear/guilt subsystem*. This subsystem embodies the universal human dread of personal annihilation and the similarly universal quota of *unconscious guilt*. Communicative studies indicate that death anxiety is managed by having much of its representations relegated to unconscious experience, while unconscious guilt seems to have evolved as a means of diminishing our natural tendencies towards violence towards each other (Langs, 1995b, 1996).

There are many clinical ramifications to these clinically based communicative formulations of the architecture of the emotion-processing mind. These realizations indicate that with the exception of the communicative approach, current forms of therapy deal with *conscious system* issues and adaptive responses – intrapsychic and relational – to the exclusion of those issues that impinge on patients unconsciously and are processed by the deep unconscious system. It is for this reason that other therapies pay little or no attention to therapists' ground rule related interventions and neglect the ever-present, ongoing impact on their patients of every nuance of their behaviors and communications, while the communicative approach sees these efforts as constituting the critical trigger events that affect unconscious experience and on that basis, deeply influence the emotional lives of both patients and their therapists.

6 *The science of emotionally pertinent contexts, frames, rules and settings.* This level of observation and theory could be incorporated into the systems theory level of this hierarchy because all systems have boundary issues and follow rules. However, the exploration of these issues appears to merit a level of its own because it is an area which requires very distinctive observations and theoretical formulations which contribute significantly to psychoanalytic thinking (Langs, 1992a, 1992c, 1993a, 1994a, 1995a, 1996).

This dimension is the prime concern of the deep unconscious system and it deeply affects the experience of both parties to therapy – the meanings of their exchanges, the safety and danger levels of the situation, the vicissitudes of the patient's symptoms, and much more. It is, however, only through the trigger decoding methods of the communicative approach that this dimension can be explored and dealt with in terms of both interpretation and frame-securing efforts at the behest of the patient's encoded material.

7 *The study of interactions, relating and relationships* (Gill, 1994; Langs, 1992a, 1993a, 1994a; Slavin and Kriegman, 1992). There are two ways that the important issues of interacting and relating have been explored by psychoanalysts. The first is in terms of recent revisions of the intrapsychically focused classical theory which has moved towards object relations and relational issues – for example, defining repression as the result of relational nonconfirmation. However, these approaches remain focused on the

patient's inner experience without full attention to the nature of relational, adaptation-evoking realities. These investigators also have failed to recognize the existence of deep unconscious processing and adapting, and the nature of trigger-evoked unconscious communication – they rely on manifest content/evident implications, ways of listening and formulating which greatly limit their purview and resultant ideas.

The second approach to relating and interacting is communicative and, for psychotherapy, it begins with a careful assessment of the conscious and unconscious implications of the therapist's interventions as they constitute his or her contribution to the therapeutic interaction and the patient's experiences in the treatment situation. The patient's conscious and unconscious experiences of these trigger events are assessed and interpreted in this light – a very different approach from those taken by other treatment modalities. The results of these efforts have been described above.

8 *The science of emotionally related personal development and personal genetics.* This is the familiar realm of personal and developmental history, which includes tracing of the history and nature of a given individual's psychosexual and cognitive development and critical life events and experiences, especially as they pertain to later emotional health or dysfunction (Wilson and Gedo, 1993). This is a level that clearly has its own, distinctive means of observing both within and outside of the therapy situation, as well as its own methods of formulating and theorizing. It is helpful to see how contributions from this level of the analytic hierarchy are distinctive and add to those made at other levels – they provide critical information about and insight into current adaptations and maladaptations unavailable through any other means. In principle, then, each level of the psychoanalytic hierarchy of subsciences contributes distinctive insights and theoretical constructs to the overall theory that are unique to its own methods and formulations.

9 *The exploration of psychodynamics.* This includes many familiar elements – issues of conflict, self and identity, conscious and unconscious fantasies and wishes, problems of sex and aggression, etc. All in all, this level entails investigations of the operations of the ego, id and superego, and the conflicts and issues that arise within and between the agencies of the mind (Gill, 1994; Lloyd, 1990; Nesse, 1990b; Nesse and Lloyd, 1992; Slavin and Kriegman 1992).

There are many competing subtheories of psychodynamic psychoanalysis, such as classical analytic, object relations, relational, self-psychology and the like. Together with personal genetics, this level occupies almost all of the thinking theorizing of today's psychoanalysts and psychotherapists.

10 *The investigation of human emotions and affects.* This is the study of human feelings and affects, especially anxiety, depression, guilt and shame (Badcock, 1994; Darwin, 1872; Nesse, 1990a; Tooby and Cosmides, 1990b). Heretofore, therapists have not sharply distinguished the vicissitudes of

affective states, which tend to be without verbalized or verbalizable meaning (though often accompanied by narratives) from the operations of the emotion-processing mind – the cognitive mental module for emotional adapting. These are, however, two very different levels of observation and theorizing within the science of psychoanalysis and each contributes in its own way to the full theory of the field.

This, then, is the currently fashioned communicative hierarchical theory of psychoanalysis. Notice that the ordering of this hierarchy affords its formal science the fundamental position and places evolution, the basic biological science, next in line. Systemic aspects follow, then psychoanatomy and frames. All of these levels are seen as more fundamental and powerful than the current levels at which therapists formulate and base their interventions – psychodynamics and personal genetics.

Given that nested hierarchies posit that the propositions from a given sub-science cannot violate an established postulate from a subscience in a more basic position, this gives pause for much thought in respect to psycho-analytic and nonanalytic theories of the mind, and in regard to the basis for existing forms of therapy. Many cherished theoretical constructs, such as transference and the nature of resistances, need to be reconsidered in light of the contributions made from the various subsciences of the field – especially those from formal science, evolutionary psychoanalysis, systems theory and psychoanatomy.

As for the clinical arena, this hierarchy suggests that formulations of patients' material and the nature of their emotional dysfunctions currently are being made at relatively unempowered levels of cogency and meaning. Indeed, communicative studies have shown that the conscious mind is naturally drawn to thinking in terms of psychodynamics and personal genetics because of their relative lack of immediate potency, and that it has a much less natural inclination to think in terms of the more powerful aspects of this hierarchy, especially formal science, evolution, and rules, frames and boundaries.

Overall, then, the hierarchical structure of the communicative approach, as it informs the techniques of psychotherapy, both validates its own postulates and speaks for the uniqueness of its contributions to the field. When thera-pists begin to regularly use trigger decoding in formulating their patients' material and, when necessary, their own interventions, they will at last have the opportunity to evaluate and appreciate the power of this paradigm of therapy and make use of its many important and distinctive features.

Some issues taken with the communicative approach

Personally, I am convinced that communicative psychotherapy has the best cost-benefit ratio to be found among therapeutic approaches. This implies that almost every patient – exceptions being individuals in acute psychotic

states – deserves to have an opportunity to undergo communicative psychotherapy (Langs, 1992a) and its recent offshoot, empowered psychotherapy
(Langs, 1993a). This does not imply that every patient will accept or tolerate communicative treatment, largely because secured frames and decoded
unconscious meaning are terrifyingly threatening for some individuals. For
example, some psychotic and borderline patients, those who need medication or whose deep unconscious perceptions and experiences of secured
frames are especially horrifying, will find conscious rationalizations for
fleeing the very kind of communicative therapy they unconsciously advocate
and most need.

In addition, because the approach intensely pursues deep unconscious
meaning and secured frames, individuals with extremely traumatic early life
experiences may become unbearably anxious in a communicative form of
treatment because, for them, a secured frame is felt to be dangerously
entrapping and annihilating. Some of these patients will abandon communicative modes of therapy, unable to manage both deep unconscious
meaning and the secured frames and constructive holding that they offer –
for them, too, their greatest dread is connected with their greatest therapeutic need.

Empirical study also has revealed that patients suffering from what is
termed *the syndrome of overintense exposure to death anxiety*, whether in
childhood or as an adult, often flee communicative therapies for much the
same reasons – they too are terrified of both secured frames and unconscious
meaning. Indeed, *secured-frame anxieties* are the most pervasive unrecognized unconscious source of resistances in psychotherapy – the deep fear of
personal mortality looms large on the deeper levels.

Oddly enough, I have yet to hear an outside criticism of the communicative approach that is supported by empirical observation or persuasively
calls for rethinking and revising the approach. On the other hand, as communicative observations unfolded and were refined over the years, there
were many periods of reassessment and revision. One example is the early
shift from seeing triggers both within and outside of therapy as equally critical adaptation-evoking events for patients' unconscious experiences in
therapy, to recognizing that the triggers within therapy, and especially
frame-related triggers, are by far the most powerful evocative stimuli for the
patient's deep unconscious system and for the patient as a whole.

Another change in the aforementioned revisions in how communicative
therapy is framed and carried forth. The original treatment paradigm
evolved from the classical forms of psychodynamic psychotherapy and kept
the parameters or frame intact, even as it stressed the importance of establishing and maintaining secured frame conditions for therapy whenever
possible – and working with the patient's unconscious responses to modified frames when they become a factor.

The new paradigm arose from two sources: first, clinically, from dream
study seminars and realizations about how to maximize access to deep
unconscious experience, especially by associating to manifest dream

elements (so-called, guided associating; Langs, 1993a); and secondly, from our formal science studies which revealed the power and importance of narrative communications. These investigations also showed that left to its own proclivities, the conscious mind will tend to move towards low energy states. This means that patients (and therapists) will naturally tend to move away from the relatively powerful narrative mode of expression and towards intellectualizing and the avoidance of encoded imagery. Indeed, empowered psychotherapy is the first therapy modality to be based on and designed in light of mathematically based, formal science findings.

The result is a mode of therapy in which the ground rules require that the patient begin each 90-minute session with a dream and develop narrative guided associations to the elements of the dream imagery – a way of maximizing and sustaining the expression of encoded material. This effort is complemented by an intense search for frame-related behaviors by the patient and the critical, adaptation-evoking, frame-related interventions of the therapist. And finally, the process culminates in the linking of the narrative themes to the active trigger events and formulating the connections in terms of the patient's unconscious experience of these interventions. Such are the kinds of changes that have eventuated from within the communicative approach.

A common criticism of the approach is the claim that it is rigid, inappropriately inflexible about securing the frame, and erroneously confined to one type of formulation. The problem with these critiques is that they are offered by therapists who have never trigger decoded their patients' material. As a result, they are based on a manifest content view of the therapeutic situation and experience, while the communicative approach is based on a view that includes information derived from trigger-decoding narratives – a decoded, latent content view (supplemented by manifest readings) of the same conditions and events. These are two very different ways of understanding the communications from and the experiences of patients and therapists in psychotherapy, and one method cannot be used to criticize the other because it cannot fathom the basis on which it has evolved.

In addition, there are in principle, aspects of nature that are consistent and unswerving. We breathe in oxygen and exhale carbon monoxide, and we think of this as a biological regularity and not as rigidity. Psychoanalysts have not appreciated the universals and regularities that prevail in the emotional domain (Langs, 1995a; Slavin and Kriegman, 1992; Tooby and Cosmides 1990a). The finding that narratives carry two messages, one conscious and the other encoded and unconscious, is a universal property of human language, just as there is a universal design to the emotion-processing mind, as there are to human brains and arms and such. Individuals do, of course, vary, but they do so within the limits posed by these universal constraints – *individuality constrained by universals* is a key biological precept and it applies to the emotion-processing mind and the operations of its two systems, conscious and deep unconscious.

Thus, it can be shown that patients universally respond to modifications in the ideal, secured frame with encoded images of assault, seduction, other forms of harm, and a host of other negative images and themes. The therapist who trigger decodes these images in light of a given frame deviant intervention has no choice but to see that his or her effort has been harmful to the patient. In addition, the patient's narratives will contain encoded directives to the therapist to secure the frame, and again, the conscientious therapist will have no choice but to do so lest he or she continue to damage the patient (and himself or herself as well). This consistency is supported by the finding that quite without exception, once the frame has been rectified and secured, images of well-functioning, trustworthy, wise people will appear, and the patient's symptoms are likely to be resolved (and those of the therapist too).

The deep unconscious mind consistently directs therapists to secure frames and sees harm in altered frames. If the therapist wishes to not harm the patient and to be helpful, he or she has no choice but to secure the frame and maintain it as such. This is no more rigid than setting a fractured bone in a plaster cast in the same manner that has been the practice thousands of times before or, to use a psychological example, no more rigid than a therapist never having sex with a patient – what heals, heals, and what harms, harms.

Existing confusion on this critical point comes from the failure to appreciate that the conscious system and a patient's manifest experience and direct comments are extremely unreliable guides to the deep and most telling effects of their therapists' interventions. In the emotional realm, direct communication is strongly colored by self-harmful needs, while encoded communication consistently expresses what is best for the patient. Indeed, patients speak the truth far more when they know not what they are saying than when they are aware of what they mean to convey.

Some additional questions

In part due to its failure to embrace the communicative approach, the field of psychotherapy presently is without a clear, scientifically grounded theory that stands at the basic level of the hierarchy of theories of emotional adaptation with compelling and validated explanatory powers and insights. Similarly, no form of treatment has established itself as most efficacious and least costly than its competitors. The question of why such comparable results have materialized with very diverse forms of psychotherapy has puzzled therapists for many years.

There undoubtedly are many reasons for this clinical situation. However, the communicative approach has developed a perspective on this issue that is both unique and fraught with implications for the field. From its vantage point, there appear to be two basic reasons that no type of therapy, including psychoanalysis, has established itself as the ideal form of therapy. They are:

1   *All forms of therapy address conscious system issues, without affect-
ing the deep unconscious system which most strongly empowers emotional
life.* As I have suggested, all forms of therapy, analytic or otherwise, operate
in terms of a weak adaptive viewpoint and address the manifest contents –
and their implications – of patients' communications. These surface communications are only rarely connected to manifest, known triggers, and
seldom, if ever, connected to *repressed* evocative triggers and defined in
terms of deep unconscious experience and processing. Without trigger
decoding, manifest content therapists fail to reach the most powerful deter-
minants of the patient's emotional dysfunctions.

There are many ways of working with the surface of a patient's communications and experiences, and evidently each has had a modicum of
success – and of failure as well. The communicative approach is distinctive
in being the only mode of therapy that addresses the encoded meanings of
a patient's material in light of specific therapist related adaptation-evoking
trigger events. It is therefore the only approach that addresses deep unconscious meanings and the operations of the deep unconscious system. And
while there has been no study of the clinical results achieved in this way,
they are probably superior to, and more lasting than, the results obtained
by other methods of treatment.

An important similarity and difference between communicative and noncommunicative therapies comes to the fore in this connection. Both communicative and noncommunicative forms of treatment share a focus on the
dynamics and other issues that pertain to the *outputs* of the emotion-processing mind. Although there are significant differences between cognitive
restructuring and the interpretation of adaptive, relational, psychodynamic,
or personal genetic issues, all such interventions address the results of the
operations and adaptations of the emotion-processing mind. Even though
the communicative approach stresses unconscious perception and the
outcome of unconscious processing, it too is dealing with output and its consequences in symptomatic cures or remissions. In essence then, all presently
known forms of psychotherapy address *foreground concerns* – their nature,
dynamics and personal genetics.

As we know, emotional dysfunction may arise because of a traumatic
trigger event that fails to receive conscious processing and is relegated to
unconscious processing and adaptation – a situation that often leads to
emotional dysfunction. Here, the issue is one of meaning, conscious and
unconscious, and of environmental impingements and the results of the maladaptive processing of these impingements and their meanings. In these situations, the deeper processing mechanisms are intact and operating as well
as can be expected in light of the evolved structure of the emotion-processing mind. It is the consciously and unconsciously experienced meaning of
events and the anxieties, issues and conflicts that they evoke that are at issue.

But there is another level of operations and transactions in the emotional
domain, hierarchically more fundamental than these output phenomena,
conscious and unconscious. This second level involves *the design and*

operations of the emotion-processing mind itself – the mental module that orchestrates and constrains all of our adaptive efforts. Once the communicative approach identified and modeled the structure of this cognitive module, and defined its architecture, it became clear that it had reached a new and basic level of exploration and influence. I have already indicated some important features of this design – for example, the defensive alignment of the conscious system, the use of subliminal or unconscious perception by the deep unconscious system, the outputs from this system through encoded narratives, the frame attitudes of each system, etc.

This brings us, then, to another, more fundamental source of emotional disturbance – *dysfunctions of the emotion-processing mind*. This is an area with many unforeseen and unexpected problems, not the least of which is the aforementioned discovery, made in exploring the evolution of this language-based adaptive module, that natural selection repeatedly has selected for defensiveness for the conscious system via the basic mechanisms of denial, repression and displacement – for knowledge reduction for the conscious system in respect to emotionally charged information and meaning. This knowledge reduction spares the conscious system considerable overload and turmoil, but it does so at considerable expense. Thus, dysfunctions of the emotion-processing mind begin with its evolved, natural structure and processing capabilities (Langs, 1996).

In psychotherapy, this means that patients (and therapists) naturally deny and repress many crucial trigger events and the most disturbing meanings of those triggers that do register in awareness. But in addition, there is a natural tendency to automatically invoke the use of displacement, not only psychologically, but even more critically, in behavior as well.

For example, in the brief vignette described above, Ms Reddy consciously accepted Dr Lake's taking her cousin into therapy with him. Her direct reaction to this consciously recognized frame-related trigger event and the meanings that had registered consciously was one of complete acceptance – for example, that Dr Lake was being helpful in seeing her cousin. At the same time, the most critical meanings of this deviant trigger event were perceived unconsciously and processed by the patient's deep unconscious wisdom subsystem, and then encoded into her brief narrative. The images were displaced from Dr Lake to Ms Reddy's boyfriend, Doug, and the experience with Dr Lake contributed to her possibly hasty reaction to the boyfriend's infidelity which may have been set up by her own actions – as was the case with Dr Lake's seeing the cousin.

But matters did not rest there. In addition to this situation, another problem arose on her job where Ms Reddy's boss brought another woman into the department in which they worked. Ms Reddy took an immediate dislike to this woman and for no apparent reason tried to get her fired. Whatever the direct and conscious sources of this maladaptive reaction – there was no sound basis for Ms Reddy's behavior – its deep unconscious source lay with the frame deviation made by her therapist who had accepted an intruder into her therapeutic space.

Without trigger decoding, there is no way that Ms Reddy could pick up and consciously become aware of this displacement. Furthermore, her insistence on getting rid of this new employee jeopardized her own job – this corrective belonged in her therapy and not at work. In general, the consequences of these unconscious and design-caused displacements are often quite harmful – many social relationships have been ruined through these unconscious displacements.

Notice too that a manifest content therapist would be restricted to working over Ms Reddy's behaviors with her boyfriend and the immediate situation at work. Some of these therapists would accept her conscious rationalizations for her actions and support her evident decision to stand up for her beliefs. Other therapists would see Ms Reddy's behavior as irrational and trace it to such proposed factors as a mother transference, latent homosexual issues, poor self-image, disturbances in self-regulation, and the like. Still others would use the incident to train Ms Reddy in assertiveness or in relaxation, etc.

But the key problem here lies with the evolved, inherited design of the emotion-processing mind. Clinical studies have shown first, that the design of this mental module is badly compromised and so defensive in respect to conscious registrations that it is evidently inherently dysfunctional – that is, everyone needs to find ways to improve on the architecture of his or her emotion-processing mind or he or she will suffer emotionally.

But in addition, as is true of all biological entities and organs of adaptation, the emotion-processing mind can be damaged psychologically and rendered even more dysfunctional for brief or long periods of time. By and large, every death-related emotional trauma causes some *alteration in the processing capacities* of this module of the mind, usually by rendering it defensive to an extreme in respect to encoded expressions and their trigger decoding. In response to these traumas, the processing of information and meaning is blocked even in the deep unconscious system and acting out, usually in self-hurtful forms, intensifies as a consequence – when language-based adaptations fail, maladaptive actions are likely to ensue. These people suffer considerably from the dysfunctions of their emotion-processing minds, and analysing and interpreting surface relations, psychodynamics and unconscious experiences have little if any effect on their basic structural pathology. The therapeutic work must be done with the emotion-processing mind itself by finding ways to modify its overdefensiveness so that adaptive processing returns to a more open and constructive mode.

The means by which this is accomplished is another unsolved puzzle and unanswered question unearthed by the communicative approach. There are indications that for the moment all we have available to help patients with these processing dysfunctions is a dynamic form of retraining of a kind that is possible only in empowered psychotherapy. However, the recognition of this very common syndrome of the dysfunctional emotion-processing mind which is inaccessible to change via present modes of therapy helps to clarify a previously unrecognized reason that all of today's treatment forms claim to have about the same degree of seemingly curative power – none of these touch the fundamental structure of the emotion-processing mind, the basic mental module for emotional adaptation.

2   *Current forms of psychotherapy essentially are instructionistic rather than selectionistic in nature.* A second unrecognized reason that no therapy modality stands out has been alluded to earlier. I refer to the fact that evolutionary research has shown that human organs of adaptation follow the universal Darwinian principles of selectionism and basically, are not instructionistic in their operations. At times mixed principles are in operation, but often what seems to be instructionistic on the surface is selectionistic on deeper levels (Gazzaniga, 1992).

For psychotherapy, instructionism implies that a therapist tries in some manner to direct a patient's mode of response or adaptation, rather than select from the modes of adaptation that are available within the patient. This principle is modeled on Lamarckism and the concepts of the inheritance of acquired traits and of use and disuse. The idea is that the environment – here, in the form of a therapist – directs the patient as to how to create and use an adaptive resource, and how to understand, behave and respond.

Instructionism was the first model of the immune system, in that it was thought that when a foreign substance or microbe enters the human body, the body's immune system responds by reading out the nature of the intruder and then creating an antibody response that will eliminate the invader. In 1967, Jerne showed that this instructionistic picture is in error, in that human beings are born with some 30 to 40 billion antibodies in its immune system. When an invader enters the body it *selects* from these billions of antibodies those that will best adapt to its unwanted presence – that is, best function to rid the body of its presence. In keeping with Darwinian principles, these selected antibodies are then favorably reproduced – and they will be reproduced again and again whenever the particular invader returns (Gazzaniga, 1992; Plotkin, 1994).

Translating these principles into the means of emotional adaptation, the selectionistic model indicates that an adaptive or maladaptive behavior (emotional dysfunction) is a response selected by the environment among potentials within a given individual and then favorably reproduced and repeated on similar occasions of adaptive challenge. Even when it is maladaptive, this mode of responding is fixed until it is rendered extinct and replaced by a new selection.

Instructions cannot alter selected responses, but they can at times override them to some extent. Selectionism is a far more basic and powerful principle than instructionism, so instructed effects tend to decay quickly and to fall aside when selected responses are mobilized.

All efforts by therapists, then, to tell patients how to behave or what their material means, or to introduce ideas and behaviors that are not part of a patient's fundamental psychological *armamentarium*, can have only weak effects on the patient. The deeper, inherited resources of the patient, including the design and operations of his or her emotion-processing mind, and most importantly, a patient's maladaptive selected responses, will continue to prevail in some way despite directives to think or behave otherwise. This is why, when one form of instruction fails, there is usually a shift to another form – the move from one kind of intervention to another kind by therapists, and the move from one kind of therapy to another kind by patients. Instructions come in countless forms and are easily substituted for each other.

Instructions, however, cannot affect the deep unconscious system which is not open to directives of any kind. When a therapist instructs a patient on how to think positive thoughts, the patient *consciously* works over the advice that he or she is being given. But all the while, the deep unconscious system is processing the fact that the therapist is offering a directive and is experiencing the intervention as an intrusion, a violation of interpersonal boundaries, a manipulation, a deprivation of autonomy, and if the directive violates a ground rule, as a frame break as well. No matter what the therapist says or does, the deep unconscious experience will take form in ways that the therapist cannot affect through instructionistic interventions.

Much the same goes for the architecture of the emotion-processing mind. You cannot instruct a brain or breathing reflex to change how it operates; if it malfunctions, you must help it to find more adaptive selections for its operations. Similarly, we need to develop psychotherapy techniques that can alter dysfunctional selected designs and modes of operation of the emotion-processing mind, changing them for the better; we need to learn how to modify environmentally selected dysfunctional adaptations.

In terms of evolution, once a design has been selected, it tends to last for very long periods of time. Evolution *per se* cannot change that design; it can only, through the mindless algorhythm of natural selection (Dennett, 1995), allow the response to become extinct and be replaced by a more favorable adaptation. Once more we come upon a newly discovered but critical problem for psychotherapists – finding the means of favorably modifying maladaptive *selections* which pertain to human emotional adaptations.

One last point: studies of adaptive strategies from the evolutionary vantage point stress the finding that adaptations are designed to deal first and foremost with immediate environmental impingements – external events of significance to the organism. This concept supports observations and postulates developed on the basis of communicative studies that see the immediate interventions of therapists as the prime trigger events for patients' deep unconscious responses.

The evolution of language and the conscious ability to be aware of our own subjective responses, bodily states and overt behaviors have enabled the conscious system to deal with a variety of triggers – immediate and remote events as well as its adaptive responses to these stimuli. Thus, internal physical and mental states and affects do function as *secondary* adaptation evoking triggers in humans, although they emerge initially as part of our *primary* adaptive reactions to external events. The fact that noncommunicative forms of therapy operate without an appreciation for these factors also helps to account for the similarities in their results – they all are missing a great deal.

The future of psychotherapy

Working in the area of evolutionary psychoanalysis dramatically alters your concept of time. Thus, I believe that the near-term picture of psychotherapy, whether we are speaking of 50 or 100 years from now, is likely to be very much as it is today, even though the evolution of a healing endeavor like psychotherapy is subject to many more forces than natural evolution and natural selection – individual and shared intelligence, culture, invention, and other social and personal factors all come into play. The rate of change in psychotherapy is likely to be unusually slow.

Among the reasons for this expectation, there is the general human resistance to change and the conservatism of the centrists who dominate teaching and control publications in the field. The problem too is that ultimately, psychotherapy is the pursuit of emotional truths; emotional truths are terrifying and mostly unconscious rather than conscious (regardless of whether or not a given form of therapy addresses the unconscious level, that level has the power); the human mind is designed to preclude awareness of unconscious meanings and experience; so as a result, psychotherapy and psychoanalysis ultimately are endeavors which must acquire their new insights and evolve by going against the natural grain of nature.

Psychotherapy is the search for emotionally relevant knowledge, but natural selection has opted against the conscious realization of such knowledge. Psychotherapy is a field that must ultimately deal with the universal dread of personal mortality, a dread we have evolved to cope with almost entirely through denial (Becker, 1973; Langs, 1995c, 1996). And denial is another form of knowledge reduction, one that precludes insight and change. Lastly, psychotherapy is a pursuit that entails the realization through trigger decoding that secured frames are health-giving while deviant frames are harmful. But the conscious mind prefers altered frames and opposes the pursuit of secured frames as much as it opposes accessing deep unconscious experience – additional reasons for the existence of enormous resistances to change within the field because it is so entrenched with therapy forms which routinely show a preference for and operate under deviant frame conditions and which deal with consciously, rather than unconsciously, registered experiences and their meanings.

But there is another side to this futuristic picture – selection pressures that are goading the field to make changes. In this regard, first, there are the many therapeutic failures and just about every psychotherapist has had his or her share of them – in both their own personal therapy and their work with their patients. There are conscious wishes in therapists to be helpful to all of their patients and themselves, and in addition, both conscious and unconscious guilt evoked by therapeutic failures – unconscious perceptions of consciously unrecognized harmful interventions actually plague most psychotherapists. And there is as well the personal lives of therapists which tend to be unwittingly damaged because of displacements of self-punitive needs caused by the unconscious guilt evoked by the unconscious experience of the errors of their ways – another (unconscious) motive for change.

Above all, there is the realization that *homo sapiens sapiens*, our species, may well be moving towards massive self-extinction (Leakey and Lewin, 1992; Ward, 1994). This possibility is the result of the design flaws of the emotion-processing mind and the resultant emotional dysfunctions they cause – chief among them the incapacity to manage conspecific violence. This means that it may well be that only psychoanalysis can save our species – mainly by becoming a true science and finding the means of improving the design of the mind. Rescuing our species implies completely changing how we do psychotherapy, so here too we have a very compelling motive for change awaiting its full impact on psychotherapists.

On balance, there is an enormous need to change the accepted precepts and forms of psychotherapy, but at present the forces opposing change appear to have the upper hand. Basic to these opposing forces are our fears of death, guilt-related needs to suffer, and poor capacity for self-observation and for being able to fully appreciate the consequences of our actions and choices (Ornstein, 1991; Langs, 1995a). These many natural obstacles to change suggest that it will take hundreds if not thousands of years for the field of psychotherapy to change significantly.

However – and I very much wish to end this chapter on an optimistic note – it is my belief that the communicative approach has built a foundation of theory and practice that could sponsor deep and extremely constructive changes in the field of psychotherapy. It is my fervent hope that this opportunity is seized sooner than later.

References

Badcock, C. (1986) *The Problem of Altruism: Freudian–Darwinian Solutions*. London: Basil Blackwell.

Badcock, C. (1990a) Is the oedipus complex a Darwinian adaptation? *Journal of the American Academy of Psychoanalysis*, 18, 368–77.

Badcock, C. (1990b) *Oedipus in Evolution*. London: Basil Blackwell.

Badcock, C. (1994) *PsychoDarwinism*. London: HarperCollins.

Becker, E. (1973) *The Denial of Death*. New York: Free Press.

Bickerton, D. (1990) *Language and Species*. Chicago: University of Chicago Press.

Corballis, C. (1991) *The Lopsided Ape*. New York: Oxford University Press.

Darwin, C. (1872) *The Expression of the Emotions in Man and Animals*. London: Murray.

Dawkins, R. (1976a) Hierarchical organization: a candidate for ethology. In P. Bateson and R. Hinde (eds), *Growing Points in Ethology*. Cambridge: Cambridge University Press.

Dawkins, R. (1976b) *The Selfish Gene*. New York: Oxford University Press.

Dawkins, R. (1983) Universal Darwinism. In D.S. Bendall (ed.), *Evolution from Molecules to Man* (pp. 403–25). Cambridge: Cambridge University Press.

Dennett, D. (1995) *Darwin's Dangerous Idea*. New York: Simon & Schuster.

Edelman, G. (1987) *Neural Darwinism*. New York: Basic Books.

Edelman, G. (1992) *Bright Air, Brilliant Fire*. New York: Basic Books.

Eldredge, N. (1995) *Reinventing Darwin*. New York: Wiley.

Eldredge, N. and Salthe, S. (1984) Hierarchy and evolution. *Oxford Surveys in Evolutionary Biology*, 1, 182–206.

Freud, S. (1895) Project for a scientific psychology. *Standard Edition*, 1, 283–397.

Freud, S. (1900) *The Interpretation of Dreams. Standard Edition*, 4 and 5, 1–627.

Freud, S. (1923) *The Ego and the Id. Standard Edition*, 19, 1–66.

Gazzaniga, M. (1992) *Nature's Mind*. New York: Basic Books.

Gill, M. (1994) *Psychoanalysis in Transition*. Hillsdale, NJ: The Analytic Press.

Glantz, K. and Pearce, J. (1989) *Exiles from Eden*. New York: W.W. Norton.

Goleman, D. (1985) *Vital Lies, Simple Truths*. New York: Simon & Schuster.

Gould, S. and Lewontin, R. (1979) The spandrels of San Marco and the Panglossian paradigm. A critique of the adaptationist programme. *Proceedings of the Royal Society of London*, 250, 581–98.

Grene, M. (1987) Hierarchies in biology. *American Scientist*, 75, 504–10.

Jerne, N. (1967) Antibodies and learning: selection versus instruction. In G.G. Quarton, T. Melnechuck and F.O. Scmitt (eds), *The Neurosciences: A Study Program* (vol. 1, pp. 200–5). New York: Rockefeller University Press.

Kuhn, T. (1962) *The Structure of Scientific Revolution*. Chicago: The University of Chicago Press.

Langs, R. (1978) *The Listening Process*. Northvale, NJ: Aronson.

Langs, R. (1982) *Psychotherapy: A Basic Text*. Northvale, NJ: Aronson.

Langs, R. (1986) Clinical issues arising from a new model of the mind. *Contemporary Psychoanalysis*, 22, 418–44.

Langs, R. (1987a) A new model of the mind. *The Yearbook of Psychoanalysis and Psychotherapy*, 2, 3–33.

Langs, R. (1987b) Clarifying a new model of the mind. *Contemporary Psychoanalysis*, 23, 162–80.

Langs, R. (1988) *A Primer of Psychotherapy*. New York: Gardner Press.

Langs, R. (1992a) *A Clinical Workbook for Psychotherapists*. London: Karnac Books.

Langs, R. (1992b) 1923: the advance that retreated from the architecture of the mind. *International Journal of Communicative Psychoanalysis and Psychotherapy*, 7, 3–15.

Langs, R. (1992c) *Science, Systems and Psychoanalysis*. London: Karnac Books.

Langs, R. (1993a) *Empowered Psychotherapy*. London: Karnac Books.

Langs, R. (1993b) Psychoanalysis: narrative myth or narrative science? *Contemporary Psychoanlaysis*, 29, 555–94.

Langs, R. (1994a) *Doing Supervision and Being Supervised*. London: Karnac Books.

Langs, R. (1994b) *The Dream Workbook*. Brooklyn, NY: Alliance.

Langs, R. (1995a) *Clinical Practice and the Architecture of the Mind*. London: Karnac Books.

Langs, R. (1995b) Psychoanalysis and the science of evolution. *American Journal of Psychotherapy*, 49, 47–58.

Langs, R. (1995c) *The Daydream Workbook*. Brooklyn, NY: Alliance.

Langs, R. (1996) *The Evolution of the Emotion Processing Mind: With an Introduction to Mental Darwinism*. London: Karnac Books.

Langs, R. and Badalamenti, A. (1992a) Some clinical consequences of a formal science for psychoanalysis and psychotherapy. *American Journal of Psychotherapy*, 46, 611–19.

Langs, R. and Badalamenti, A. (1992b) The three modes of the science of psychoanalysis. *American Journal of Psychotherapy*, 4 (6), 163–82.

Langs, R. and Badalamenti, A. (1994a) A formal science for psychoanalysis. *British Journal of Psychotherapy*, 11, 92–104.

Langs, R. and Badalamenti, A. (1994b) Psychotherapy: the search for chaos, the discovery of determinism. *Australian and New Zealand Journal of Psychiatry*, 28, 68–81.

Langs, R., Badalamenti, A. and Thomson, L. (1996) *The Cosmic Circle: The Unification of Mind, Matter and Energy*. Brooklyn, NY: Alliance.

Leakey, R. and Lewin, R. (1992) *Origins Reconsidered*. New York: Doubleday.

Liberman, P. (1991) *Uniquely Human*. Cambridge, MA: Harvard University Press.

Lloyd, A. (1990) Implications of an evolutionary metapsychology for clinical psychoanalysis. *Journal of the American Academy of Psychoanalysis*, 18, 286–306.

Mayr, E. (1983) How to carry out an adaptationist program. *American Naturalist*, 121, 324–34.

Nesse, R. (1990a) Evolutionary explanations of emotions. *Human Nature*, 1, 261–89.

Nesse, R. (1990b) The evolutionary functions of repression and the ego defenses. *Journal of the American Academy of Psychoanalysis*, 18, 260–85.

Nesse, R. and Lloyd, A. (1992) The evolution of psychodynamic mechanisms. In J. Barkow, L. Cosmides and J. Tooby (eds), *The Adapted Mind* (pp. 601–24). New York: Oxford University Press.

Ornstein, R. (1991) *The Evolution of Consciousness*. New York: Prentice Hall.

Peterfreund, E. (with J. Schwartz) (1971) *Information, Systems, and Psychoanalysis: An Evolutionary Biological Approach to Psychoanalytic Theory. Psychological Issues*, Monograph 25/26. New York: International Universities Press.

Pinker, S. (1994) *The Language Instinct*. New York: Morrow.

Pinker, S. and Bloom, P. (1990) Natural language and natural selection. *Behavioral and Brain Sciences*, 13, 707–84.

Plotkin, H. (1994) *Darwin Machines and the Nature of Knowledge*. Cambridge, MA: Harvard University Press.

Rosenblatt, A. and Thickstun, J. (1977) *Modern Psychoanalytic Concepts in a General Psychology. Psychological Issues*, Monograph 42/43. New York: International Universities Press.

Salthe, S. (1985) *Evolving Hierarchical Systems*. New York: Columbia University Press.

Shulman, D. (1990) The investigation of psychoanalytic theory by means of the experimental method. *International Journal of Psycho-Analysis*, 71, 487–97.

Slavin, M. and Kriegman, D. (1992) *The Adaptive Design of the Mind*. New York: Guilford Press.

Smith, D. (1991) *Hidden Conversations: An Introduction to Communicative Psychoanalysis*. London: Tavistock/Routledge.

Tooby, J. and Cosmides, L. (1990a) On the universality of human nature and the uniqueness of the individual: the role of genetics in adaptation. *Journal of Personality*, 58, 17–67.

Tooby, J. and Cosmides, L. (1990b) The past explains the present. *Ethology and Sociobiology*, 11, 375–424.

Ward, P. (1994) *The End of Evolution*. New York: Bantam.

Wilson, A. and Gedo, J. (1993) Hierarchal concepts in psychoanalysis. In A. Wilson and J. Gedo (eds), *Hierarchal Concepts in Psychoanalysis* (pp. 311–24). New York: Guilford Press.

7

Experiential Psychotherapy: An Unabashedly Biased Comparison with Some Other Psychotherapies

Alvin R. Mahrer

I want to express my appreciation to the editor, Colin Feltham, for inviting the contributors to answer a set of questions that are refreshingly bold, provocative, in-depth, challenging, and appealing. This chapter is organized around these questions. I have also tried to accept his invitation to answer the questions in a way that may be, in Colin Feltham's words, explicit, edifying, yet perhaps outspoken.

What were the factors leading you to choose, found, or adopt the approach you currently espouse and practice?

Experiential psychotherapy grew out of a search for some way of undergoing a lifelong journey of deep-seated personal change. From some time before I thought seriously about becoming a psychotherapist, it seems that I was drawn toward trying to find some way of becoming a continually evolving, qualitatively new and better person, and also free of painful scenes and situations I always seemed to get myself into. Psychoanalysis did not seem to do the trick, even though it was appealing to spend years talking about myself with a nice old fellow who granted me much more listening time than I got from people in my family.

After being the patient, I tried lots of different ways to have my own sessions, by myself or occasionally with a trusted partner. Very gradually, over about 40 years, what evolved was a way of working from my own dreams (Mahrer, 1989c) and from the especially painful daily events that were bothering me. What has come to be this experiential psychotherapy is the product of many years of looking for and trying to develop a way that enables me to continue this lifelong journey.

Experiential psychotherapy grew from studying tapes of impressive changes, to try to learn how to do psychotherapy. When I began doing psychotherapy, I felt unskilled and incompetent largely because I had not studied skilled and competent practitioners doing what I was paid to do. It would probably be hard to be a reasonably competent surgeon, plumber, boxer, sculptor, or pianist if you had not studied the actual work of a fine surgeon, plumber, boxer, sculptor, or pianist. Yet I was supposed to do psychotherapy without any kind of apprenticeship or opportunity to study fine psycho-therapists doing the work I wanted to learn. When I graduated, I still did not know what to do in the actual moment-to-moment session.

That was when I started a 40-year search for tapes of sessions. I got tapes from therapists who knew what they were doing, some of whom were well known, and many of whom were just well esteemed as fine therapists by their local colleagues. The initial frenzied phase of my search was to find out how to do psychotherapy. But then something wonderful hap-pened.

I began getting inspired, or challenged, or jealous, because of what seemed to be very impressive changes in some special sessions by some special thera-pists. This patient was no longer so terrified. Notice how that patient's head-ache was gone. See how this woman seemed to go from being helpless and hopeless to being sure of herself and happy. This withdrawn and quiet man is, later in the session, open and animated. I was inspired by seeing what kinds of impressive changes could occur within a session, or between one session and the next one, if I was fortunate enough to be able to listen to back-to-back sessions.

Several kinds of patient changes seemed especially compelling. One was when the patient seemed to become a qualitatively new person, a person who seemed much happier, much better put together, much different from the person who was there at the beginning of the session, or in the last session. The second inspirational change was when the patient seemed to be free of the bad feelings, the painful and troubling bad feelings, and the scenes or situations in which these bad feelings seemed to occur. These 'bad-feelinged scenes' were no longer in the person's world. My question was: How did the therapist help to accomplish that? I certainly wished that I could accomplish these two changes. These two changes were my inspira-tional aims, objectives, outcomes. Psychotherapy was a way to achieve these two changes.

I did not set out to develop a new therapy. I spent decades trying to study tapes of other therapists, and some of my own, to discover how these two impressive changes might be accomplished. Only gradually, with lots of groping mistakes and errors, did I manage to accomplish what some of these fine therapists were able to accomplish in their sessions. My quest was to try to learn how to do psychotherapy by studying tapes of lots of therapists from many different approaches.

Gradually I began to discover four in-session steps that seemed to enable patients to become qualitatively new persons, relatively free of the bad-feelinged scenes of the old person. I concentrated on studying tapes in which patients seemed to undergo these two remarkable changes. Some of these were tapes of my own sessions. Most were tapes of other therapists repre-senting lots of different approaches. Much of the study was simply listen-ing to these special tapes by myself or with a colleague or two. Increasingly,

I studied tapes, especially of other therapists' sessions, with a research team, to make my examination even more careful (Mahrer, 1996b).

What slowly seemed to emerge was a series of four steps. When a session went through these four steps, the apparent consequence was that the patient was able to become a qualitatively new person who was free of the bad-feelinged scenes and situations. In the first step of these special sessions, the patient seemed to find some scene or situation in which the feeling was rather strong. When the patient seemed to enter into this scene, what was uncovered was some actual instant or precious moment when the feeling was especially strong, and then what appeared to be accessed or opened up or brought forward was something deeper inside the patient, some inner, deeper potentiality or way of being. The first step accessed this inner deeper potentiality from within the person. In a second step, the patient seemed to welcome and appreciate this newly discovered inner experiencing or potential. The person actually came to feel good about it. In a third step, the patient was able to 'be' this inner, deeper potentiality. The person could undergo this new way of experiencing or being. This was a remarkable shift into actually being an apparently new person, even just for a few minutes or so. In a final step, the new person tried out what it could be like to be this new person in the present, in the extratherapy world.

It took a long time to find and to clarify these four steps that seemed to occur in the remarkable sessions of some therapists, and in some of my own attempts to try them out. I was learning how to attain these four steps in each session. I was discovering a way that I could work with a patient so that a session could enable the person to become a qualitatively new person who was relatively free of the bad-feelinged scenes. This way of doing therapy grew from careful and consistent study of the special sessions of many fine therapists, and from consistent study of my own tapes where I tried to apply and use what I was gradually learning.

What started out as just a way to do therapy was received as a distinctive psychotherapy by other psychotherapists. When I first taught and wrote about this way of doing therapy, I saw it as a product of lots of tapes of special sessions from lots of therapists from lots of approaches. I did not regard it as especially distinctive or unique from many aspects of many other approaches.

What may have been somewhat distinctive or unique is the way this therapy originated and evolved. It did not start out from some new conceptualization of human beings. It did not come from some variant of an established family of psychotherapies. It did not originate from a distinctive way of combining common or effective elements from a variety of therapies. It did not grow as a distinctive specialty to treat some defined problem or mental disorder. It did not originate from some new wrinkle in philosophy or theory or practice. It did not develop from the application of a body of thought such as systems theory, physics, semiotics, or neurology.

However, once this psychotherapy gained a form and shape, it seemed to be regarded as rather distinctive by many other psychotherapists. What was apparently somewhat distinctive was that this therapy seemed able to accomplish some specific changes that were distinctive from many other therapies, and that this therapy relied upon a sequence of in-session steps that again were perhaps distinctive from many other therapies. It was distinctive as a practice. It was hard to compare it to other therapies in terms of some abstract conceptualization or theory of how change occurs or of some theory of human beings, mainly because this applied practice had no respectable theory of psychotherapy or human beings.

If this practice were somewhat distinctive, what is it to be called? I called it 'experiential' because it seemed this word made sense of what went on in the practical steps of in-session change. But this was a fumbling designation that seemed better than calling it a way of doing therapy derived from loose study of what lots of fine therapists seemed to be doing in impressive sessions. Only later did I appreciate that this particular 'experiential' psychotherapy was perhaps also distinctive from other experiential psychotherapies (Mahrer and Fairweather, 1993).

The experiential theory of psychotherapy and model of human beings were developed on the playing field of actual practice. As I was developing this new way of doing psychotherapy, I probably had some dim sense of what might be dignified as a theory of psychotherapy and perhaps a theory of human beings. It was not so much that I had no theory. It was more that I was not at all clear as to what it was.

While I was learning how to do this therapy, I was also trying to find a way of picturing human beings and change in a way that both came from and made sense of the practice. I was looking for the theory that I somehow was following or working from.

The first clarification was that I was trying to define a model of human beings and psychotherapy, rather than some theory of truth. This was freeing, because I was free to modify and refine the model, depending on whether or not it proved useful, rather than to try to find some theory that was supposedly true or right. The important thing was the practice. If the model seemed to fit the practice, and even helped to make sense of the practice, then the model was useful.

I spent about 11 years trying to develop a thorough, comprehensive, and useful experiential model of human beings (Mahrer, 1989b). It is a model of what human beings are like, of how we feel good or bad, of how we organize our worlds, of how we act and behave, of how we originate and come about in the first place, of how we then become what we are, of what we can become, of how social events come about and how they change. I tried to provide an experiential model of just about everything that other theories deal with.

Trying to develop a model of psychotherapy was perhaps harder. My first attempts were rather fumbling efforts to organize what seemed to occur in this form of psychotherapy. Only recently (Mahrer, 1996a) does it seem that the experiential model of psychotherapy has taken shape.

My aim was to develop a model of human beings and a model of psychotherapy that fit the practice, that came from and could help make sense of the practice. I was not trying to develop a new or distinctive theory of human beings or psychotherapy. The worth of my model of human beings and psychotherapy was in its usefulness in and for the practice, not to devise a better theory of human beings or psychotherapy.

Do you consider this approach to be simply one among many others, and equally valid, or more effective, elegant or comprehensive?

I consider the experiential approach to be more effective and more comprehensive, in being able to bring about what it is designed to bring about, than any other approach.

Experiential psychotherapy may be so different that it falls outside the club of most psychotherapies. There are some explicit ways that experiential sessions differ so significantly from what is generally understood as psychotherapy that experiential psychotherapy perhaps falls outside the club of what is ordinarily called psychotherapy (cf. Prochaska and Norcross, 1994). Therapist and patient do not look much at one another. There is no intake, no case history, no assessment or evaluation, no diagnosis of a problem or mental disorder. There is no attempt to value, bring about, or use what is ordinarily understood as a relationship. The therapist has little or no stream of private thoughts or clinical inferences. There is no treatment plan or agenda. There is no pre-post determination of outcome. Most of the technical terms of most psychotherapeutic vocabularies make little or no sense. Each session is regarded as a complete mini-therapy. It is a therapy for virtually any, or all, persons.

There may be other therapies that likewise fall outside the club of most psychotherapies. Experiential psychotherapy is probably one of this group. *Some theories come closer to what is real and true versus some models may be more useful than others.* In one sense, the experiential approach is simply one among many. We do not believe in the reality of what is called mental disorders, ego, ambivalence, schizophrenia, or most of the things that most psychotherapists accept as real and true. We do believe that just about any approach can make its own sense of what is referred to as a mental disorder or ambivalence or ego strength. We believe that there are 'events' that you can describe in terms of chemistry, economics, sociology, or in cognitive terms, Adlerian terms, experiential terms, or psychoanalytic terms. When you ask the patient how her mother feels about her, and the patient seems to pause and look away for some seconds, you can describe that set of events with cognitive, Adlerian, experiential, psychoanalytic, communication, sociological, chemical, or physiological terms. We believe that most events in psychotherapy are open to description from lots of perspectives. We do not believe that a physiological description is more valid or true than a Jungian description. We do not believe that the ego or schizophrenia are real things so that a chemical description gets closer to its real, true, basic nature than a Gestalt description. In this sense, experiential descriptions and terms are about as valid and accurate as most other descriptions and terms when it comes to most of the actual events we deal with in psychotherapy.

However, things can change drastically when we talk about usefulness. Experiential terms, descriptions, and constructs are not especially useful if you want to predict the fetus's eye color or the amount of weight the bridge can hold. But I do believe that experiential terms, descriptions, and constructs are far more useful and effective than most others if you want to attain the four steps of an experiential session and enable this person to become a qualitatively new person who is free of the bad-feelinged scenes. Then this approach is not just one among many others.

It is one of very few therapies that enable the person to undergo profoundly deep change toward becoming a qualitatively new person. A small group of therapies have a picture of the person that includes a rich interior world, an inner deeper world of which the person has little or no awareness. It is a deeper world of possibilities, dimensions and qualities, ways of being, potentials, a world that is essentially beyond what the person knows of himself or herself. Psychoanalysis and Jungian analysis are among this small group of therapies. So are experiential psychotherapy and a few more therapies. But not many.

These therapies hold out the possibility that the person can undergo a deeply profound change toward becoming a qualitatively new person. This qualitative change includes new ways of behaving, seeing oneself and the world, new thoughts and attitudes, new feelings and emotions, changes in the way the person is. But the change goes much deeper to include inner, deeper possibilities, potentialities, dimensions, qualities. The direction is toward being a qualitatively new person, from inside out. It is a qualitative change in the very core person, the one who has the sense of self, the continuing sense of who you are from moment to moment.

In experiential psychotherapy, each session offers the person an invitation to undertake this change. In each session, the person can taste, sample, undergo a qualitative change into attaining this higher plateau, into becoming this new person.

It is one of few therapies that provide the practitioner with an organized framework of working steps to follow in the session. Experiential psychotherapy provides the practitioner with a sequence of four steps that are the framework for each session. This four-step sequence is for virtually every session, from the initial to the final session, and enables the practitioner to be programmed toward attaining each step in turn until the session is completed.

This organizational framework is more than, and different from, a predetermined treatment plan for this particular session. It is more than an agenda of topics that the practitioner intends to cover.

A few therapies likewise provide an organized, stepwise program or framework for the practitioner to follow in carrying out a session. Rational emotive behavior therapy and a few other therapies provide their own series of steps to be carried out in just about every session.

It is one of few therapies with a distinctive, comprehensive model or theory of human beings. It is hard to say how many different kinds of psychotherapy there are. There are over two dozen different therapies that call themselves experiential psychotherapy (Mahrer and Fairweather, 1993). Estimates of the number of different psychotherapies run upwards into the hundreds.

How many of these therapies are linked to their own distinctive, comprehensive theories of human beings? I am referring to theories that deal with the structure of personality, explanations of pleasant and unpleasant feelings, mind–body issues, understandings of the human body, of how and why a person thinks this way or that way, of how a person organizes the external world, how the person interacts and relates to the external world, how social phenomena come about and change, what accounts for human behavior and change, the origin and explanation of painful and anguished feelings, the nature of the optimal state and what a person can become, the origins of infants, how infants grow and develop and behave, the development of the child, and the plateaus of human development.

Experiential psychotherapy has its own model of human beings (Mahrer, 1989b), one that is perhaps relatively distinct from virtually all other theories. There are a few other psychotherapies that are linked to a fully fledged, comprehensive, distinctive theory of human beings, but the heavy preponderance of most other therapies are not. They typically share family kinship with the relatively smaller number of distinctive, comprehensive theories of human beings. Virtually all of the integrative and eclectic psychotherapies likewise have no distinctive, comprehensive theories of human beings. There are dozens of cognitive therapies, dozens of family therapies, dozens of biological therapies, dozens of behavioral therapies, dozens of psychodynamic therapies, dozens of humanistic–existential therapies, and dozens of systems therapies, with each group generally sharing one or more of the relatively few distinctive, comprehensive theories of human beings.

Besides any subjective preference for your approach, is there any objective (research or other) evidence or rationale which you consider compelling in its favour?

From the very beginning, continuous study helped this therapy gradually to take shape and improve. Many therapies seem to have simply appeared from the writings of master thinkers and clinicians. Once these therapies were born, researchers then set to work poking and testing them to see if they were any good. For example, Freud created psychoanalysis, and, years later, researchers go about researching it. On the other hand, some behavior therapies may have evolved from bodies of research on how animals learn, on social change, on human thinking and behavior change, and other areas of research outside the field of psychotherapy.

Experiential psychotherapy did not just appear, nor did it come from other areas of research. This therapy had its origin in years of careful study of tapes to try to discover the secrets of psychotherapy (Mahrer, 1996a, 1996b). Instead of testing this therapy after it somehow appeared, clinical and research study were the parents of what slowly emerged as experiential psychotherapy.

I trust a therapy that gradually appears from such careful study of what therapists actually do in sessions, of what therapists seem to help accomplish in their actual sessions, of what therapists seem to do to help bring about impressive in-session changes. I trust experiential psychotherapy because of the way it originated through the careful study of so many tapes of so many therapists.

In just about every session you can actually witness a sequence of four impressive, objective changes. Every session is designed to go through a sequence of four steps. You can see the sequence unfolding. They are objective because it is easy to tell whether or not these four steps have been attained.

1   *The person is living and being in a moment of strong feeling, and a deeper potential is accessed.* In each session, the person looks for a scene or time of strong feeling. The feeling may be good or bad, but it is to be strong. Once this scene of strong feeling is found, the person is to enter into the scene, to live in it, to undergo the strong feeling. Inside the scene, the person searches for the actual moment or instant in which the feeling is strong. Then the therapist and patient are in a precious position to access something deeper, something that is inside, something that is opened up or activated in this moment of strong feeling. The inner something is called a deeper potential for experiencing. Both therapist and patient can access, sense, feel, receive, be in touch with, whatever deeper potential for experiencing is now accessible. For example, in this person, in this moment of strong feeling, the deeper potential may be described as a deeper potential for experiencing freedom, liberation, spontaneity.

It is impressive to witness the person actually living and being in a moment of strong feeling, and especially impressive to access or discover some inner, deeper potential. That inner deeper potential was not present or accessed earlier in the session. Yet here it is. That is objective and impressive.

2   *The person is actually able to welcome, appreciate, and have good feelings about the inner deeper potential for experiencing.* In the second step, the person is shown how to move from having kept down, sealed off, been distant from this inner deeper potential, to a new state in which the person welcomes it, appreciates it, has good feelings toward it. The person actually is warm and friendly about the formerly deeper potential for experiencing freedom, liberation and spontaneity, or whatever is the content of the inner deeper potential for experiencing. This change is objective and impressive.

3   *The person actually disengages from being the ordinary continuing*

person, and literally becomes a qualitatively different person who is the deeper potential for experiencing. The therapist shows the person how to step out of, let go of, the ordinary, continuing person that the person is. Instead, there is a radical change into being a qualitatively new and different person who is this formerly deeper potential for experiencing. Here is a whole new person, a person who is experiencing, for example, freedom, liberation, spontaneity. Actually witnessing this objective change can be impressive.

4   *This qualitatively new person is ready to live and be in the extratherapy world.* In the final step of the session, what had been an inner, deeper potential is now a part of who and what this qualitatively new person is. Furthermore, it is this new person who is ready to go out into the extratherapy world, and to live and be in this perhaps new and different extratherapy world. Here is a magnificent change that is objective and usually quite impressive.

Taken together, it is quite impressive that these four objective changes occur in just about each experiential session. It is also impressive that this four-step sequence leads to the big consequences of a successful session.
You can actually witness the two big consequences of a successful session. It can be quite compelling to see the changes that are present at the end of this session and hopefully are still present in the beginning of the next session.

You can see that the person is free of the bad-feelinged scenes that were at the front and center in the previous session. In the previous session, what was so very troubling was a scene in which his parents are at him once again, coldly dissecting his faults. Now, in the opening of the subsequent session, the person seems free of these awful scenes. They are gone, or perhaps much less bothersome or troublesome. It is compelling when the person seems to be free of the bad-feelinged scenes that had been so central in the previous session.

You can see that the person is the new person. It is impressive to see that the person who is here in this session is qualitatively different from the person who was there at the beginning of the last session. It is compelling to see that the new person who was present at the end of the last session is still here. There has been a shift in who this person is, a shift that seems very substantial, as if there truly is a new person.

In the beginning of the last session, the deeper potential was deep inside, sealed off. In the course of the session, the deeper potential was accessed, and the person was actually able to disengage from the ordinary continuing personality, and to live and be as the deeper potential. Now, in the opening of this session, here is a qualitatively new person, including the potential for experiencing that had been accessed in the last session. There is a qualitative change in who and what this person is. That can be compelling evidence.

Taken together, these are relatively objective indications that just about any practitioner or judge can use to tell whether or not the four steps were achieved in the session, and whether or not the next session revealed a qualitatively new person who was free of the bad-feelinged scenes. It is relatively easy to see if this session was successful, and if the two consequent changes were present in the subsequent session. When even a fair proportion or most of the sessions yield these changes, when most sessions go through the four steps, and when most subsequent sessions indicate the valued consequences, it is easy to be compelled by this therapy.

Do you think this approach is particularly suited to certain clients or client problems more than to others?

This approach is useful to help enable a qualitative change in the person that the person is, and to free the person of the scenes of bad feeling, almost regardless of the ways in which therapists label clients or the categories of 'problems' that clients are supposed to have. In other words, experiential psychotherapy is for just about any person.

Experiential psychotherapy is for just about any person whatsoever. There are a few ways to clarify what is and is not meant by claiming that this therapy is for just about any person whatsoever.

Just about any person can have a successful experiential session. For an experiential therapist, the question is whether this particular person can have a session that enables the person to be able to have a touch of what it can be like to be a qualitatively new person, and free of the bad-feelinged scenes. I picture a single session, rather than five or 30 or 100 sessions. Thinking mainly in terms of a session, whether it is the initial session or any other session, changes the meaning of the question dramatically. Picture asking a psychodynamic therapist, an eclectic, a Jungian, a systems, client-centered or cognitive behavioral therapist: 'If you have only one session with this person, do you think your approach is particularly suited to certain clients or client problems more than to others?' Most therapists might graciously decline to enter the contest. The experiential answer is that just about any person can gain what an experiential session is designed to provide.

Experiential psychotherapy is 'suited' to any person who is ready and willing to go through the steps in this particular session. If you ask if a therapy is 'suited' to particular persons, the word 'suited' can have lots of meanings. From the experiential perspective, 'suited' means that the person is ready and willing to do what the experiential method invites the person to do. If the person is ready and willing to play the game and to follow the steps in the session, then this therapy is suited to this person in this session.

However, having a sufficient degree of readiness and willingness can ebb and flow. In most of the sessions, a person may be quite ready and willing. In an occasional session, the person is quite entitled to be not especially ready and willing. Readiness and willingness are not some kind of permanent inherent characteristic of the person.

Experiential psychotherapy enables qualitative change in the person and freedom from the bad-feelinged scenes: it is not a 'treatment of problems and mental disorders'. It is relatively common to ask if a therapy is suited to treat patients with defined problems and mental disorders. Typically, the questioner has already defined something as a problem or mental disorder. Then the question is whether this psychotherapy is suited to patients who are schizophrenic, incest survivors, have Bruxism, have this phobia, are sexually dysfunctional, suffered this or that kind of abuse, are truant, are conduct disorders, have repressed aggressive impulses, poor study habits, borderline conditions, a depressive mental disorder, an eating disorder.

The 'yes' answer is that experiential psychotherapy is for just about any person, including those whom someone has labelled as having this problem or mental disorder. The 'yes' answer is that this psychotherapy can enable qualitative change in the person and a freeing from the scenes of bad feeling so that, ordinarily, this means a change in the way the person is, perhaps including what led others to say that the person was schizophrenic, or an incest survivor, or has this or that kind of problem or mental disorder.

The 'no' answer is that each experiential session enables the person to focus on whatever scenes of strong feeling are front and center for this person in this session. Many of these scenes are accompanied with feelings that are strong and good, happy, pleasant. Almost all of these strong-feelinged scenes are the ones that are front and center, are important, for the person. These scenes may or may not have anything to do with schizophrenia or poor study habits.

The 'no' answer is that our aim is to open up whatever is truly deeper within the person so that the person can become a qualitatively different person, and so that the person can be free of explicit bad-feelinged scenes. This therapy is not designed to treat what others refer to as mental illness, mental disorders, psychopathology, or what is ordinarily called 'problems'. So alien are those terms and concepts that the experiential psychotherapist would usually have no idea of what to label as this person's diagnosis, mental illness, psychopathology, or 'problem'. The closest we could come is to say that here are the explicit scenes of bad feeling that are at the front and center for this person.

Experiential psychotherapy is distinctive in not including itself in the many therapies that say they are good for treatment of particular mental disorders or problems. In a sense, this may also apply to client-centered therapy, meditative-contemplative approaches, or perhaps some psychoanalytic and analytic therapies.

This particular session is not likely to be successful if (a) the person is not ready and willing to carry out the work, or (b) attends mainly to the therapist. The experiential therapist shows the person what to do and how to do it. However, it is up to the person to be ready and willing to undertake the work or to be not especially ready and willing. In the beginning of the session, if the person is not especially ready and willing to carry out the work, there is no law that we have to have a session. Occasionally, this happens after a fair number of sessions. Sometimes this happens in the initial sessions. When this happens, we may pause for a while and then continue the session. Or we may decide not to try to continue this particular session. This is perfectly fine.

With some persons, in some sessions, it may be important for the person to attend fully, directly, and continuously on the therapist, rather than on something out there, on the focal center of work in this session. When the person attends mainly at the therapist, experiential work is unable to move forward. We may stop for a bit, or we may decide to not continue in this particular session.

Being less than ready and willing to do the work, or attending mainly to the therapist, are descriptions of how this person seems to be in this particular session. They are not regarded as entrenched qualities or characteristics of the person. Nor are they regarded as indications that this person is or is not suitable for experiential psychotherapy. Since we work one session at a time, the person is quite free to have a later session in which we can see if the person is now ready and willing to carry on the work, including attending mainly to what is out there, to the focal center of concern, rather than attending mainly to the therapist.

Do you think this approach is particularly suited to certain therapists more than to others?

The answer is an overwhelming yes. This therapy is open to and useful for just about any patient, but it takes a particular kind of therapist to be able to do this psychotherapy. In terms of suitability, my concern is far more about therapists than about patients.

It is for psychotherapists who share the experiential model of human beings and psychotherapy. Most therapists have a deeply rooted, almost generic, inflexibly anchored set of basic beliefs about what human beings are like, how a person got to be the way the person is, what causes the person to think, feel, and act the way the person does, how psychotherapy must work, what is to change, and the direction in which the person is to change. These beliefs are typically so entrenched that they are almost absolute truths – inflexible, rigidly unvioluateable, and beyond question. They comprise many theories of personality and theories of psychotherapy, but they deserve to be called basic truths about people and about psychotherapy.

There is an experiential model of how human beings may be pictured and how changes can be understood as occurring in psychotherapy. This model is just a model, one of perhaps lots of other models, a provisional picture rather than a theory that tries to approximate the true nature of things. If a therapist shares the experiential model of human beings and psychotherapy, the therapist can do this therapy. However, if the therapist clings to some other set of fundamental truths about human beings and psychotherapy, if the experiential model fails to conform to or violates the therapist's absolutely entrenched truths, then the therapist is almost certainly unable to do experiential psychotherapy.

Almost as soon as a therapist begins talking about people, about this patient, about what is happening in work with this person, it can be relatively clear whether or not the therapist shares the experiential way of thinking about human beings and psychotherapy. If the answer is yes, then the therapist can probably do this therapy. If the answer is no, and if the therapist holds to some well-anchored theory of truth, then the therapist probably cannot do experiential psychotherapy.

It is for therapists who can be 'aligned' with the person rather than gaining personal experiencings in face-to-face therapist roles. For the experiential therapist, it makes considerable sense that the person's attention is almost fully and unwaveringly concentrated on whatever is centrally compelling for this person. Accordingly, the person is fully attending to important scenes, things, situations, images, events, on whatever is of concern for this person, on living and being in scenes and worlds that are first and foremost for this person right now and throughout this session (Mahrer, 1996a, in press; Mahrer et al., 1994). The person's attention is mainly out there, or whatever it is, rather than on the therapist.

In the same way, the therapist's attention is mainly out there, focused on whatever is so important for the person – looking at it, seeing it, living and being here with it. There is a therapist, a patient, and a third important focal center of attention. Both therapist and patient are attending mainly to it, and this is the way they are throughout most of the session. So allied and conjoined are therapist and patient that the words of the patient seem to come from within the therapist. It is as if the patient's voice is coming from within the therapist, as if patient and therapist are two parts of the person who is attending mainly to that third thing. This is the stance or posture of the experiential therapist. This is what is meant by a therapist who is 'aligned' with the person. It means that the therapist shares what is occurring in the person, and shares living and being in and with whatever is out there for the person.

Therapists can do this therapy if it makes sense to be aligned with the patient, if it makes sense for both of them to be fully attending to what is out there, living and being here with it, seeing it, relating to it, and having feelings and experiencings that go with fully attending to it. Being aligned with the patient must make sense.

But this is a massive shift for most therapists. Most therapists have to be external to the patient, with both of them attending mainly to one another. In almost every therapy, therapist and patient are essentially face-to-face, attending mainly to one another. Most therapists would probably have a hard time trying to do experiential psychotherapy.

From my perspective, it is almost inevitable that face-to-face therapists and patients will encompass one another in mutual roles (Mahrer, 1989b, 1996a). Once therapist and patient attend mainly to one another, they are engaging in a grand game of role-playing. Each partner is working out a role for oneself and for the other. You can assert that you are doing psychoanalytic therapy or eclectic therapy. You can claim that you are developing a relationship or using a behavioral intervention. All of that may be accurate, from one perspective. However, from the experiential perspective, you are merely fulfilling some sort of therapist role in relating to this patient who is outfitted into a complementary patient role.

From the experiential perspective, face-to-face psychotherapy is merely a situation in which you can have special moments of highly personal, important, precious experiencings. Psychotherapy is a situation in which the therapist and the patient are mainly attending to one another, each fulfilling a role in which each undergoes moments of preciously personal experiencings. From this perspective, the therapist gains wonderful moments of experiencing a sense of being a fountain of psychic wisdom, or being the one whom the patient trusts above all others, or being a truly mature person, or being the one who can be singularly close to this patient, or the one who can lead the way to salvation, or who is genuinely seductive, or who is the safe haven for this poor patient, or whose pronouncements are taken so very seriously, or who has moments of wonderful intimacy that do not get out of hand, or who feels like an exemplar of mental health, or the one who can spout wise truths about life.

How willing are most therapists to let go of these precious experiencings? It is quite understandable that most therapists would cling to being face-to-face with patients, each attending mainly to one another. It is quite understandable that most therapists would confess that it is the 'relationship' (read as the precious experiencings in the therapist role) that is too valuable to consider giving up. Most therapists would rarely run out of reasons for attending mainly to their patients, for being essentially face-to-face, for being 'in a relationship'.

It seems that therapists have to give up this posture in order to do experiential psychotherapy. They must find it eminently sensible to adopt a radical posture in which both are attending mainly to the third focal center of attention, both relating to what is so personally important to the patient, both aligned as they are seeing the cancer, hearing the raspy voice of the attacker, both swimming in the horrible terror, both giggling at what flushed down the toilet.

Experiential psychotherapy is for therapists for whom being aligned with the person makes exceedingly good sense, is powerfully useful in helping to accomplish what the therapist finds important to help accomplish.

It is for psychotherapists who are not especially inclined to highlight their own conspicuous physical features or conspicuous differences from their patients. Some therapists may find it quite important to highlight their conspicuous physical features or their conspicuous differences from their patients. The therapist may be conspicuously beautiful, and this feature presents itself as something that is exceedingly present. As soon as the patient sees the therapist, the dominant feature is that this is a beautiful therapist, compellingly attractive, stunning. What does the therapist do? Try to hide the sheer beauty? Many physical features or conspicuous differences from patients will present themselves because they are so conspicuous. The therapist is nearly seven feet tall or well under five feet, is confined to a wheelchair, is blind, has a bulbous nose, a withered arm, is very white-skinned with black-skinned patients, is very male with female patients, is very young with old patients. These conspicuous physical features and differences from their patients will be highlighted whether the therapists like it (and some do) or not.

If anything, experiential therapy tends to interfere with these therapists' highlighting of these physical features or differences from their patients. On the other hand, if therapists want a therapy in which these conspicuous physical features do not seem to count for much, or in which their conspicuous differences from their patients do not play much of a role, then experiential therapy can be suitable.

There are at least four reasons why this therapy can be attractive to such therapists: (a) the patient and therapist usually have their eyes closed, rather than attending to one another; (b) their attention is generally on that third thing, out there, rather than mainly on one another; (c) the therapist gets so close to the patient that they are just about aligned or conjoined with one another, rather than attending mainly to one another; (d) they generally go through the four in-session steps, rather than working each other into a relationship about which they talk with one another.

Accordingly, therapists are drawn toward this therapy if they want to have a successful session without emphasizing that they are exceedingly tall or short, fat or skinny, young or old, attractive or ugly, have one arm or leg, are conspicuously pregnant, have a head that shakes or an arm that is withered, are albino, are blind, are in a wheelchair, or any other kind of conspicuously compelling physical feature.

In the same way, the therapist can have successful sessions when there are conspicuous differences between the therapist and the patient. In addition to therapists who have the above conspicuous physical features and patients who do not, the oriental therapist can work with the caucasian patient, the black therapist with the white patient, the female therapist with the male patient, the young therapist with the old patient, the Catholic therapist with the Jewish patient, the homosexual therapist with the heterosexual patient, the beautiful therapist with the ugly patient.

It is for therapists who are willing to learn the requisite competencies and skills. In many therapies, a beginning therapist can quickly get the hang of it, and do a passable job with patients. Take a course in the therapy. Try it out with a partner, perhaps in role-play, probably being watched through a one-way mirror. Then, after doing it with a real client, you are doing the therapy, especially if a teacher or supervisor heads off the glaring mistakes and helps you to do it better.

In rather stark contrast, in experiential therapy and a few others, it is almost immediately conspicuous that the therapist knows what to do or does not know, that the therapist is skilled or not skilled. It is conspicuously clear that the experiential psychotherapist is or is not achieving the four steps, that the experiential therapist has or does not have the skills to help bring about each of the steps.

When you are sufficiently skilled, you can achieve the steps, and your skill level and competence are evident. If you are not sufficiently skilled, you will essentially be unable to achieve the steps, and this too is quite evident. The experiential therapist must be willing to go through a period of actually learning the skills, of slowly developing competence. Experiential therapy is suited to therapists who are willing to go through this period of actual skill learning. Experiential therapy is not especially suited to therapists who are inclined to 'get the idea', try it out a bit, and then do a somewhat adequate session. In many therapies, a journeyman level of adequacy can be achieved rather quickly. In experiential therapy, and a few others, it takes a much longer period of actual practice until the therapist has sufficient competency in the skills to achieve the steps and goals of the session.

It is not for therapists who try to combine experiential psychotherapy with other therapies. Lots of therapists believe that if one therapy is good, then two or three therapies must be better. Lots of therapists believe that if two or three therapies are fairly good, then it is better to combine the best or the effective common parts of all the therapies. Lots of therapists believe that each therapy may be of some good, so a better therapy is to combine them.

In actual practice, these therapists either tend to switch back and forth between therapies, or they combine parts of various therapies into a super-therapy (Mahrer, 1989a). These are the therapists who say that after six or seven systemic sessions, they had a couple of experiential sessions, because of the client's inability to show adequate feeling, and then back to the family systems work. These are the therapists who describe their therapy as inte-grative: 'I combine cognitive behavioral with some experiential and a little psychodynamic, with a dash of primal screaming.'

It is almost impossible to combine the four steps of an experiential session while simultaneously using the session to attain psychoanalytic under-standing of her infantile sexual impulses toward her father, trying to build a trusting, helping relationship, and using the session to attack a central irrational idea that the patient has. It is almost impossible to hold to an experiential model of human beings and of therapeutic change and, at the same time, to hold to theories of psychoanalytic insight, cognitive perme-ability, birth traumas, mental diseases, and conditioned learning.

It may sound appealing on the surface, but experiential therapy is not especially for therapists whose deeply rooted way of thinking is that psy-chotherapies are best combined and integrated with one another (Mahrer, 1989a). There are plenty of other therapies for therapists whose thinking is like that.

Which criticisms of your approach by other therapists do you believe contain some validity?

Here are what seem to be the most common criticisms of experiential psychotherapy. They identify how this therapy is bad because it does not conform to the criticizer's own therapy. I am inclined to agree with each of the criticisms, but I am not inclined to change experiential therapy so it will become more like the criticizer's therapy.

Experiential psychotherapy does not fit into the managed care system as a treatment of standard 'problems' and 'mental disorders'. One very practical criticism is that if I do experiential psychotherapy, I would probably have very few clients because this therapy does not conform to the ordinary way of diagnosing and treating problems and mental disorders. This therapy does not fit in to what is referred to as the managed care system, health care delivery systems, health maintenance organizations, preferred provider plans, managed fee-for-service plans, or employee assistance plans.

This criticism is accurate. The experiential therapist works toward enabling the person to become a qualitatively new person, and to be free of scenes of bad feeling. The experiential therapist would have little or no idea what to call the patient's 'problem' or 'mental disorder'. This therapist could produce no statistics about his or her success in treating that problem or mental disorder. This therapist would not do an intake evaluation to diagnose the patient's problem or mental disorder. This therapist would not estimate the number of sessions to treat this problem or mental disorder. This therapist would not approach each session with a treatment plan for treating some diagnosed problem or mental disorder. This therapist would not gauge success by getting indications of the reduction of the supposed problem or mental disorder.

It is very likely that the managed care system would find no place for the experiential therapist. Indeed, the experiential therapist would probably be asking for trouble by even trying to gain acceptance into a club whose rules make so little sense to the therapist. In other words, this criticism of experiential psychotherapy seems to be quite accurate.

The experiential therapist goes through the same steps in each session with each person. This is an accurate criticism by critics who like selecting the treatment to fit the patient's pathological problem. Each session goes through the same four steps already described. However, the criticism does not say that we work with the very same content for each patient in each session. Indeed, what is front and center, the specific scenes of strong feeling, the specific accessed deeper potential, are almost certainly different for each person in each session (step 1). The deeper potential that is welcomed and appreciated is almost certainly only for this particular person in this particular session (step 2). It is almost certain that the person is being a different deeper potential for experiencing in different earlier life scenes in each particular session (step 3). And the new way of being, the new behavior, and the new extratherapy present and prospective scenes are almost certainly different for each person in each session (step 4). So, in this crucial sense, the criticism loses much of its steam.

The four steps seem to be the very best way to achieve enabling this person, in this session, to become the qualitatively new person that the person can become, based upon this session, and to be free of the bad-feelinged scenes that were front and center for this person in this session. If there were better ways of accomplishing these goals for this person in this session, I would adopt these other ways. Until I find these better ways, I will rely on these four steps.

Experiential psychotherapy declines the cherished truths that most therapists insist are universally true. Most therapists utterly and unquestionably believe in a bedrock of cherished truths that they know are universally true. These are general truths about psychotherapy, so firmly entrenched and so unquestionably known to be true that any therapist who dares to decline or to be in violation of these universal truths risks being labelled as suspect, wrong, bad, unscientific, cultish, unprofessional, immoral, and perhaps dangerous. If you do not know these universal truths, you are in danger of not graduating from your training program, of failing your internship or residency, of not being licensed, accredited, or accepted as a qualified professional.

Here is a small sample of the cherished truths in the field of psychotherapy: when you see depression, you are to check for signs of suicidal tendencies. You have to know the signs of psychosis and be able to check them out if they appear. First you diagnose the problem and mental disorder, and then you apply the appropriate treatment. You must be able to determine which problems are most appropriately treated by psychological therapy and which by other, non-psychological treatments. You should be able to diagnose neurological disorders. Egos vary in integrative capacity. If a patient has a weak ego, some treatments can be dangerous because they involve too much stress. A therapy can be dangerous if it opens up unconscious impulses in a patient with weak defenses. There are universal basic needs, drives and motivations. There are stages of development. A person may be arrested or fixated at certain stages of development. Each mental disorder has characteristic signs, patterns and clusters of symptoms. Psychotherapeutic change requires a helping alliance or relationship. The brain is a basic determinant of behavior. Strong emotional expression is dangerous for patients with fragile personalities, weakened defenses, or heightened impulses. Psychopaths do not do well in intensive psychotherapy. Psychoanalysis is the deepest form of psychotherapy. Patients come to therapy for treatment of their problems and relief of their suffering. Insight and understanding are essential for psychotherapeutic change.

The experiential model does not accept any of these cherished truths, does not believe in them, and is wholesomely guilty of violating all of them. Even worse, the experiential model does not believe in the usefulness of trying to state universal truths like the ones above. What may be true in and for some approaches is held, in the experiential model, as universally true only for those approaches that believe in universal truths. In the experiential model, we look for working principles and psychotherapeutic models that are useful, not parts of the storehouse of universal truths. The criticism is apt.

To have a successful experiential session the therapist needs a substantial period of skill-development, skill-training, skill-practice and skill learning.

It is rather common that trainees will get some didactic background about a therapy, learn about its basic techniques and methods, try these out with a partner, be supervised in some sessions, and be reasonably able to get the hang of having a passable session of that therapy. The criticism is that at the point where most beginners can do a minimally passable job of doing many therapies, they cannot accomplish this with experiential psychotherapy. This criticism is quite appropriate. Here are some reasons why.

It is eminently clear that you have or have not attained each of the four steps. It is eminently clear that you are or are not on the right track toward attaining each step. It is, therefore, rather hard to fake your way through an experiential session, to try to convince yourself that you did achieve the four steps, because it is so clear that you either did or did not achieve them.

It is hard to do this therapy because you have to have a reasonable degree of competence in quite particular skills. Many beginning trainees accurately complain that the ordinary 'basic skills' that they are taught are not especially helpful for doing an experiential session. Furthermore, they complain, again accurately, that achieving a working level of competence in the experiential skills seems to require actual practice, a period of sheer learning how to do it passably, like learning how to play the piano or to remove an appendix or to fly an airplane. Practicing a skill to reach a level of proficiency is rather alien to the field of psychotherapy. I agree that you must have working-level competence in the experiential skills, and that this takes time, training, practice, actual development of specific competencies.

It is hard to mix and match experiential psychotherapy with other therapies. Many therapists like to mix and match different therapies to integrate and combine them. The criticism is that it is hard to include experiential therapy as one of these. I agree.

Some therapists like to do a therapy that is an integrative blend of several therapies, or of bits and pieces from several therapies. The therapist says, 'I do a combination of cognitive and behavioral, with some psycho-dynamic . . .' 'My therapy is mainly humanistic, with some Jungian and transpersonal . . .' 'I do client-centered therapy, with some Gestalt methods, and flooding . . .'. These therapists accurately complain that it is hard to include experiential as one of the combining ingredients, largely because its model of therapy, its goals, and its in-session steps are not especially cordial to being blended into other models and in-session aims and goals.

Some therapists do one kind of therapy for a number of sessions, switch over to another therapy for a few sessions with this patient, and then either return to the original brand or move on to a third therapy. The justification for having a few sessions of some particular therapy is that the therapist decides the patient needs a little couples work, or to help her express her resentment, or he needs to control his impulses, or this other therapy would help deal with the stress, or he needs to go through the stages of grief-expression, or she could profit from some assertion training right here. The trouble is that experiential psychotherapy has little chance of 'working' when you choose this therapy to try to achieve the immediate goal that you have in mind. It simply will not work if you have an experiential session so that your client can start having the resentment you know is blocked, or to try and get the patient to get into that awful scene in which his mother abused him so mercilessly when he was a child, or to get this controlled and unemotional fellow to be more uncontrolled and more emotional.

In general, experiential psychotherapy does not seem to conform to the rules of therapies that mix and match with one another, that nicely blend with one another. The criticism is quite appropriate.

There is no research on whether experiential psychotherapy achieves the ordinary meanings of successful outcome. Why do researchers do research on psychotherapy? What are the aims and purposes of doing research on psychotherapy? You can do research to show that your theory of personality or your theory of psychotherapeutic change is solid, sound, good. You can do research to see if your favored method, such as a desensitization method or focusing or the two-chair technique, is better than other methods and techniques for accomplishing this or that kind of outcome. You can do research to see if this kind of client or problem or mental disorder has those other characteristics, dimensions, qualities, common-abilities. You can do research to see if your therapy is effective and successful, or is more effective and successful than these other therapies, especially in treating this kind of problem or mental disorder, as indicated in that kind of outcome.

If there are four or six quite different reasons, purposes, or aims for doing research on psychotherapy, which one or ones do you select?

My reason for doing research is to try to discover more about how to do psychotherapy, how to help improve and develop this therapy. I do a fair amount of research aimed at discovering how to do psychotherapy, to do it better (Mahrer, 1996b). In just about all of these studies, the conclusion is not that experiential psychotherapy works, or works better than other therapies, or is effective and successful in achieving its aims and goals. That is not why I do research on psychotherapy. Instead, my choice is to do research on psychotherapy so that the conclusion lets me say: 'So that is how to do psychotherapy better'; 'so that is how to accomplish these two ultimate aims and goals'; 'so that is a better way to accomplish these in-session steps that pave the way toward achieving these two aims and goals!' I study sessions that are effective and successful to try to discover the secrets of psychotherapy, to try to discover how to help make experiential psychotherapy better and better.

I do not do research to see if experiential psychotherapy is effective or successful in the traditional meanings of those words. Such research would have little payoff for me. In other words, the criticism is quite appropriate.

Which other therapists and approaches command your respect or strike you as especially effective or promising?

Just about everything that is experiential psychotherapy has come from studying tapes of many other therapists using many different approaches. A general answer is that I have an especially high regard for those many thera-pists, using many approaches, from whom I borrowed the important bits and pieces of what I tried to put together as experiential psychotherapy. But there are some more direct answers to this question.

Therapists who can help enable the person to become a qualitatively new person. There are therapists who are able to help enable the person to undergo a qualitative change into becoming a qualitatively new person. The person seems to be a whole new person, and this applies to the way the person is both on the outside and on the inside. The change applies to the way the person seems to behave, affect others, think, and also to the very inner person that the person now is. Furthermore, the new person seems to be happier, better put together, more solid, more of the kind of optimal person I value. It is a qualitative change, and it seems to be a good change. These therapists command my respect.

These therapists may have similar or different models of what human beings are like, the structures of personality. I think in terms of deeper poten-tials for experiencing, and relationships among these potentials. Other models may be somewhat similar or strikingly different. These therapists may have similar or different pictures of what a person can be, the direc-tions of change. Their pictures of optimal change may be similar to or differ-ent from that of experiential psychotherapy. Yet all of us are characterized by the intent of enabling qualitative changes in who and what this new person can be. I have high regard for these therapists.

My respect is for the *therapists* rather than for particular kinds of thera-peutic approach. It is hard for me to respect psychoanalysis, hypnotherapy, Jungian analysis, meditation, or any other approach. It is much easier for me to respect those therapists who use these or any other approaches to open up the very real possibility of becoming a qualitatively new person.

Approaches that can be carried out by oneself or with a partner. Every week or so, I have an experiential session by myself or with a partner. When I work with a partner, we alternate who is patient and who is therapist. In either case, whether I work by myself or when it is my turn to be the patient, or when I am the therapist, I follow the same four steps of therapeutic change. Almost always, the session starts with a recent dream (Mahrer, 1989c) or with some recent scene of strong feeling, usually a scene of bad feeling. My aim, just as with patients with whom I work, is to enable me to move in the direction of becoming a qualitatively new person, and to be free of the scenes of bad feeling.

Undergoing my own self-change is precious to me. I have very high regard for other approaches that likewise can be carried out by oneself or with a partner. I include here the many different approaches that have many differ-ent aims and goals but share in being used by oneself or with a partner. There are ancient practices of meditation and contemplation. There are lots of behavior change programs, self-change programs, ways of working with dreams, and other programs designed for use by oneself or with a partner. I have a high regard for the whole range of such programs, especially those whose aims and purposes are similar to those of experiential psychotherapy.

**Which approaches do you find particularly unhelpful,
unappealing, ineffective, misleading, or dangerous? Why?**

It seems to me that the problem lies more with the therapists than with the various approaches. Here are some of the main ways in which I see many therapists as unhelpful, unappealing, ineffective, misleading, or dangerous. *When therapists and clients are mainly attending to one another, therapy is a way for therapists to undergo precious personal experiencings.* For most therapists, most of what is called therapy consists of therapists and clients attending mainly to one another as they talk to one another. Therapists usually call this a 'relationship'. I prefer to call this two people attending mainly to one another as they are talking to one another.

From the experiential perspective, when therapists are attending mainly to their clients and when they get clients to attend mainly to them, it is almost inevitable that therapists are thereby gaining some kind of personal experiencings. Quite aside from the many ways that therapists like to describe what is called psychotherapy, ways of describing what they like to say they are doing, the experiential perspective sees the therapist as working hard to create a situation in which they are able to have some kind of precious personal experiencing. For a few moments here and there in the session, or even for longer stretches, the therapists enjoy the tasty fruit of the session, namely some precious personal experiencing.

With this patient, in this session, there are special moments when the therapist has a wonderful sense of being the one who manages, who controls, who makes the important decisions in this patient's life. Or the therapist enjoys special experiencings of intimacy, closeness, togetherness. Or she has pleasant moments of being sexually appealing, attractive, sought after. Or she experiences being the wise one, the sage, the one who knows about life. Or there is an inner sense of being the solid rock, the anchor to reality. Or he has a delicious experiencing of being the one whom the person trusts, confides in, entrusts himself to. Or the therapist gains some precious moments of being the stronger one, the one in better psychic shape, the one who is sounder and better put together. Or the therapist has moments of almost revelling in the patient's admiration, worship, adoration. Or the therapist experiences the sense of being the patient's best friend, the real buddy, the loved companion. Or the therapist swells with pride in special moments of experiencing a sense of being the consummate professional, expert, authority. Or there are wonderful moments of being the omnipotent God with magical healing powers. Or the therapist tingles with being the model of mental health, the exemplar, the kind of person the patient can become. Or the therapist has moments of thrilling with the experiencing of being the main one who offers understanding, sheer interest, unwavering concern and prizing.

Is this kind of personal experiencing just a minor side issue? Isn't there so much more to psychotherapy? Doesn't this apply only to a few extreme therapists? The answer to all these questions is no. From the experiential perspective, most of what is called therapy is little more than therapists constructing situations that provide precious personal experiencings as they and their clients are attending mainly to one another.

How and why is this unhelpful, unappealing, ineffective, misleading, or dangerous? First, psychotherapy is dressed up as being for the welfare of the client, as a way of 'helping' the client. Not from this perspective. Looked at in this way, therapy is predominantly a way for the therapist to gain precious personal experiencings. Psychotherapists believe they should get paid for their 'service', for treating problems. Psychotherapists regard themselves as dedicated and noble because they are helping clients. Not from this perspective. I see most therapists as using the therapy situation as a means of having highly personal, self-centered, preciously personal experiencings, and therapists quietly collude with one another to disguise 'psychotherapy' as a noble profession dedicated to the welfare of the clients.

Secondly, in what is called psychotherapy, virtually everything the therapist does is in the service of providing for the therapist's own precious personal experiencings. In almost flagrant camouflage, most of what therapists do is disguised as 'doing psychotherapy', as practicing a sophisticated profession, as requiring years of training, as restricted to qualified and licensed and accredited professionals, as based on a foundation of science. Strip away much of this disguise, and the therapist is more simply getting the patient to look up to and trust the therapist, or putting the patient down so that the therapist has a sense of being mean, nasty, tough. Doing what the therapist does to gain these kinds of precious personal experiencings can be quite far from the typical technical, abstruse, academic, professional justifications for what the therapist is doing and why the therapist is doing it. 'I am desensitizing her conditioned response to stress associated with a poorly differentiated ego structure in situations involving loss of identity.' Perhaps, but the observer may adopt another perspective and say, 'Well, it seems like you're just holding her hand, getting her to tell you about her sex life.' A psychotherapist can get away with what many ordinary people would like to achieve. Most of what most therapists do requires professional training mainly in the vocabulary for what therapists call it and how therapists justify why they do it.

Thirdly, I am not so concerned when therapist and patient have mutual and complementary personal experiencings that feel good, and when this is occurring between two consenting adults who are up front about what they are getting from one another. The patient may have fine experiencings of being important in someone's eyes, of being valued as special, and the therapist has complementary experiencings of being admired, seen as a valued confidante. They are providing for each others' personal experiencings. What does bother me is when the therapists's personal experiencing is obtained at the expense of the patient. The therapist gains the experiencing of safe sex and adoration, and the patient writhes in the pain of unfulfilled longings. The therapist gains a sense of being the superior one who scolds the patient for seeking from the therapist what the therapist does not wish to provide. The patient is promised unconditional love and acceptance that is really full of restrictive conditions. The therapist gains whiffs of being the rescuer at the painful expense of the patient's being pushed into a maelstrom of whirling pathology. The therapist gains the personal experiencing of being the all-powerful one at the expense of others in the person's life who are forced into accompanying the patient in having sessions, or whose lives are bent out of shape by the therapist who tells the sister why she is to let the patient live with her for the patient's welfare.

I believe that for most therapists therapy is mainly a situational context that allows therapists to undergo precious personal experiencings, and I regard that as unhelpful, unappealing, misleading, and dangerous. But very common, and effectively disguised.

I object to dominant approaches forcing their universal truths on approaches that do not believe in universal truths. The philosophy of science that goes with experiential psychotherapy is one of useful models, not theories of universal truths. This means that experiential psychotherapy has one model of what human beings are like and how change is described as occurring. A 'model' means that there may be other models, that the experiential model is used because it is useful, not because it is somehow 'true'. It means that the experiential model can be played with, modified, or even replaced with another that seems more useful.

What bothers me are dominant approaches who know unquestionably that there are universal truths, who know what these universal truths are, and whose messianically self-arrogated relentless right is to force these universal truths on to weaker approaches who believe in models rather than believing in those universal truths. Because I believe in varying models, each one trying to become increasingly useful, I am vulnerable to dominant approaches who inflict their universal truths on to me. This is bad enough because I do not believe in universal truths. It is even worse when I am forced to conform to their particular, universal truths.

These dominant theories of universal truths force weaker approaches to recite that there are basic skills and here they are; there are mental disorders, and therapists have to know what they are and how to treat them; therapy requires a relationship and insight; therapists have to know about the brain because the brain is the basis of behavior; there really is psychopathology and therapists have to know the various signs; therapy requires an initial assessment-evaluation and here is what you are to assess and evaluate; experiments using control groups are the highest form of science; psychotherapies are successful and 'validated' if they get the right 'outcome'; there is a research foundation underlying psychotherapeutic practice; there are sexual and aggressive impulses in everyone; and hundreds of other assertions of universal truths to which all approaches are to abide.

Most approaches, and just about all the dominant approaches, are full of asserted truths that are assumed to be universal, and therefore all weaker approaches are forced to obey and salute the dominant universal truths. I object both to the particular catechism of current universal truths to which

I am to conform, and also to there being dominant approaches with their universal truths to which all other approaches are to conform.

How do you account for research which suggests that no one approach seems more effective than any other?

It seems to me that the statement, 'Research suggests that no one approach seems more effective than any other', makes fairly good sense under some relatively specific conditions. Here are a few of these relatively specific conditions.

It makes sense when the contestants are probably very similar to one another in order to abide by the contest rules and enter the contest. If the contest is to see which approach is more effective at treating this particular problem or mental disorder, then the contestants probably believe that they are pretty good at treating whatever it is. If the aim of the contest is to see which approach is able to treat an infected wisdom tooth, or miasma, or a simple phobia, or second-degree Bruxism, then each contest might attract a somewhat different group of contestants. The very nature of the contest probably means that the contestants who enter are more similar to one another than are all the approaches, some of which do and some of which do not enter the contest. Experiential psychotherapy, for example, would probably not enter any of the contests. The net result is that most of the contestants are relatively effective in being able to do what the contestants are judged as being able to do.

Most studies of the effectiveness of various approaches tend to use therapists who are at or below the journeyman level of competence rather than the pinnacle of expertise at that particular approach. When the therapists are at relatively similar levels of journeyman competence it makes sense that the findings will reflect more similarity than differences in overall effectiveness.

In order to be in the contest, the contestants probably agree on the rules or criteria for whom is to be declared the winner. The contestants would have to agree that the winner is the one who gets this change on the MMPI, or who promotes the largest number of orgasms, or who has the fewest recurrences of the original symptoms in the termination phase of long-term psychoanalysis. If the contestants all agree on the criteria of who wins, the chances are that the contestants are already quite similar to one another. And that is what many studies find.

It makes sense that research suggests no one approach is more effective than any other when the contestants are already very similar to one another in order to abide by the contest rules and to be in the contest. In other words, the research findings tend to corroborate what the design shapes as the expected research findings.

It makes sense when the major approaches have their own dedicated researchers. Just about all of the major approaches have their own dedicated researchers, and their own favorite journals. It is understandable that cognitive behavioral researchers might find how effective cognitive behavior therapy is, and psychodynamic researchers might be inclined to lean toward psychodynamic therapy as fairly effective. Some integrative-eclectic researchers might find that integrative-eclectic therapy is king of the mountain, and other integrative-eclectic researchers might well find that most approaches have something in their favor. It therefore seems no special surprise when reviewers conclude that most approaches can show proof of their effectiveness.

It makes sense when you get down to the level of what most therapists actually say and do in most of their sessions. I have listened to hundreds of sessions by hundreds of therapists from dozens of approaches. My impression is that if you leave out tell-tale terms such as archetype, superego, thought-stopping, and other give-away terms, much of what most therapists actually say and do is impressively similar. Down at the level of what therapists and patients actually say and do, there is a remarkable commonality across the approaches therapists claim to be carrying out. All in all, it makes sense that most approaches fare about the same in what is called effectiveness.

What are your views on eclecticism and integrationism? How do you account for the vast number of different approaches and their continuing proliferation?

I am combining these two questions because my answers to each are so similar. For example, it seems to me that (a) it is mainly an illusion to believe that whatever eclecticism and integration are, they can be achieved in an impressively rigorous, systematic, careful way, and (b) perhaps the main consequence of the eclectic-integrative movement is to contribute to the proliferation of what is already a vast number of different approaches (Mahrer, 1989a).

Here is how to produce a new approach, especially if you are integrative-eclectic. I know of no rules for what qualifies as a truly new approach. Therefore, it seems that you can claim to have produced a new approach in at least the following 'integrative-eclectic' ways: (a) add, modify, or use a somewhat different set of terms or vocabulary. Take words and terms from communication theory, or postmodern constructivism, or hindu philosophy, physics, mathematics, engineering, social systems theory, semiotics, chemistry, or epidemiology; (b) assemble your own package of methods. Take a particular kind of therapist–patient relationship, one or two behavioral methods, and a couple of Gestalt games. Or combine past life experiences, guided imagery, and focusing; (c) slightly alter the popular notions of what personality structure is like, what makes people be the way they are, how people change from birth to death, and what is important in how and why people change; (d) modify popular notions of how and why change occurs in psychotherapy. Combine some common notions in a new way, or slightly revise some current theory of psychotherapy. Here are only four of the workable ways to get loads of new approaches.

The integrative-eclectic movement provides a powerful added wrinkle that can produce new approaches with the ease of a popcorn machine. There is an almost endless number of possible combinations of terms and vocabularies, methods and procedures, theories and conceptualizations of personality, and explanations of how and why psychotherapeutic change can occur. If you put all of these into a computer and ask the computer to spin out all possible permutations and combinations, the sheer number of possible new approaches would likely far exceed the number of present and future practitioners.

Here is one test of the usefulness of integrationism-eclecticism for experiential psychotherapy. In each session of experiential psychotherapy, one aim is to enable the client to become a qualitatively new person, based upon the deeper potential for experiencing that had been discovered in this session. A related aim is for the qualitatively new person to be essentially free of the bad-feelinged scenes that were troubling for the old person. The four steps are designed to help bring about these two aims or goals.

The general test is to see if the integrative-eclectic movement can help achieve those two aims or goals. More specifically, here are two questions: Is there some integrative-eclectic therapy that can achieve these aims and goals better than experiential psychotherapy can? Is there something that the integrative-eclectic movement can offer that can improve the way in which experiential psychotherapy tries to achieve these aims and goals? If the answer is yes to either or both of these questions, then the integrative-eclectic movement is helpful for experiential psychotherapy. Since I am usually on the lookout for better ways of achieving these two aims and goals, and also for improving the four steps, I think I might be pleased if the integrative-eclectic movement passed this test.

There seems to be something a little sad about the popularity of integrationism-eclecticism and the easy proliferation of new approaches. What seems a little sad to me is that with all of our licensings, accreditations, professional associations, standards and qualifications, with all of the fighting among the psychotherapy-related professions, with all of our chest-pounding about science and research, we still seem to know so very little about how to help bring about impressive changes in psychotherapy sessions. We sputter about, posture and pose, but we cannot produce impressive changes as a genuine science should. After more than a century of trying to pretend we belong among the sciences, our actual accomplishments seem more nugatory than laudatory.

Because there are so few impressive changes that we can accomplish, the stage is ripe for lots of new approaches. After all, what is to say that this new approach is not as good as the more popular approaches? It is easy to be drawn toward the eclectic use of lots of different methods, procedures, and techniques, when few if any can be shown to be much more impressive than others. That is a little sad.

It also seems a little sad that so many different ways of thinking about human beings, what they are like and how they change, make some sense. Every decade or so, a bunch of new theories, conceptualizations, explanations, can become fashionable, partly because we have no good way of showing how and why one is truly better than another.

Finally, it seems sad that along with the cascading proliferation of varying approaches there is a symmetrical rigid clinging to dogmatic truths, an insistence that we know how to do psychotherapy, that we have basic knowledge to teach, that there are fundamental truths on which the field of psychotherapy rests. Psychotherapists know the truths about psychotherapy because they truly believe there are truths to be known, and because psychotherapists are trained to know these truths. Partly because we are not especially able to point toward impressive changes that we can bring about, we too easily believe in basic truths, in dogma, in group-constructed illusions that become what you supposedly need to accept to be a psychotherapist. This strikes me as somewhat sad.

How would you advise people seeking therapy to choose a therapist and a therapeutic orientation?

This question is just a little bit sneaky because it has a number of pictures that are smuggled inside the question. One picture is that the person will be signing up for an extended series of sessions. There may be five or ten or two years' worth of sessions. I picture one experiential session at a time, each being a mini-therapy, and therapist and patient deciding whether to have another session. A second picture is that the person has some problem or mental disorder, and some treatments are better than others for the particular problem or mental disorder. I do not believe in either part of this picture. A third picture is that when a therapist says he or she is eclectic or Jungian or cognitive, I would have a fairly good idea of how he or she works in the session. I do not believe that much at all. A fourth picture is that I would have some first-hand knowledge of the therapist's work, such as I might have in choosing a secretary, chef, writer, architect, or photographer. I practically never have any first-hand knowledge of that sort. With all this, I prefer to try to be clear about the pictures that are smuggled inside the innocuous-looking question. Those pictures make the question hard to answer.

Ordinarily, I work hard to avoid advising someone on how to choose a therapist. When I am inclined or pressured to give some advice, I use a few guidelines. First is to choose an experiential psychotherapist, preferably someone I have helped train or whose work I have studied in cassettes of their actual sessions. Secondly, if the therapist uses the traditional face-to-face stance, I suggest that the person might consider trying out a few sessions with that therapist and also with one or two others. Then see which one seems to be more enjoyable, to appeal to you more – the one you feel best with. It is very much like dating. If the person is looking for some safe sex, a little safe intimacy with an attractive other person, there are therapists who suit that purpose. If the person is lonely, seeking a friendly confidante, have a few sessions and try to judge whether you are less lonely, have found a friend in whom you can nicely confide. The third guideline is to avoid signing a contract for the duration, and to include a clause that you reserve the right to end the sessions when you are not especially getting what you signed up for, in spite of the therapist's likely pressure for you to continue.

What would you guess the field will look like in, say, 50 years' time? Which approaches will thrive and which will decline?

Quite aside from the names of the approaches, I believe that there will be large and popular clusters of patients and therapists fulfilling mutually important personal roles and getting mutually important personal experiencings. There will be large groups of patients who seek a few precious moments of closeness and intimacy, and large groups of therapists who want to provide and share in precious moments of closeness and intimacy. There will be patients who get excited about stroking their precious selves, and therapists who love being the provider of such fascinating personal attention. There will be patients searching for truth and wisdom, and therapists eager to provide it. There will be patients looking for exemplars and models, and therapists loving to fulfil such roles. Each providing what the other seeks is now, and probably always will be, the working basis of whatever future therapies will enable groups of patients and therapists to find and provide for one another. I do not think much of this, but it fuels most of our therapies, for now and, probably, 50 years from now.

Approaches flourish in part because they rest on an underlying model of human beings that is held by a large proportion of practitioners. What we dignify as theories is, I believe, a scientifically dressed version of what most therapists believe humans are like, how they come about, how change occurs, and so on. My guess is that in 50 years the popular approaches will be those that consist of the popular 'theories' that most people will be holding in 50 years. The popular approaches will be whatever theories are present in high school students, politicians, athletes, and those who become psychotherapists.

I believe that my experiential psychotherapy will be viable, but not popular. Its model of human beings is not the commonly held model. It violates too many of the cherished beliefs of most therapists. It counts too much on actual skills that require learned and practiced competence. It deprives too many therapists of the precious in-session personal experiencings that are so important for so many therapists. In 50 years' time, I hope that my experiential psychotherapy will have developed far beyond what it is today, and will still be around. In 50 years I will see whether or not this is so.

References

Mahrer, A.R. (1989a) *The Integration of Psychotherapies: A Guide for Practicing Therapists*. New York: Human Sciences.

Mahrer, A.R. (1989b) *Experiencing: A Humanistic Theory of Psychology and Psychiatry*. Ottawa: University of Ottawa Press. (Original work published 1978.)

Mahrer, A.R. (1989c) *Dream Work in Psychotherapy and Self-Change*. New York: W.W. Norton.

Mahrer, A.R. (1996a) *The Complete Guide to Experiential Psychotherapy*. New York: Wiley.

Mahrer, A.R. (1996b) Discovery-oriented research on how to do psychotherapy. In W. Dryden (ed.), *Research in Counselling and Psychotherapy: Practical Applications* (pp. 233–58). London: Sage.

Mahrer, A.R. (in press) Empathy as therapist–client alignment. In A.C. Bohart and L.S. Greenberg (eds), *Empathy and Psychotherapy: New Directions to Theory, Research and Practice*. Washington, DC: American Psychological Association.

Mahrer, A.R. and Fairweather, D.R. (1993) What is 'experiencing'? A critical review of meanings and applications in psychotherapy. *The Humanistic Psychologist*, 21, 2–25.

Mahrer, A.R., Boulet, D.B. and Fairweather, D.R. (1994) Beyond empathy: advances in the clinical theory and methods of empathy. *Clinical Psychology Review*, 14, 183–98.

Prochaska, J.O. and Norcross, J.C. (1994) *Systems of Psychotherapy: A Transtheoretical Analysis*. Pacific Grove, CA: Brooks/Cole.

8

Multimodal Therapy

Stephen Palmer

Too often therapists discuss factors that led them to espouse and practise a particular approach but this is usually from an academic or clinical perspective. Instead, I've decided to give the reader a personal account starting from my childhood interests and specific events that possibly influenced my decision to practise Multimodal Therapy. Currently, I am a leading exponent of Multimodal Therapy in Britain and well known in the field of counselling, counselling psychology and stress management. However, there are probably less than 150 practising multimodal therapists in Britain and so it is easy to see how one can become a leading exponent! Also I regularly practise Rational Emotive Behaviour Therapy but my colleague, Albert Ellis, has written very eloquently elsewhere in this book about this approach so I will limit myself to why it still commands my respect.

Experiences that have influenced my approach to therapy and stress management

I remember as a child reading my father's medical and psychology books. No, he was not professionally qualified but read books suitable for the layperson. For some reason these books fascinated my sister Jayne and me. I recall when Sara, my youngest sister, was born undertaking developmental experiments with her. Of course, at the time (I was about nine years old) I had little concept of what I was actually doing and could hardly utter such complicated words. However, Jayne and I remember sitting my baby sister in between us. We sat at either end of the hall and waited for Sara's reaction. She slowly crawled her way towards me. She had responded to her name. Later we repeated the experiment without calling names or making any gesticulations. Experiments continued and at about the same time I read, with great difficulty, the section in my father's medical book about hypnosis. We plucked up courage and gave it a go. Using self-hypnosis my arm levitated. I was in awe! I then inflicted hypnosis upon Jayne. Perhaps Jayne was my first client? When I was 12 years old I and the rest of my classmates had to give a presentation. Of course, my paper was on hypnosis. Still to this day I remember being criticized by the English teacher for reading from my notes.

As an adolescent I was interested in how my younger cousins responded to any punishment meted out by their parents. I discovered that they held on to different belief systems and this appeared to affect how they would react. Therefore a simple belief such as, 'I'm not going to let them see that they have hurt me' would stop one of my cousins from crying.

From the age of 17 onwards I regularly read books about different forms of therapy. At about the age of 18, a friend introduced me to *The Primal Scream* (Janov, 1973). With self-help groups we suffered many ear-bashing experiences. In hindsight this was potentially dangerous. (I'm glad I did not suffer from an unknown cardiac condition.) I started to realize that catharsis could help one to retrieve long-forgotten memories. In my case I could always ask Jayne for confirmation about the accuracy of most memories. Sometimes she would remember different aspects about the same event – an interesting time but probably very difficult for my parents. However, my main goal of reducing my symptoms of hayfever through 'therapy' was not achieved. In fact, if anything, the problem escalated. I became disillusioned about 'therapy' but still retained an interest in the hope that one day I would find a psychological cure to my somatic problems. Stress management was another possible avenue to investigate.

I studied for my BA degree with the Open University on and off over many years as my business commitments came first. I studied psychology, biology and management, with a year spent on art and environment. However, one of the modules I studied included Personal Construct Psychology. This rekindled my curiosity and with the encouragement from my tutor, Ray Bull, I undertook a course at The Centre for Personal Construct Psychology, London. Metaphorically speaking, this kick-started me back into therapeutic motion. I finished my ordinary BA degree course and then went on with the higher level psychology credits to complete my BA(Hons), majoring in psychology. Simultaneously, I went into overdrive and attended a variety of courses. I concentrated on those approaches that took my fancy. These included hypnosis, psychodynamic therapy and more traditional stress management. I chose the psychodynamic course because the Open University programme was not very complimentary about Freud's approach, and as I recognized that I was heavily influenced by this I decided to find out the truth for myself. In counselling I found that hypnosis and Personal Construct Therapy appeared to help some of my clients. However, the psychodynamic approach was less effective for helping clients to overcome the stress-related problems I tended to see working in a health clinic and a stress centre.

My course of training in behaviour therapy at the Institute of Psychiatry, London, heavily influenced my subsequent approach to stress management, counselling and psychotherapy as the strategies were particularly suited to helping clients deal with stress-related problems such as anxiety and phobias (Palmer, 1991a). My enthusiasm for the approach was probably one of the factors that persuaded clients to undertake the unpleasant exposure programmes. However, occasionally clients did not wish to comply with the relatively strict behavioural programmes and this increased the rate of attrition (i.e., early termination from therapy).

It was at this stage I wanted to offer my clients more. In fact, I wanted to offer the students attending my stress management courses more skills, techniques and strategies too. I wanted them to have a simple but thorough assessment procedure which would guide them through the client's maze of problems without overlooking any important aspect. I wanted more durable results.

I became aware that I tended not to consider clients and their diversity of problems from a holistic perspective. I thought I did but in actuality I did not regularly undertake a comprehensive assessment. For example, I only occasionally asked clients to describe the negative, self-defeating pictures they generally held about particular stressful situations such as public speaking (Palmer, 1990a). I usually focused on their cognitions, behaviours and physiological reactions (Palmer, 1988, 1989, 1990b, 1991a, 1991b) even though I could still clearly see in my mind's eye my English teacher commenting on my lack of lecturing prowess.

I decided to undertake a more thorough examination of different approaches to therapy and I came up with a number of conclusions. First, I would start undertaking comprehensive and systematic assessments of clients and their presenting problems (Palmer and Dryden, 1991). I decided to use the assessment template devised by Arnold Lazarus (1981, 1989) in which seven discrete but interactive dimensions or modalities are routinely examined. The modalities are: behaviour, affect, sensation, imagery, cognition, interpersonal, drugs/biology. The useful acronym BASIC ID arises from the first letter of each one (Palmer and Lazarus, 1995). I agreed with Lazarus that the entire human personality could be included within the seven modalities and this approach was exactly what I was looking for (Palmer, 1992; Palmer and Dryden, 1991). The multimodal framework was also underpinned by a broad social and cognitive learning theory (Bandura, 1977, 1986; Rotter, 1954), to which I already subscribed. In fact, I now realize that the early observations I made during childhood and adolescence probably influenced my painless acceptance of learning theory. For me, the theory had ecological validity. In addition, Multimodal Therapy examined the biological dimension and this was one area that I believed was important since my childhood. Perhaps I could relieve my hayfever! Perhaps I could manage my Type A behaviour too.

Secondly, I wanted to improve my cognitive disputation skills. I decided that advanced training in Rational Emotive Behaviour Therapy would be perfect as the techniques used would suit the hard-headed business people I tended to see for stress counselling and it would be the ideal approach for running industrial stress management workshops. The cognitive therapy training I had previously received tended to play down forceful disputation and I quickly discovered that clients who held their self-defeating beliefs and attitudes for many years were very unlikely to jettison them without good cause and reason.

As, in Britain, few psychotherapists have much, if any, knowledge or understanding about Multimodal Therapy, in the next section I will briefly describe the basic approach.

The comprehensive nature of the multimodal approach

Before I cover some of the pertinent aspects of the multimodal approach, for the uninitiated, this is probably the best place to drop a proverbial bombshell. 'Multimodal Therapy' *per se* does *not* exist. Multimodal therapists, as technical eclectics, draw from as many other approaches or systems as necessary. To be precise, there is a multimodal assessment format and a multimodal framework (Lazarus, 1989). The comprehensive assessment and extensive framework enables therapists to choose, with negotiation with their clients, the most appropriate therapy programme.

Many approaches to psychotherapy are trimodal, focusing on affect, cognition and behaviour, and may overlook important areas such as the imagery and biological modalities. In addition, clients are often 'helped' by therapists practising in a social void. In other words, the interpersonal modality is not directly addressed during therapy and short-term therapeutic gains by the individual may be sabotaged by their family, friends or work colleagues. Even if all of the BASIC ID modalities are considered by therapists adhering to other approaches, the therapist may not always systematically address them, thereby overlooking vital information. The polar opposite of the multimodal approach is the Person-centred or Rogerian orientation which is generally conversational and essentially unimodal (Bozarth, 1991; Thorne, 1990). From the multimodal perspective, a good relationship, a constructive working alliance and adequate rapport are usually necessary but often insufficient for effective therapy (Fay and Lazarus, 1993; Lazarus and Lazarus, 1991a). The therapist–client relationship is considered as the soil that enables the techniques to take root. Hopefully, the experienced multimodal therapist offers a lot more by assessing and treating the client's BASIC ID, endeavouring to 'leave no stone (or modality) unturned'.

One of the criticisms often directed at Multimodal Therapy is that it really is 'multi-muddle therapy' in which the therapist selects any technique and applies it at random. For experienced multimodal therapists this is far from the truth, and I would like to encourage the reader to follow carefully the rest of this section in the hope that it will become apparent what technique is selected, when, and for what particular client. I wish to return to the 'multi-muddle' debate later in this chapter.

Assessment procedures

At the initial therapy session the multimodal therapist derives 13 determinations (based on 12 determinations of Lazarus, 1987; adapted in Palmer and Dryden, 1995: 19):

1 Are there signs of 'psychosis'?
2 Are there signs of organicity, organic pathology or any disturbed motor activity?
3 Is there evidence of depression, or suicidal or homicidal tendencies?
4 What are the persisting complaints and their main precipitating events?
5 What appear to be some important antecedent factors?
6 Who or what seems to be maintaining the client's overt and covert problems?
7 What does the client wish to derive from therapy or training?
8 Are there clear indications or contra-indications for the adoption of a particular therapeutic style (e.g., is there a preference for a directive or a non-directive style)?
9 Are there any indications as to whether it would be in the client's best interests to be seen individually, as part of a dyad, triad, family unit and/or in a group?
10 Can a mutually satisfying relationship ensue, or should the client be referred elsewhere?
11 Has the client previous experience of therapy or relevant training? If yes, what was the outcome? Was it a positive, negative or neutral experience, and why?
12 Why is the client seeking therapy/training at this time and why not last week, last month or last year?
13 What are some of the client's positive attributes and strengths?

In the beginning phase of therapy the multimodal therapist is collecting information and looking for underlying themes and problems. Additionally, the therapist endeavours to ascertain whether a judicious referral may be necessary to a psychiatrist or medical practitioner if the client presents problems of a psychiatric or organic nature. A referral may also be recommended if a productive match between the therapist and client is not possible. As more data is gleaned it may become apparent that the client would benefit from, for example, group therapy or couples therapy. This issue is then explored with the client.

By carefully observing the client's reaction to various tactics, statements and strategies, the multimodal therapist determines the most suitable interpersonal approach to take. Thus the counsellor needs to:

1 Monitor the client's response to directive and non-directive interventions.
2 Discover whether the client responds well to humour.
3 Decide whether the client prefers a formal or informal relationship.
4 Establish how the client responds to counsellor self-disclosure.

(Palmer and Dryden, 1995: 24)

Matching therapist behaviour with client expectations will generally ensure a good therapeutic alliance and may prevent early termination of therapy. The multimodal therapist will also consider what they wear with a particular client; for example, suits or formal jackets may be unnerving to adolescents who associate them with authority figures (Palmer and Dryden, 1995). In essence, the multimodal therapist attempts to be an authentic chameleon who decides the relationship of choice (see Lazarus, 1993).

The essential ingredients of a thorough systematic assessment may include the following range of questions (Palmer, 1997).

Behaviour

- What would you like to start or stop doing?
- What behaviours are preventing you from being happy?
- What do you avoid doing?
- What skills would you like to develop further?
- When do you procrastinate?
- Are 'significant others' doing things you would like to do?
- What is preventing you from doing things that you want to do?
- How does your behaviour affect your relationships (or emotions, or images, or sensations, or thoughts, or health)?

Affect

- What are your most predominant emotions?
- What appears to trigger these negative emotions (e.g., particular images, cognitions, interpersonal conflicts)?
- What do you cry/laugh about?
- What do you get angry/anxious/depressed/sad/guilty/jealous/hurt/envious about?
- How do your emotions affect your relationships (or behaviour, or images, or sensations, or thoughts, or health)?

Sensation

- What unpleasant sensations do you suffer from, if any (e.g., chronic pain, tremors, tics, tension, light-headedness, etc.)?
- What do you like to taste/see/touch/hear/smell?
- What do you dislike tasting/seeing/touching/hearing/smelling?
- How do you feel emotionally about any of your sensations?
- How do your sensations affect your relationships (or behaviour, or images, or thoughts, or health)?

Imagery

- Can you describe your self-image (or body-image)?
- What images do you have that you like/dislike?
- When you have these negative images, do you feel less or more depressed (or anxious, or guilty, etc.)?
- Describe any recurrent daydreams/dreams/nightmare you may have.
- Describe any pleasant/unpleasant flashbacks (or memories) you may have.
- Can you picture any scene that you find relaxing?
- What do you picture yourself doing in the immediate future (and/or six months', and/or one year's, and/or two years', and/or five years', and/or ten years', time)?

- In moments of solitude, do you picture any particular event from your past or have any fantasy about your future?
- How do these images affect your emotions (or behaviour, or thoughts, or sensations, or relationships, or health)?

Cognition

- If you could use one word to describe yourself, what would it be?
- If you could use one word to describe your main current problem, what would it be?
- What are your main musts, shoulds, oughts, have tos, got tos?
- What are your main wants, wishes, desires and preferences?
- What are your main values that you believe are important?
- What are your main beliefs that you believe are important?
- In key areas of your life what basic philosophy do you hold?
- What perfectionist beliefs do you hold?
- What are your major intellectual interests?
- How do your thoughts and beliefs affect your emotions (or behaviour, or sensations, or relationships)?

Interpersonal

- What expectations of others do you have?
- What expectations do you think they have of you?
- What expectations do you believe society has of you?
- How assertive (or aggressive, or passive) are you?
- When are you most likely to be assertive (or aggressive, or passive)?
- What people are important in your life?
- What people have been important in your life?
- Who has been the most significant person in your life?
- How do the significant people in your life affect you (e.g., emotionally, practically, etc)?
- How do you affect the significant people in your life?
- What social situations do you prefer (and/or avoid)?
- To what extent are you either highly gregarious or a loner?

Drugs/biology

- What are your main concerns about your health?
- Are you on medication?
- Do you take drugs (and/or smoke)?
- Have you ever undergone major surgery?
- How much alcohol do you drink in a week?
- Can you describe your typical diet?
- Have you tried to lose weight? (Were you successful?)
- What type of exercise do you do?

- Do you have any problems sleeping? If so, what problems?
- Are you interested in improving your general health?
- Do you believe that if you are taking regular exercise and eating a balanced diet, you will feel better about yourself?
- Have significant others set you a good/poor health-related role model?

The questions highlight some of the main issues that multimodal therapists cover while assessing the client's BASIC ID. Some clients only need an in-depth assessment of key modalities in which they are experiencing difficulties, for example, a client suffering from a simple phobia. Any competent therapist would first investigate the presenting problems or issues: for example, 'You said that you were really angry about your boss. What exactly are you getting angry about?', 'Can you tell me more about the physical pains you've been experiencing recently?' However, a multimodal therapist goes one stage further. He or she will observe which specific modalities are being discussed and what ones are being omitted or avoided. The modalities which are 'overlooked' often provide useful information when specific enquiries are made by the therapist. In addition, when examining a particular issue, the therapist rapidly traverses the entire BASIC ID to ensure that 'no stone (or modality) is left unturned'. I have found this procedure very useful when assessing clients suffering from post-traumatic stress disorder or occupational stress.

A comprehensive assessment is normally made straightforward by the client completing the Multimodal Life History Inventory (MLHI) (Lazarus and Lazarus, 1991b). This 15-page questionnaire aids the therapy programme when conscientiously completed by clients as a homework assignment, and avoids the therapist asking too many questions in the therapy session. This process helps to speed up the assessment and routine history-taking. It readily provides the therapist with a BASIC ID analysis and also helps to give further clues on how to interact with the client as it asks relevant questions. On completing the 'Expectations Regarding Therapy' section of the MLHI, one of my clients, Sue, responded to the questions as below:

Q: In a few words, what do you think therapy is all about?
A: Having the opportunity to talk through problems with a non-partial listener. Hopefully be given a new way of thinking about things/rationalizing problems.
Q: How long do you think your therapy should last?
A: As long as it is useful to me and productive.
Q: What personal qualities do you think the ideal therapist should possess?
A: Warmth and friendliness, and be non-judgemental, sincere and professional.
(Palmer and Dryden, 1995: 24)

This information helped me to adjust my interpersonal style accordingly. It facilitated the therapeutic alliance and also initially focused on the cognitive modality which she favoured. She revealed in the initial therapy session that she was unhappy about the psychodynamic therapy received previously. I decided that it was crucial to use an approach that she could relate to, otherwise she may have terminated prematurely. (For an in-depth session-by-session report of this case, see Palmer and Dryden, 1995: 181–99.)

From assessment to an individual therapy programme

Arnold Lazarus (Dryden and Lazarus, 1991: 132) has briefly summarized the 'main hypothesized ingredients of change' when using a multimodal approach:

> *Behaviour*: positive reinforcement; negative reinforcement; punishment; counter-conditioning; extinction.
> *Affect*: admitting and accepting feelings; abreaction.
> *Sensation*: tension release; sensory pleasuring.
> *Imagery*: coping images; changes in self-image.
> *Cognition*: greater awareness; cognitive restructuring.
> *Interpersonal*: non-judgemental acceptance; modelling; dispersing unhealthy collusions.
> *Drugs/biology*: better nutrition and exercise; substance abuse cessation; psychotropic medication when indicated.

This list gives a flavour of the type of interventions used. An in-depth description, including indications and contra-indications, of over 50 techniques and strategies I regularly use in my particular field of work are covered in *Counselling for Stress Problems* (Palmer and Dryden, 1995). Table 8.1 summarizes these interventions (adapted from Palmer, 1996: 55–6).

The information obtained from the initial session and a completed MLHI helps the therapist to produce a comprehensive Modality Profile (or a chart of the BASIC ID). The Modality Profile initially consists of a break down of the indentified problems into each related modality. Many clients are able to compile their own Modality Profile if they are given written instructions describing each modality (see Lazarus, 1989: 76–7). Then the therapist and the client discuss and negotiate a therapy programme and the Modality Profile is completed. Table 8.2 shows John's completed profile (Palmer, 1997).

The Modality Profile is modified as new relevant information is obtained. It is important for clients to be involved with developing the therapy programme to ensure that they understand the rationale for each intervention recommended and take ownership of their own programme. Often clients will suggest interventions that will be helpful, such as joining an exercise, assertion, self-hypnosis or meditation class. The therapist always takes these ideas seriously. Lazarus (1973a) found that if client expectations are met, then this will usually lead to a better outcome. He demonstrated that if clients believe that hypnosis will help, then this method is more effective than another technique named 'relaxation', even though the latter was still

Table 8.1   Frequently used techniques in Multimodal Therapy and training

Modality	Techniques/interventions
Behaviour	Behaviour rehearsal
	Empty chair
	Exposure programme
	Fixed role therapy
	Modelling
	Paradoxical intention
	Psychodrama
	Reinforcement programmes
	Response prevention/cost
	Risk-taking exercises
	Self-monitoring and recording
	Stimulus control
	Shame-attacking
Affect	Anger expression
	Anxiety management
	Feeling-identification
Sensation	Biofeedback
	Hypnosis
	Meditation
	Relaxation training
	Sensate focus training
	Threshold training
Imagery	Anti-future shock imagery
	Associated imagery
	Aversive imagery
	Coping imagery
	Implosion and imaginal exposure
	Positive imagery
	Rational emotive imagery
	Time projection imagery
Cognition	Bibliotherapy
	Challenging faulty inferences
	Cognitive rehearsal
	Coping statements
	Correcting misconceptions
	Disputing irrational beliefs
	Focusing
	Positive self-statements
	Problem-solving training
	Rational proselytizing
	Self-acceptance training
	Thought-stopping
Interpersonal	Assertion training
	Communication training
	Contracting
	Fixed role therapy
	Friendship/intimacy training
	Graded sexual approaches
	Paradoxical intentions
	Role play
	Social skills training
Drugs/biology	Alcohol reduction programme
	Lifestyle changes, e.g., exercise, nutrition, etc.
	Referral to physicians or other specialists
	Stop smoking programme
	Weight reduction and maintenance programme

Source: adapted from Palmer, 1996: 55–6.

Table 8.2 John's full Modality Profile (or BASIC ID chart)

Modality	Problem	Proposed programme/treatment
Behaviour	Eats/walks fast, always in a rush, hostile, competitive: indicative of Type A	Discuss advantages of slowing down; disadvantages of rushing and being hostile; teach relaxation exercise; dispute self-defeating beliefs
	Avoidance of giving presentations	Exposure programme; teach necessary skills; dispute self-defeating beliefs
	Accident-proneness	Discuss advantages of slowing down
Affect	Anxious when giving presentations	Anxiety management
	Guilt when work targets not achieved	Dispute self-defeating thinking
	Frequent angry outbursts at work	Anger management; dispute irrational beliefs
Sensation	Tension in shoulders	Self-massage; muscle relaxation exercises
	Palpitations	Anxiety management, e.g., breathing relaxation technique, dispute catastrophic thinking
	Frequent headaches	Relaxation exercise and biofeedback
	Sleeping difficulties	Relaxation or self-hypnosis tape for bedtime use; behavioural retraining; possibly reduce caffeine intake
Imagery	Negative images of not performing well	Coping imagery focusing on giving adequate presentations
	Images of losing control	Coping imagery of dealing with difficult work situations and with presentations; 'step-up' imagery (Palmer and Dryden, 1995)
	Poor self-image	Positive imagery (Lazarus, 1984)
Cognition	I must perform well otherwise it will be awful and I couldn't stand it. I must be in control. Significant others should recognize my work. If I fail then I am a total failure	Dispute self-defeating and irrational beliefs; coping statements; cognitive restructuring; ABCDE paradigm (Ellis et al. 1997); bibliotherapy; coping imagery (Palmer and Dryden, 1995)
Interpersonal	Passive/aggressive in relationships	Assertiveness training
	Manipulative tendencies at work	Discuss pros and cons of behaviour
	Always put self first	Discuss pros and cons of behaviour
	Few supportive friends	Friendship training (Palmer and Dryden, 1995)
Drugs/biology	Feeling inexplicably tired	Improve sleeping and reassess; refer to GP
	Takes aspirins for headaches	Refer to GP; relaxation exercises
	Consumes ten cups of coffee a day	Discuss benefits of reducing caffeine intake
	Poor nutrition and little exercise	Nutrition and exercise programme

essentially the same hypnosis intervention. I have also reported a similar experience with a client (Palmer, 1993a; Palmer and Dryden, 1995: 28–9). This possibly raises the issue of whether all therapy is an act of faith on behalf of the therapist and the client.

Other strategies

In addition to the Modality Profile, multimodal therapists use a number of strategies to enhance their effectiveness. For example, Structural Profiles are drawn to elicit more relevant clinical information (see Figure 8.1; Palmer, 1997). This is obtained by asking clients to rate subjectively, on a score of 1–7, how they perceive themselves in relation to the different modalities. For example, when investigating the behaviour modality the therapist may ask: 'On a scale of 1–7 how much of a "doer" are you?' These scores are usually derived from a section of the MLHI. Then, with negotiation with the client, a Desired Structural Profile is drawn, highlighting how the client would like to change his or her profile (see Figure 8.2; Palmer, 1997). This helps to keep both the client and therapist focused on the client's goals.

A second order Modality Profile assessment is undertaken when the most obvious techniques or strategies have not helped to resolve a problem. The second order assessment concentrates in greater detail on the specific problem, as opposed to the initial assessment which looks more at the overview or 'big picture'. Often clients have preferred modalities which they may use to communicate with the therapist, for example, talking about the images or the sensations they may experience. Multimodal therapists will intentionally use a 'bridging' procedure to initially 'key into' the client's pre-

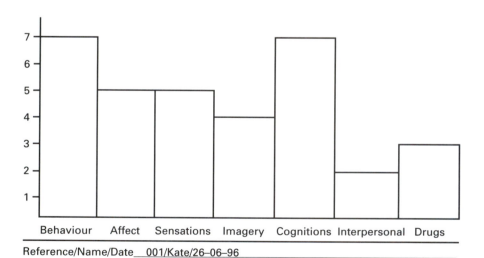

Figure 8.1 *Kate's Structural Profile*

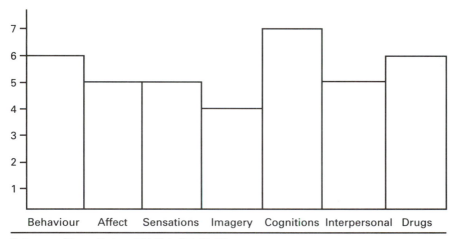

Reference/Name/Date___001/Kate/26–06–96

Figure 8.2 *Kate's desired Structural Profile*

ferred modality, before gently exploring a modality that the client may be avoiding, such as the affect/emotions (Lazarus, 1987). Bridging is undertaken if the avoided modality may be clinically useful to examine.

'Tracking', in which the 'firing order' of the different modalities is noted for a specific problem, is another procedure often used in Multimodal Therapy. For example, one client first had the cognition, 'I can't stand crowded places', closely followed by the physical sensations of extreme anxiety, and then an image of publicly vomiting and collapsing. This would happen in under ten seconds and the client would then behaviourally escape from the situation. This was a C–S–I–B sequence. The client was instructed to match the firing order of the modalities with a C–S–I–B sequence of interventions, thus ensuring a quick reduction of the stress response.

The strategies described in this section help the therapist to tailor the approach to each individual client and unconditionally accepts the uniqueness of each person. Clients are actively involved in their own therapy programme if they so wish.

Do I consider this approach to be simply one among many others and equally valid, or more effective, elegant or comprehensive?

An interesting question! Let us briefly consider one other therapy that has received much attention and research over the years and has repeatedly been shown to be effective. I, like many other practitioners, have found straightforward behaviour therapy to be reasonably successful for a range of anxiety-based disorders. It is beneficial for 10 per cent of adult psychiatric patients and about 25 per cent of all neurotic clients as the primary therapeutic intervention (Marks, 1982). Clients on waiting lists can successfully treat themselves by using bibliotherapy (e.g., Marks, 1978) and can often render the therapist redundant. Behaviour therapy has even been used to help clients deal with depression (Lewinsohn, 1974). However, let's be realistic. Many clients refuse to undertake an exposure programme or rapidly drop out of therapy after only one or two exposure sessions. Behavioural techniques and strategies alone are only likely to work if the client follows the therapist's (or author's in the case of bibliotherapy) instructions.

In my opinion, Arnold Lazarus' great contribution to therapy came in 1971 when he wrote *Behaviour Therapy and Beyond*, and he advocated a broad but systematic range of effective cognitive-behavioural techniques and later went on to describe multimodal behaviour therapy in 1973 (Lazarus, 1971, 1973b). Multimodal Therapy finally came of age in 1981 when Lazarus published *The Practice of Multimodal Therapy*. Why do I think this is relevant? Multimodal therapists are trained not to assume immediately that clients are 'resistant' if they do not wish to undertake an agreed assignment, such as an exposure exercise. Among other things, they are encouraged to understand why the client is reluctant to do the task, and examine whether they are expecting too much too soon and/or whether or not they have inadequately prepared the client. The Modality Profile usually highlights a number of skills deficits that the client may have which need to be tackled before or in tandem with other problems. Therefore, a client may need coping imagery, relaxation skills and cognitive restructuring before undertaking an apparently simple exposure assignment, especially if they have a low tolerance to discomfort, a particular problem many clients suffering from phobias possess. Unlike behaviour therapists, the multimodal therapist will probably consider the other modalities just as important as the behaviour modality. By preparing the client in this systematic manner, he or she is more likely to undertake the assignment and not leave therapy prematurely, thereby increasing his or her chances of overcoming his or her problem(s).

Essentially, by taking a comprehensive approach, multimodal therapy is considerably more supportive and helpful to anxious clients attempting to overcome difficult anxiety-provoking situations. Therefore, in my clinical experience, Multimodal Therapy is more effective than behaviour therapy as there are lower rates of attrition. But, of course, this is all relative. Let's not beat around the bush! Behaviour therapy is better than person-centred and psychodynamic therapy if an individual wishes to overcome anxiety-related disorders.

Besides any subjective preference for Multimodal Therapy, is there any objective evidence (research or other) or rationale which I consider compelling in its favour?

There are literally hundreds of studies that show the effectiveness of cognitive, imaginal, sensory and behavioural techniques and strategies (e.g. Blackburn et al., 1981; Eisen and Silverman, 1993; Fairburn, 1985; O'Sullivan and Marks, 1990; Rush et al., 1977; Teasdale et al., 1984). This is Multimodal Therapy's strength as multimodal therapists will use techniques from 'all walks of life', or, to be more precise, techniques drawn from a variety of approaches that the current research highlights as useful for specific problems.

It is interesting to observe the recent published academic literature focusing on the treatment of a range of disorders such as post-traumatic stress, phobias, etc. There has been a tendency to concentrate on the specific procedure used to treat the problem as opposed to stating that just cognitive or behaviour therapy was applied. Not only does this allow the studies to be replicated, it accurately reflects what techniques work for particular disorders. These findings also ensure that multimodal therapists do not have to apply the meta-belief systems of the different 'schools' of psychotherapy which may or may not be correct. Although Multimodal Therapy is underpinned by social and cognitive learning theory (Bandura, 1977, 1986), it is relatively atheoretical, pragmatic and empirical. I would agree with London who noted that 'however interesting, plausible and appealing a theory may be, it is techniques, not theories, that are actually used on people. Study of the effects of psychotherapy, therefore is always the study of the effectiveness of techniques' (London, 1964: 33).

I suppose this leads us to the crucial question of whether or not there is evidence that a multimodal approach is superior to more narrow or targeted therapy or treatment programmes? A strong argument for combined treatments was made by Blake (1965) who found that individuals suffering from alcoholism who were only treated by aversion therapy were more likely to relapse than other subjects who had also received relaxation training. In 1974 Sherman, Mulac and McCann reported a synergistic effect of rehearsal feedback and relaxation training for speech anxiety. Garson's (1978) controlled study highlighted the superiority of broad-spectrum treatment in smoking reduction. Several studies have indicated that a combination of exposure and imipramine is more effective in treating panic disorder with agoraphobia than either exposure treatment or drug treatment alone (Telch and Lucas, 1994).

One of the mainstays of Multimodal Therapy is 'tracking', as described earlier. The research indicates that interventions tend to be more effective when 'matched' to the particular modality response (e.g., Eisen and Silverman, 1993; Mackay and Liddell, 1986; McKnight et al., 1984; Michelson, 1986; Nelson-Grey et al., 1989). Phobic clients can be divided into two broad classes: physiological reactors and behavioural reactors. Clients with social phobias who are 'physiological reactors' respond better to applied relaxation than to social skills training, whereas the latter proved more effective with 'behavioural reactors'. Likewise, clients who suffer from claustrophobia respond better to exposure if they are 'behavioural reactors', while relaxation is more effective with the 'physiological reactors' (Ost et al., 1981; Ost et al., 1982).

Another assessment procedure used in Multimodal Therapy is the Structural Profile Inventory (SPI) which provides a quantitative rating of the extent to which clients favour specific modalities (Lazarus, 1989: 257–8). This instrument has been shown to have good factorial stability, and the reliability and validity has been borne out by research (Herman, 1992a; Landes, 1991). Herman (1992b, 1994; Herman et al., 1995) has undertaken extensive research into the SPI. Interestingly, he has discovered that when therapists and clients have wide differences on the SPI, therapeutic outcomes are unfavourably affected (Herman, 1991). This indicates that the SPI could be used to match client to therapist in a counselling centre. An intriguing thought!

Do I think Multimodal Therapy is particularly suited to certain clients or client problems more than to others?

Let's put the record straight. The multimodal orientation is not yet another system of therapy to be added to the many hundreds already in existence (Karasu, 1986). Rather, it is an approach that takes Paul's (1967) mandate very seriously: '*What* treatment, by *whom*, is most effective for *this* individual with *that* specific problem and under *which* set of circumstances?' (Paul, 1967: 111). But in addition to applying the strategies or techniques of choice, as discussed earlier, the multimodal therapist also attempts to be an authentic chameleon who also considers the *relationships of choice* (Lazarus, 1993). In the first therapy session the multimodal therapist may tentatively experiment with different styles of interaction with the client to discover the interpersonal approach that may benefit the therapeutic relationship. Decisions are made on when and how to be directive, non-directive, supportive, cold, warm, reflective, gentle, tough, formal, informal or humorous. Would the client prefer the therapist to take the stance of a coach or trainer rather than that of a warm, empathic counsellor? These issues are all considered important in forming a good therapeutic alliance with the client (Bordin, 1979).

So I would like to suggest that the limitations of the multimodal orientation rests in the particular proclivities of each therapist – to be even more precise, his or her individual abilities and aptitudes, creativity and intelligence, strengths and weaknesses, inclinations and predilections. These all affect the therapeutic alliance and whether the therapist can zero-in on the best-fit intervention at a particular time for a specific problem, underpinned by an acceptable rationale that the client both agrees with and understands. (Of course, the rationale is not explained when using paradoxical intention, but this would be a strategy usually applied as a last resort when every other technique has failed and a good therapeutic relationship exists.)

Perhaps the key concept is 'flexibility'. If the assessment reveals the need to take a directive stance involving role-playing or other directive strategies and techniques, then this will be implemented. If the client wants support through a recent stressful event such as a close family bereavement, then the therapist may become non-directive and listen attentively to the client and reflect his or her thoughts and feelings in the session. However, a therapist should always be aware that the client's needs may change during the course of therapy. Essentially, the multimodal therapist is unlikely to place clients on a Procrustean bed and treat them alike, but will look for broad, tailor-made combinations of effective techniques and strategies to bring to bear upon the problem. The methods are carefully applied within an appropriate context and delivered in a manner or style that is most likely to have a positive impact and a good long-term outcome.

It would be foolish to deny that YAVIS clients, in other words Young, Active, Verbal, Intelligent and Successful, tend to do well in many forms of therapy, including Multimodal Therapy. However, there are now many case studies of a range of clients being treated for a variety of different problems in Multimodal Therapy. As the multimodal therapist will tend to be flexible in his or her approach, there is likely to be a lower rate of attrition (i.e., early termination of therapy). In my clinical experience I have found that clients who would have left other forms of therapy I have practised, such as behaviour therapy, stay in Multimodal Therapy and overcome their difficulties. Multimodal Therapy has been particularly helpful when a client has previously 'suffered' at the hands of other forms of therapy. I regularly see clients who have had such negative experiences (see p. 169). If, for the moment, I just stick to the treatment of phobias, the usual complaints are as follows: person-centred counselling made them feel better about having the phobia but they still had it; they are generally confused about how the psychodynamic counselling they received was going to help them as the counsellor seemed more interested in their own childhood (Palmer and Dryden, 1995); and lastly, they have tended to find behaviour therapy 'too brutal'. Although these experiences could reflect the inexperience of the counsellor, I believe that the flexible multimodal therapist is ideally suited to helping these clients overcome their problems.

Multimodal Therapy, counselling and training have been applied successfully to a range of clients in different settings, including: helping alcohol abuse (Lazarus, 1965); schizophrenia (Lazarus, 1973b); career education (Gerler, 1977); children (Keat, 1979); agoraphobia (Blasucci, 1985); somatization disorder (Roborgh and Kwee, 1985); anorexia nervosa (Kwee and Duivenvoorden, 1985); post-traumatic stress disorder (Slowinski, 1985); depression and obesity (Brunell, 1985); enuresis (Keat, 1985); encopresis (Gumaer, 1990); clinical and industrial stress management (Palmer and Dryden, 1995); generalized and social anxieties (Gross, 1989); tortured political prisoners (Agger, 1988); older client groups (Weikel, 1990); rehabilitation (Weed and Hernandez, 1990); borderline patients (Stone, 1990); and airsickness (Jackson, 1994). In addition, I have applied the multimodal approach to the field of sports psychology, focusing on performance anxiety. Due to space restrictions I have not provided a comprehensive list of the areas and client groups to which the multimodal orientation has been applied (see Psyc.LIT). Hopefully, the list is sufficient to illustrate that a large amount of research and practice has been and still is being carried out in Multimodal Therapy and the approach can be applied to clients from a wide range of backgrounds suffering from a variety of problems.

Which criticisms of Multimodal Therapy by other therapists do I believe contain some validity

I will now return to the 'multi-muddle' debate. Quite rightly, Owen has noted that '. . . any integrative approach could end up as multi-muddle therapy, when it is not clear which aspect should take preference at any one stage in the proceedings' (Owen, 1996: 17). Many other practitioners have raised this subject too. However, when they have directed these comments at the practice of multimodal therapy I believe that this notion has been put forward by psychologists who have little idea how the approach is applied by experienced practitioners. Perhaps if they have only dipped into a book, chapter or article which explains how the therapy is applied, it would be possible to believe that we use a wide range of techniques almost at random. This is far from the truth. I hope that the first part of this chapter has given the reader an insight into how we tailor the approach to each client. In fact, I wonder how many other therapies have a whole book devoted to the indications and contra-indications of each major technique most commonly used by their therapists. Blowing my own trumpet, I played a key role in ensuring that we do have such a handbook for Multimodal Therapy, based on clinical experience and published research (Palmer and Dryden, 1995).

I want to take this complex issue a stage further. Multimodal therapists are encouraged to consider five fundamental factors when deciding how to respond and what techniques to use with each unique client in therapy:

1 Client qualities.
2 Therapist qualities.
3 Therapist skills.
4 Therapeutic alliance.
5 Technique specificity.

If there is a large mismatch between the client and the therapist qualities, we may refer the client elsewhere. However, the therapist is encouraged to be an authentic chameleon to help the therapeutic relationship and reduce the rate of attrition. The client may have a specific modality which may be the best place to intervene with a suitable technique or strategy (see 'tracking' and 'bridging'). The therapist may lack certain therapeutic skills and will consider referring the client elsewhere for a specific treatment (e.g., biofeedback or hypnosis). Conversely, the therapist may negotiate a different technique with the client. Depending upon the strength of the therapeutic alliance, the therapist may choose an effective, empirically validated but more anxiety-provoking strategy to deal with a problem. For example, with a good therapeutic alliance the client may be easily persuaded to undertake an *in vivo* exposure programme, whereas with a weaker alliance imaginal exposure and relaxation may be necessary before the client would even consider *in vivo* exposure. Trust, and possibly faith, in the therapist and the approach is undoubtedly an important factor. Thus, technique selection is not straightforward.

Returning to the 'multi-muddle' debate, I can understand why some counsellors may be confused by how we choose a particular technique for a specific problem for each unique client. But this just highlights their lack of understanding of Multimodal Therapy. We do not use techniques just because it feels right. When I supervise trainees, they know that I want a clear, concise reason for whatever they do in therapy, based on the five issues just discussed.

I suppose I would have to agree to a certain extent about one criticism of Multimodal Therapy: a lot is expected from practitioners. In my experience, many therapists do not possess the necessary skills and may avoid reading the academic literature that guides empirically validated treatment. They also may lack good therapist qualities such as flexibility, creativity, open-mindedness, acceptance of others, adequate intelligence, wide-ranging general knowledge, humour, assertiveness, communication skills, ability to think quickly, life experience, and an interest in helping people. If I discount my childhood experiences, my therapeutic training took over ten years, learning about different forms of therapy and the relevant techniques. Yet many trainees want to learn about Multimodal Therapy in a relatively short space of time (e.g., from as little as a two-day primary certificate course). Many therapists claim to be practising their own version of Multimodal Therapy. If I supervised their work, I wonder if I would cry 'multi-muddle therapy'! I hope not but I suspect that I would.

Another criticism I sometimes hear is that the assessment procedure may alienate many clients, especially those in acute distress. There may be some truth in this if the multimodal therapist is being rigid and inflexibly applies the full assessment procedure to every client who walks into his or her counselling room. Once again, this reflects the therapist and not the therapy, which is supposed to be applied in a flexible manner. The BASIC ID framework can be used by therapists as a guide and does not have to be shared with the client or used to overwhelm a client.

There are a number of other criticisms I've also heard but due to space restrictions I will not cover them in this chapter.

Which other psychotherapeutic approaches besides my own command my respect or strike me as especially effective or promising?

Cognitive-behavioural therapies command my respect, especially if the therapist undertakes a comprehensive assessment. However, in my experience too many therapists overlook particular areas because they do not adhere to a systematic assessment procedure such as BASIC ID framework. Generally, the therapies based on the work of Aaron Beck, Donald Meichenbaum and David Barlow have my support.

Rational Emotive Behaviour Therapy (REBT) is multimodal in its approach in that therapists may use a wide range of techniques, although underpinned by REBT theory (i.e., theoretically eclectic). I think highly of the forceful cognitive disputation techniques and strategies that Albert Ellis has pioneered over many years (Ellis, 1994, 1995). In my own field of work in stress counselling and stress management, cognitive appraisal is seen as a major factor that influences whether a person perceives a situation as either threatening or innocuous. Hence my continued interest in REBT.

I am also a supporter of problem-management and life-skills models which are effective with a range of problems (e.g., Egan, 1994; Nelson-Jones, 1994; Palmer and Burton, 1996). Also person-centred therapy has its place in supporting people through bereavement and other problems too.

Which approaches do I find particularly unappealing, ineffective, misleading or dangerous?

Answering this question is one way to lose friends and colleagues, and with guidelines suggesting that psychologists should not bring the profession into disrepute, I will carefully give my views. Therapies that only make people feel better either by catharsis or helping them get difficulties 'off their chest' are ones I would not recommend my family or friends to attend. Often these are therapies that focus on only one or two modalities for intervention. I agree with Albert Ellis that there are potentially three stages in the client's therapeutic progress: 'feeling better', 'getting better' and finally 'staying better'. The last two stages usually involve clients changing their philosophy of life, in other words, their attitudes, core schemas and irrational beliefs. As their philosophy and appraisal of life becomes more realistic, in my clinical experience they become more able to deal with stressful events such as hardships at work and at home. With a constructive philosophy they are more likely to use a range of coping skills to deal with problems, especially if the therapist has taught the client how to apply them.

Therapies that reinforce dependency on the therapist, the group, some 'higher being' or different substance can help clients through a difficult period of their lives but later can lead to new problems. In particular, the addictions field is replete with clients and ex-clients who have substituted one need for another as opposed to looking at and modifying the underlying core philosophies that drive them to take drugs or whatever. Let us take a simple example. The average smoker who stops smoking replaces nicotine addiction with food and consequently puts on weight. The underlying 'I can't stand it itis' philosophy with its associated discomfort anxiety is not altered. A similar thing happens with clients suffering from more extreme forms of addiction. In this case we could say that proof of the pudding (or success of the intervention) literally is in the eating!

Many therapies use techniques which may be iatrogenic, that is strategies which inadvertently exacerbate existing problems or induce new problems. I believe in the freedom of therapists to practise and for people to choose with informed consent whatever therapy they wish. However, the therapists should be aware of the limitations of their approach or the specific techniques they use. Too often they carry on with therapy and watch their clients become worse without referring them elsewhere or ensuring they receive adequate medication (Palmer and Lazarus, 1995). Although this may lead to litigation, in some cases the damage done is permanent. Instead of discussing the numerous examples of this I have observed during my clinical practice, I'd rather discuss an example closer to home. I've personally seen a friend spend time in therapy keeping to the therapist's agenda, in this case exploring childhood, while her work and love life became overwhelmingly difficult. What's more, she had entered therapy wanting to look at her current problems. I remember her words about her therapist quite clearly: 'He's a nice chap. I want to give him another chance.' Unlike myself, the therapist had never asked her about her suicidal ideation. As I noted in my diary at the time, I was far more concerned about her chances of survival if she stayed in this therapy. She committed suicide days later. Of course, this may reflect poor training or supervision and not the therapeutic approach.

How do I account for the research which suggests that no one approach seems more effective than any other?

I believe that this really shows the limitations of the published research and also perhaps researchers finding what they were looking for. Let us put this into a historical context. This popular myth has permeated the field of counselling and psychotherapy outcome studies ever since Luborsky, Singer and Luborsky (1975) claimed that no single treatment is more effective than any other. They called this the 'Dodo Bird' verdict, everyone has won and all must have prizes! This crazy notion was then reinforced by Smith, Glass and Miller's (1980) meta-analysis which was a flawed study with conceptual shortcomings and with a surprising failure to include a large number of relevant studies (see Paul, 1985; Wilson and Rachman, 1983). I would concur with Lazarus that 'if you reinterpret a lot of the meta-analyses more carefully you will see that behavioural approaches are the ones that are superior to all others across the board (e.g., Shapiro and Shapiro, 1983)' (in Dryden and Lazarus, 1991: 50). Other studies have highlighted the limitations of meta-analysis in the evaluation of the effects of psychological therapy (e.g., Wilson, 1985). Yet do the proponents of the Dodo Bird verdict ever refer to these studies? All I can say is that when I've attended their seminars or corresponded with them they seldom refer to these studies.

Research has established the effectiveness of cognitive-behavioural strategies and therapies for a range of disorders (e.g. Butler et al., 1991; White et al., 1992). In recent years, how many studies exist that clearly show the effectiveness of other popular therapies such as person-centred or psychodynamic in dealing with obsessive-compulsive and other anxiety related disorders? Not many! No wonder there has been a recent outcry among practitioners when service purchasers want to see the evidence for the effectiveness of their particular approach. Excuses are given such as 'it is totally against the philosophy of our approach to offer time-limited or brief therapy'. Yet, when we survey clients at our Centre in London, they invariably state (on the MLHI) that they see therapy as short term. So what explains the resistance to change? I would suggest that for practitioners to accept that their particular approach is ineffective when dealing with specific disorders would cause extreme cognitive and emotive dissonance, especially if they have spent years in training.

Returning to Multimodal Therapy, controlled outcome studies have supported the benefits of multimodal assessment and counselling programmes (e.g., Williams, 1988). In addition, Kwee's (1984) outcome study on 84 hospitalized patients suffering from phobias or obsessive-compulsive disorders resulted in substantial recoveries and durable nine-month follow ups. Ninety per cent of these patients had previously received therapy which was unsuccessful and 70 per cent had suffered from the disorders for more than four years. More recent research has continued to confirm these findings (Kwee and Kwee-Taams, 1994). Certainly, my clinical experience has highlighted the effectiveness of Multimodal Therapy when clients have not overcome their disorders after months or even years of previous person-centred, psychodynamic or even behaviour therapy they had received elsewhere. (In a few cases they had received other forms of therapy from me and on changing to Multimodal Therapy, their problems improved. This is interesting as it overcomes the problem of therapist variance.)

How do I account historically for the vast number of differing approaches and for their continuing proliferation?

I'm going to answer this question somewhat tongue in cheek. I put it all down to what makes us essentially human compared to other animals: the size of our homo sapiens cortex. Literally translated, 'Man wise'. Humans are always seeking new ways to overcome problems, often inspired by sheer boredom, just killing time between birth and death, or are pursuing ways of remaining immortal by leaving their mark on this planet. There may also be the need to be recognized. It certainly keeps some practitioners occupied. And, of course, the crusading gurus receive positive reinforcement from their trainees and clients. This maintains the whole process.

How do I advise distressed people seeking therapy to choose a therapist and therapeutic orientation?

When I realized that professional bodies such as the British Association for Counselling (Palmer and Palmer-Barnes, 1993) and the British Psychological Society did not give potential clients direct and free guidance on how to choose a therapist, I started to develop a checklist with one of my colleagues at my Centre. We used it with new clients and the feedback was positive. We then published it in the *Counselling, Journal of the British Association for Counselling*, asking for feedback from counsellors (Palmer and Szymanska, 1994a). We received some very useful comments but were also astounded at the response of some counsellors who thought clients should not enquire about the service on offer. In addition, some were outraged at the prospect of new clients negotiating goals with them. This then confirmed for me that some counsellors put their approach before the interests of their clients. One of the most outraged counsellors coincidentally worked at the college attended by a friend's daughter. It now made sense. Only months previously my friend's daughter had joked about how the students did not find the counselling useful as the counsellor was obsessed with their childhood and not on helping them with their current problems such as exam anxiety. In another case, a Registrar of a *National Psychotherapy Register* wrote a letter to one of the journals stating that our checklist was not acceptable as we recommended that therapists should be in supervision. (Supervision was at that time and still is in Britain mandatory for counsellors and therapists who are members of most professional bodies.) It became apparent that many people were offering therapy in a professional vacuum. We did not realize that we were going to stir up a hornets' nest by devising a simple checklist for the benefit of clients. We continued to develop and publish the checklist in a number of professional journals (e.g., Palmer and Szymanska, 1994b, 1994c). Box 8.1 shows the final version (Palmer and Szymanska, 1994d). It is now used by many practitioners and also by a variety of counselling agencies.

I think the therapeutic orientation I would recommend clients to is probably obvious to most readers. However, experience, good interpersonal skills, appropriate qualifications and preferably acceptable accreditations to practise the therapy would be an additional guide. Last but not least, training in Brief Therapy would be essential (see Lazarus, 1997).

What are my views on eclecticism and integrationism?

The three principal routes to integration are common factors, theoretical integration and technical eclecticism. I personally prefer not to view the latter as integration. I have not been able to find any research data that supports the notion that when diverse approaches have been 'integrated' a more powerful therapy has been the outcome. When I have listened to integrative

1. Here is a list of topics or questions you may wish to raise when attending your first counselling (assessment) session:

a. Check that your counsellor has relevant qualifications and experience in the field of counselling/psychotherapy.

b. Ask about the type of approach the counsellor uses, and how it relates to your problem.

c. Ask if the counsellor is in supervision (most professional bodies consider supervision to be mandatory; see footnote).

d. Ask whether the counsellor or the counselling agency is a member of a professional body and abides by a code of ethics. If possible obtain a copy of the code.

e. Discuss your goals/expectations of counselling.

f. Ask about the fees if any (if your income is low, check if the counsellor operates on a sliding scale) and discuss the frequency and estimated duration of counselling.

g. Arrange regular review sessions with your counsellor to evaluate your progress.

h. Do not enter into a long-term counselling contract unless you are satisfied that this is necessary and beneficial to you.

If you do not have a chance to discuss the above points during your first session discuss then at the next possible opportunity.

General issues

2. Counsellor self-disclosure can sometimes be therapeutically useful. However, if the sessions are dominated by the counsellor discussing his/her own problems at length, raise this issue in the counselling session.

3. If at any time you feel discounted, undermined or manipulated within the session, discuss this with the counsellor. It is easier to resolve issues as and when they arise.

4. Do not accept significant gifts from your counsellor. This does not apply to relevant therapeutic material.

5. Do not accept social invitations from your counsellor. For example, dining in a restaurant or going for a drink. However, this does not apply to relevant therapeutic assignments such as being accompanied by your counsellor into a situation to help you overcome a phobia.

6. If your counsellor proposes a change in venue for the counselling sessions without good reason, do not agree. For example, from a centre to the counsellor's own home.

7. Research has shown that it is not beneficial for clients to have sexual contact with their counsellor. Professional bodies in the field of counselling and psychotherapy consider that it is unethical for counsellors or therapists to engage in sexual activity with current clients.

8. If you have any doubts about the counselling you are receiving, then discuss them with your counsellor. If you are still uncertain, seek advice, perhaps from a friend, your doctor, your local Citizens Advice Bureau, the professional body your counsellor belongs to or the counselling agency that may employ your counsellor.

9. You have the right to terminate counselling whenever you choose.

Footnote: Counselling supervision is a formal arrangement where counsellors discuss their counselling in a confidential setting on a regular basis with one or more professional counsellors.

© 1994d, Palmer and Szymanska

Box 8.1 *Issues for the client to consider in counselling or psychotherapy (Palmer and Szymanska, 1994d)*

counsellors in action I have noticed that some tend to 'flip-flop' like an electrical circuit: for a part of one counselling session they may be practising Gestalt and minutes later they may be cognitive. Unless this is done with care it can prove confusing to the client as there is a lack of consistency.

Some brands of therapy are easier to integrate, such as behaviour and cognitive therapy, and a simple rationale can be given to a client to explain the mechanism of therapy. In fact, I have developed a training book for managers based on two models that I have found effective for dealing with work problems (Palmer and Burton, 1996). I include Ellis's ABCDE paradigm to help managers deal with their own or their employees' emotional disturbance and a seven-stage practical problem-solving model to deal with general difficulties (Ellis, 1994, 1995; Palmer, 1994). As soon as the clients realize that they have an emotional block, such as anxiety, to dealing with a practical problem, they switch to using the ABCDE paradigm. This form of integration is easy for the layperson to understand and use. I have called this approach, 'Problem Focused Therapy' (or training). I have also included the BASIC ID framework to encourage regular self-audits. Next year a version of this approach will be available for practitioners (Milner and Palmer, in press). Therefore I am willing to experiment with a limited form of integration.

Some of the integrative forms of counselling currently being taught are attempting to be all things to all people. Realistically, how can you integrate person-centred with cognitive therapy and still be true to both forms of therapy? One claims to be non-technique based and the other is laden with techniques (Palmer, 1993b). When you closely examine a practitioner apparently integrating cognitive with psychodynamic/analytic therapy, are the active ingredients the cognitive disputation methods, or the dynamic theory? Until I can be persuaded otherwise, as I stated earlier, I still agree with London (1964: 33) who noted that it is techniques, not theories, that are actually used on clients. The effectiveness of specific techniques may not depend upon the theory from which they were created. So the systematic, technical eclectic has the best of both worlds: the use of empirically validated or seemingly effective techniques without the restriction of theories from which they were born. All this, underpinned by cognitive and social learning theory, general systems theory and group and communications theory, gives Multimodal Therapy a very firm base. Lazarus (1987) believes that these theoretical systems blend harmoniously into a congruent framework.

50 years from now

In the short term, I suspect that in Britain counsellor-bashing by the media will continue until we get our act together. I suspect that we will find that, contrary to current popular belief, counsellors attempting to integrate incompatible approaches are on a hiding to nothing. Research into discovering the most effective therapeutic interventions will flourish as the demand by cost-cutting service purchasers increases. What will this mean? Therapies that do not adapt to brief or time-limited settings will become obsolete or relegated to private practice. This may upset some practitioners, but it is a tough world out there beyond the relatively safe environment of the counselling room. Unfortunately, accountants and administrators rule the roost and this is unlikely to change. New drugs will be found that are cheaper and possibly more effective than therapy in dealing with a wide range of disorders. I suspect cognitive-behavioural forms of therapy will be here to stay for at least another 50 years. Just think how long other less effective forms of therapy have been with us.

Within the next 15 years voluntary euthanasia for adults with severe physical illness may become legal. However, what may cause a real ethical dilemma for counsellors might be in 50–100 years from now if it is legalized for any adult for any reason. I know that many clients I have helped through depression go on to lead fulfilling lives. Would I find it easy to support a young client who wishes to undertake euthanasia because he or she found university exams too difficult. This may sound crazy but society may be radically different in 50 years from now, with many new challenges for our profession, assuming that we are still allowed to practise.

I would like to thank Arnold Lazarus for his help with this and other projects.

References

Agger, I. (1988) Die politische Gefangene als Opfer sexueller Folter (The female political prisoner as victim of sexual torture). *Zeitschrift fur Sexualforschung*, 1 (3), 231–41.

Bandura, A. (1977) *Social Learning Theory*. Englewood Cliffs, NJ: Prentice Hall.

Bandura, A. (1986) *Social Foundations of Thoughts and Action: A Social Cognitive Theory*. Englewood Cliffs, NJ: Prentice Hall.

Blackburn, I.M., Bishop, S., Glen, A.I.M., Whalley, L.J. and Christie, J.E. (1981) The efficacy of cognitive therapy in depression: a treatment trial using cognitive therapy and pharmacotherapy, each alone and in combination. *British Journal of Psychiatry*, 139, 181–9.

Blake, B.G. (1965) The application of behavior therapy to the treatment of alcoholism. *Behaviour Research and Therapy*, 3, 75–85.

Blasucci, A.P. (1985) The case of Joan: the 'bipolar' agoraphobic. In A.A. Lazarus (ed.), *Casebook of Multimodal Therapy* (pp. 168–75). New York: Guilford Press.

Bordin, E.S. (1979) The generalizability of the psychoanalytic concept of the working alliance. *Psychotherapy: Theory, Research and Practice*, 16 (3), 252–60.

Bozarth, J.D. (1991) Person-centered assessment. *Journal of Counseling and Development*, 69, 458–61.

Brunell, L.F. (1985) Multimodal treatment of depression and obesity: a case of single Susan. In A.A. Lazarus (ed.), *Casebook of Multimodal Therapy* (pp. 50–69). New York: Guilford Press.

Butler, G., Fennell, M., Robson, P. and Gelder, M. (1991) A comparison of behaviour therapy and cognitive-behaviour therapy in the treatment of Generalized Anxiety Disorder. *Journal of Consulting and Clinical Psychology*, 59, 167–75.

Dryden, W. and Lazarus, A.A. (1991) *A Dialogue with Arnold Lazarus: 'It Depends'*. Buckingham: Open University Press.

Egan, G. (1994) *The Skilled Helper: A Systematic Approach of Effective Helping* (5th edn). Pacific Grove, CA: Brooks/Cole.

Eisen, A.R, and Siverman, W.K. (1993) Should I relax or change my thoughts? A preliminary examination of cognitive therapy, relaxation training and their combination with overanxious children. *Journal of Cognitive Psychotherapy*, 7 (4), 265–79.

Ellis, A. (1994) *Reason and Emotion in Psychotherapy* (Rev. and updated edn). New York: Carol Publishing Group.

Ellis, A. (1995) *Better, Deeper, and More Enduring Brief Therapy: The Rational Emotive Behavior Therapy Approach*. New York: Brunner/Mazel.

Ellis, A., Gordon, J., Neenan, M. and Palmer, S. (1997) *Stress Counselling: a Rational Emotive Behaviour Approach*. London: Cassell.

Fairburn, C.G. (1985) Cognitive-behavioural treatment for bulimia. In D.M. Garner and P.L. Garfinkel (eds), *Handbook of Psychotherapy for Anorexia Nervosa and Bulimia* (pp. 160–92). New York: Guilford Press.

Fay, A. and Lazarus, A.A. (1993) On necessity and sufficiency in psychotherapy. *Psychotherapy in Private Practice*, 12, 33–9.

Garson, E.B. (1978) The application of positive imagery in the maintenance of smoking reduction following broad-spectrum treatment. Unpublished PhD dissertation, Department of Psychology, Rutgers University.

Gerler, E.R. (1977) The 'BASIC ID' in career education. *The Vocational Guidance Quarterly*, 25, 238–44.

Gross, P.R. (1989) Multimodal therapy for generalized and social anxieties: a pilot study. *Behavioural Psychotherapy*, 17 (4), 316–22.

Gumaer, J. (1990) Multimodal counselling of childhood encopresis: a case example. *School Counselor*, 38 (1), 58–64.

Herman, S.M. (1991) Client–therapist similarity on the Multimodal Structural Profile Inventory as predictive of psychotherapy outcome. *Psychotherapy Bulletin*, 26, 26–7.

Herman, S.M. (1992a) A demonstration of the validity of the Multimodal Structural Profile Inventory through a correlation with the Vocational Preference Inventory. *Psychotherapy in Private Practice*, 11, 71–80.

Herman, S.M. (1992b) Predicting psychotherapists' treatment theories by Multimodal Structural Profile Inventories: an exploratory study. *Psychotherapy in Private Practice*, 11, 85–100.

Herman, S.M. (1994) The diagnostic utility of the Multimodal Structural Profile Inventory. *Psychotherapy in Private Practice*, 13, 55–62.

Herman, S.M., Cave, S., Kooreman, H.E., Miller, J.M. and Jones, L.L. (1995) Predicting clients' perceptions of their symptomatology by Multimodal Structural Profile Inventory responses. *Psychotherapy in Private Practice*, 14, 23–33.

Jackson, R.J. (1994) A multimodal method for assessing and treating airsickness. *International Journal of Aviation Psychology*, 4 (1), 85–96.

Janov, A. (1973) *The Primal Scream*. London: Abacus.

Karasu, T.B. (1986) The specificity versus nonspecificity dilemma: toward identifying therapeutic change agents. *American Journal of Psychiatry*, 143, 687–95.

Keat, D.B. (1979) *Multimodal Behavior Therapy with Children*. New York: Pergamon Press.

Keat, D.B. (1985) Multimodal therapy with children: Ernie the enuretic. In A.A. Lazarus (ed.), *Casebook of Multimodal Therapy* (pp. 70–80). New York: Guilford Press.

Kwee, M.G.T. (1984) *Klinische multimodale gegragtstherapie*. Lisse, Holland: Swets and Zeitlinger.

Kwee, M.G.T. and Duivenvoorden, H.J. (1985) Multimodal residential therapy in two cases of anorexia nervosa (adult body weight phobia). In A.A. Lazarus (ed.), *Casebook of Multimodal Therapy* (pp. 116–38). New York: Guilford Press.

Kwee, M.G.T. and Kwee-Taams, M.K. (1994) *Klinische gedragstherapie in Nederland and vlaanderen*. Delft, Holland: Eubron.

Landes, A.A. (1991) Development of the structural profile inventory. *Psychotherapy in Private Practice*, 9, 123–41.

Lazarus, A.A. (1965) Towards an understanding and effective treatment of alcoholism. *South African Medical Journal*, 39, 736–41.

Lazarus, A.A. (1971) *Behavior Therapy and Beyond*. New York: McGraw Hill.

Lazarus, A.A. (1973a) ' "Hypnosis" as a facilitator in behavior therapy', *Journal of Clinical and Experimental Hypnosis*, 21: 25–31.

Lazarus, A.A. (1973b) Multimodal behavior therapy: treating the BASIC ID. *Journal of Nervous and Mental Disease*, 156, 404–11.

Lazarus, A.A. (1981) *The Practice of Multimodal Therapy*. New York: McGraw-Hill.

Lazarus, A.A. (1984) *In the Minds Eye*. New York: Guilford Press.

Lazarus, A.A. (1987) The multimodal approach with adult outpatients. In N.S. Jacobson (ed.). *Psychotherapists in Clinical Practice* (pp. 286–326). New York: Guilford Press.

Lazarus, A.A. (1989) *The Practice of Multimodal Therapy*. Baltimore, MD: Johns Hopkins University Press.

Lazarus, A.A. (1993) Tailoring the therapeutic relationship or being an authentic chameleon. *Psychotherapy*, 30, 404–7.

Lazarus, A.A. (1997) *Brief But Comprehensive Psychotherapy*. New York: Springer Publishing Company.

Lazarus, A.A. and Lazarus, C.N. (1991a) Let us not forsake the individual nor ignore the data: a response to Bozarth. *Journal of Counseling and Development*, 69, 463–5.

Lazarus, A.A. and Lazarus, C.N. (1991b) *Multimodal Life History Inventory*. Champaign, IL: Research Press.

Lewinsohn, P.M. (1974) A behavioral approach to depression. In R.M. Friedman and M.M. Katz (eds), *Psychology of Depression: Contemporary Theory and Research*. New York: Wiley.

London, P. (1964) *The Modes and Morals of Psychotherapy*. New York: Holt, Rinehart and Winston.

Luborsky, L., Singer, B. and Luborsky, L. (1975) Comparative studies of psychotherapies: is it true that everyone has won and all must have prizes? *Archives of General Psychiatry*, 32, 995–1008.

Mackay, W. and Liddell, A. (1986) An investigation into the matching of specific agoraphobic anxiety response characteristics with specific types of treatment. *Behaviour Research and Therapy*, 24, 361–4.

Marks, I.M. (1978) *Living with Fear*. New York: McGraw-Hill.

Marks, I.M. (1982) *Cure and Care of Neuroses: Theory and Practice of Behavioral Psychotherapy*. New York: Wiley.

McKnight, D.L., Nelson, R.O., Hayes, S.C. and Jarrett, R.B. (1984) Importance of treating individually-assessed response classes in the amelioration of depression. *Behavior Therapy*, 15, 315–35.

Michelson, L. (1986) Treatment consonance and response profiles in agoraphobia: the role of individual differences in cognitive, behavioural and physiological treatments. *Behaviour Research and Therapy*, 24, 263–75.

Milner, P. and Palmer, S. (in press) *Problem Focused Stress Counselling: an Integrative Approach*. London: Cassell.

Nelson-Gray, R.O., Herbert, J.D., Herbert, D.L., Sigmon, S.T. and Brannon, S.E. (1989) Effectiveness of matched, mismatched, and package treatments of depression. *Journal of Behavior Therapy and Experimental Psychiatry*, 20, 281–94.

Nelson-Jones, R. (1994) Hello DASIE! Introducing the lifeskills helping model. *Counselling*, 3, 203–6.

Ost, L.G., Jerrelmalm, A. and Johansson, J. (1981) Individual response patterns and the effects of different behavioral models in the treatment of social phobia. *Behaviour Research and Therapy*, 19, 1–16.

Ost, L.G., Johansson, J. and Jerrelmalm, A. (1982) Individual response patterns and the effects of different behavioral methods in the treatment of claustrophobia. *Behaviour Research and Therapy*, 20, 445–60.

O'Sullivan, G. and Marks, I. (1990) Long-term outcome of phobic and obsessive-compulsive disorders after treatment. In R. Noyes, M. Roth and G.D. Burrows (eds), *Handbook of Anxiety Disorders* (Vol. IV). Amsterdam: Elsevier.

Owen, I. (1996) Are we before or after integration? *Counselling Psychology Review*, 11 (3), 12–18.

Palmer, S. (1988) *Personal Stress Management Programme Manual*. London: Centre for Stress Management.

Palmer, S. (1989) The use of stability zones, rituals and routines to reduce or prevent stress. *Stress News*, 1 (3), 3–5.

Palmer, S. (1990a) Uses of biofeedback techniques in cognitive behavioural therapy. *Bulletin of the Association of Behavioural Clinicians*, III, December, 29–34.

Palmer, S. (1990b) Stress mapping: a visual technique to aid counselling or training. *Employee Counselling Today*, 2 (2), 9–12.

Palmer, S. (1991a) Behaviour therapy and its application to stress management. *Health and Hygiene*, 12, 29–34.

Palmer, S. (1991b) A study of stability zones, rituals and routines used by health professionals. *Stress News*, 3 (2), 6–13.

Palmer, S. (1992) Multimodal assessment and therapy: a systematic, technically eclectic approach to counselling, psychotherapy and stress management. *Counselling*, 3 (4), 220–4.

Palmer, S. (1993a) *Multimodal Techniques: Relaxation and Hypnosis*. London: Centre for Multimodal Therapy.

Palmer, S. (1993b) Directive or non-directive. *Counselling News*, March, 9, 8.

Palmer, S. (1994) Stress management and counselling: a problem-solving approach. *Stress News*, 5 (3), 2–3.

Palmer, S. (1996) The multimodal approach: theory, assessment, techniques and interventions. In S. Palmer and W. Dryden (eds), *Stress Management and Counselling: Theory, Practice, Research and Methodology* (pp. 45–58). London: Cassell.

Palmer, S. (1997) Modality assessment. In S. Palmer and G. McMahon (eds), *Client Assessment* (pp. 134–67). London: Sage.

Palmer, S. and Burton, T. (1996) *Dealing with People Problems at Work*. Maidenhead: McGraw-Hill.

Palmer, S. and Dryden, W. (1991) A multimodal approach to stress management. *Stress News*, 3 (1), 2–10.

Palmer, S. and Dryden, W. (1995) *Counselling for Stress Problems*. London: Sage.

Palmer, S. and Lazarus, A.A. (1995) In the counsellor's chair. Stephen Palmer interviews Arnold Lazarus. *Counselling*, 6 (4), 271–3.

Palmer, S. and Palmer-Barnes, F. (1993) In the complaint's chair. Stephen Palmer interviews Fiona Palmer-Barnes. *Counselling*, 4 (2), 84–6.

Palmer, S. and Szymanska, K. (1994a) How to avoid being exploited in counselling and psychotherapy. *Counselling*, 5 (1), 24.

Palmer, S. and Szymanska, K. (1994b) Referring patients for counselling, psychotherapy or hypnosis: a cautionary note for health practitioners and a guide for patients. *International Journal of Alternative and Complementary Medicine*, 12 (6), 21.

Palmer, S. and Szymanska, K. (1994c) A checklist for clients interested in receiving counselling, psychotherapy or hypnosis. *The Rational Emotive Behaviour Therapist*, 2 (1), 25–7.

Palmer, S. and Szymanska, K. (1994d) Referral guidance for participants attending stress management training courses. *Stress News*, 5 (4), 10–11.

Paul, G.L. (1967) Strategy of outcome research in psychotherapy. *Journal of Consulting Psychology*, 331, 109–18.

Paul, G.L. (1985) Can pregnancy be a placebo effect? Terminology, designs and conclusions in the study of psychosocial and pharmacological treatments of behavioral disorders. In L. White, B. Tursky and G.E. Schwartz (eds), *Placebo: Theory, Research and Mechanisms* (pp. 137–63). New York: Guilford Press.

Roborgh, M.R.H.M. and Kwee, M.G.T. (1985) Multimodal Therapy in a case of Somatization Disorder. In A.A. Lazarus, (ed.), *Casebook of Multimodal Therapy* (pp. 147–67). New York: Guilford Press.

Rotter, J.B. (1954) *Social Learning and Clinical Psychology*. Englewood Cliffs, NJ: Prentice-Hall.

Rush, A.J., Beck, A.T., Kovacs, M. and Hollon, S. (1977) Comparative efficacy of cognitive therapy and imipramine in the treatment of depressed outpatients. *Cognitive Therapy and Research*, 1, 17–37.

Shapiro, D.A. and Shapiro, D. (1983) Comparative therapy outcome research: methodological implications of meta-analysis, *Journal of Consulting and Clinical Psychology*, 51, 42–53.

Sherman, A.R., Mulac, A. and McCann, M.S. (1974) Synergistic effect of self-relaxation and rehearsal feedback in the treatment of subjective and behavioral dimensions of speech anxiety. *Journal of Consulting and Clinical Psychology*, 42, 819–27.

Slowinski, J.W. (1985) Three multimodal case studies: two recalcitrant 'ghetto clients' and a case of post-traumatic stress. In A.A. Lazarus (ed.), *Casebook of Multimodal Therapy* (pp. 81–107). New York: Guilford Press.

Smith, M.L., Glass, G. and Miller, T. (1980) *The Benefits of Psychotherapy*. Baltimore, MD: Johns Hopkins University Press.

Stone, M.H. (1990) Multimodal therapy: applications to partial hospitalization in the light of long-term follow-up of borderline patients. *International Journal of Partial Hospitalization*, 6 (1), 1–14.

Teasdale, J.D., Fennell, M.J.V., Hibbert, G.A. and Aimies, P.L. (1984) Cognitive therapy for major depressive disorder in primary care. *British Journal of Psychiatry*, 144, 400–6.

Telch, M.J. and Lucas, R.A. (1994) Combined pharmacological and psychological treatment of panic disorder: current status and future directions. In B.E. Wolfe and J.D. Maser (eds), *Treatment of Panic Disorder* (pp. 177–97). Washington, DC: American Psychiatric Press.

Thorne, B. (1990) Person-centred therapy. In W. Dryden (ed.), *Individual Therapy: A Handbook* (pp. 104–26). Buckingham: Open University Press.

Weed, R.D. and Hernandez, A.M. (1990) Multimodal rehabilitation counselling. *Journal of Applied Rehabilitation Counselling*, 21 (4), 27–30.

Weikel, W.J. (1990) A multimodal approach in dealing with older clients. *Journal of Mental Health Counseling*, 12 (3), 314–20.

White, J., Keenan, M. and Brookes, N. (1992) Stress control: a controlled comparative investigation of large group therapy for generalised anxiety disorder. *Behavioural Psychotherapy*, 20, 97–114.

Williams, T.A. (1988) A multimodal approach to assessment and intervention with children with learning disabilities. Unpublished PhD dissertation, Department of Psychology, University of Glasgow.

Wilson, G.T. (1985) Limitations of meta-analysis in the evaluation of the effects of psychological therapy. *Clinical Psychology Review*, 5, 35–47.

Wilson, G.T. and Rachman, S. (1983) Meta-analysis and evaluation of psychotherapy outcome: limitations and liabilities. *Journal of Consulting and Clinical Psychology*, 51, 54–64.

9

Transpersonal Psychotherapy

John Rowan

Some of this material is fairly new and may be unfamiliar to some readers. It should perhaps be said, before we plunge in, that good introductions to the transpersonal approach to psychotherapy are to be found in Gordon-Brown and Somers (1988), Whitmore (1991), Rowan (1993) and of course in the old original book of readings compiled by Boorstein (1996). Those who feel a need to check up on the terms and concepts used are advised to look at such sources.

What were the factors leading you to choose, found or adapt the approach to therapy which you currently espouse and practise?

In April 1975 I went through a primal experience. I relived my own birth. I seemed to hear the voices and see the sights which surrounded it. This was quite unexpected, and the therapist I was with had no particular expertise in primal work, and was more transpersonally orientated. It was a highly emotional experience, and went on for some time. Later I wrote up what had happened. Here is the record:

> Went through whole big catharsis on this, very powerful, leaving me lying down exhausted but whole and centred. Beverly said – 'Let an image come into your mind.' My reply:
>> There is no image, it's just grey. Grey all round in every direction, and the ground is grey too. It's all grey, all round.
> Beverly said – 'What is it like?'
>> It's not like anything. There is nothing there at all. It is just grey. It is sort of grey at an equal distance all round, as if I am at the centre and the grey goes out to the horizon. Now it is like a dome. A plain grey dome, very big and covering the whole area where I am lying. I am lying in the middle of a grey plain and the grey dome is covering the whole.
> Beverly said – 'Be the dome.' I said:
>> I am protecting him. I am looking after him. I love him. He's done all these stupid things, but he's all right. He's all right. He's made some stupid mistakes, but they are the kind of mistakes that anyone might make. He confused the womb with me, and he confused the breast with me, and he confused Mother's love with me – but it's understandable. All the time he thought he'd lost me, I was there all the time, and I always will be there.
> Beverly – 'Go back to being you. Did you hear that?'

Yes. (Crying) It's all true, I know now. What a waste! (Crying) I didn't need to blame my mother, or get revenge, or create my monsters, it was all a mistake! It was all a waste! It was all a misunderstanding.
Beverly – 'Now be the dome again. Does his behaviour hurt you?'
No, it doesn't hurt me. I care, but I don't mind. I don't add to his bad feelings by having bad feelings myself. But I do really care.
We finished up by resolving to remember the dome every day. To take some time to slow down and remember the dome.
It seems to me that this puts together so much, and brings this whole episode to an end – the whole business that started with [the Gestalt group experience and what followed]. It was all about destroying my mother, and now I don't need to destroy her any more! And now maybe the whole thing about being either sloppy or hateful can just dissolve. I really hope so, and think so. I feel so good.
It seems to me that this fits very well with the idea of the transpersonal self. The dome felt as if in a sense it was me, but it was also more than me. It couldn't explain itself, because I could only understand in pictures, and no picture could get it right. But it seemed exactly like what I understand of the transpersonal self.
(Rowan, 1992: 175–6)

This was my experience in relation to the transpersonal. I had had glimpses before, but this was much more than a glimpse – it opened up a vista which I then proceeded to explore much more thoroughly, particularly in the years from 1982 to the present.

The most succinct description of the transpersonal is still that of Stanislav Grof: 'experiences involving an expansion or extension of consciousness beyond the usual ego boundaries and beyond the limitations of time and/or space' (Grof, 1975: 155). It means entering the realm of mysticism.

The characteristic thing about mystics is that they insist on having the experience for themselves; they are not willing to be told by others. But within mysticism there are some important distinctions. James Horne (1978) says that mysticism can be serious or casual. A serious experience is where we treat it as significant and try to learn from it; it often has important further results in our lives. It is usually intentional. A casual experience is one which comes unexpectedly: it may or may not be dismissed or treated lightly. It may or may not have much effect on later life or behaviour. The experience mentioned above was serious.

He also distinguishes between extravertive and introvertive mystical experiences. In the extravertive, the mystic experiences *the world* as transformed, and discovers the unity which exists in a multiplicity of external physical objects. It usually happens spontaneously, without preparation or seeking for it. The introvertive experience is quite different. Usually it takes place after much preparation and discipline, where the mind is cleared for it to take place, by meditation or by some other means, such as catharsis. Here it is *the self* which is transformed. Again, I would want to say that the experience mentioned above was an introvertive one.

Many people reading this will not have had a serious introvertive mystical experience. But most of those reading this will have had a peak experience, which in the terms just outlined is a casual extravertive mystical experience. Surveys indicate that such events have been experienced by about 60 per cent of the population. It is a spiritual event, but a commonly available one.

What is a peak experience? I have defined it as the unpredictable occurrence of some kind of ecstasy, most often triggered by nature, music or sex, where the person feels one with the Whole. The great writer on this experience is of course Abraham Maslow (1968, 1970), who in a number of books and essays argued that peak experiences tend to come thick and fast at a particular stage of development, when the person is ready for them.

But most of the people who have such experiences are not ready for them; they dismiss them as odd, meaningless or even dangerous. They try to forget them. Even those who value them do not talk about them, for three reasons: (1) they are special, intimate and personal, and to be kept to oneself; (2) others might devalue them or put them down; and (3) they are too difficult to describe in words (Davis et al., 1991). But they are still spiritual experiences, and if we take them seriously and cultivate them, they can help us to go further in our own development. They are glimpses of the divine.

There is one more distinction we must make before we go on, however, because it is so clarifying and helpful. This is a distinction which was originally suggested by Alyce and Elmer Green (1986) between the extrapersonal and the transpersonal. This is very similar to the distinction made by Wilber (1980), and also used by Grof (1988), between the Lower Subtle and the Higher Subtle.

The extrapersonal has to do with psychic states and abilities such as clairvoyance, contact with the supposedly dead, telepathy, spoon-bending, ESP, walking on fire without getting burned, piercing the skin without drawing blood and so on and so forth. There is a strong connection with the occult and parapsychology, with fakirism, and with a wide range of paranormal phenomena.

The transpersonal has to do with such things as the higher self, the inner teacher, the transpersonal self as taught in psychosynthesis, the high archetypes as taught by Jung, the soul as taught by Hillman, the creative self, peak experiences, the more advanced types of intuition, certain aspects of healing (which have to be carefully looked at because there is an overlap here with the extrapersonal), the upper chakras and subtle energy systems as taught in Yoga, and so on. Green and Green (1986) suggest that the basic distinction is that in the transpersonal there is something divine, whereas the extrapersonal is not necessarily anything to do with the divine.

In the past this distinction between the extrapersonal and the transpersonal has not been drawn so clearly, and Jung's notion of the collective unconscious includes both. But Stan Grof (1988) finds the distinction useful in his work, which is, as far as I can see, quite close to my own.

Thinking now more about psychotherapy, we can say that the underlying assumption of transpersonal psychotherapy is that each human being has impulses towards psychospiritual growth. We are all on a path of development which leads from the prepersonal life of infancy and childhood through the personal life of our everyday existence in society – developing through the stages outlined by people like Maslow (1987), Kohlberg (1981), Loevinger (1976) and Piaget (1977) – to self-actualization and on to the transpersonal life of the soul and spirit. People have the capacity for learning and growing throughout life, and this process can be facilitated and enhanced by psychotherapy. In this respect, transpersonal psychotherapy has much in common with growth-orientated humanistic approaches such as client-centred therapy, gestalt, psychodrama, body therapies and so forth, but goes beyond them in affirming the potentiality for self-transcendence beyond self-actualization.

Do you consider this approach to be simply one among many others and equally valid, or more effective, elegant or comprehensive?

In the process of psychospiritual development, we experience, at each stage along the way, a change of the self-concept. At first the self is simply a body. Then the self starts to imagine that everything has a self, everything is alive, things can happen of their own accord. Then the self becomes seen as embedded within a family – it is essentially a membership self. Then the self becomes experienced as a functioning ego, capable of playing roles and gaining a niche in society as a separate individual. At each of these stages the previous notion of the self is carried forward within the new version, so that it is like a box within a box. The next self to appear is the existential self, characterized by autonomy – the fully functioning person, the self-actu-alizing person. Next comes the transpersonal self.

The concept of the transpersonal self is as a centre of pure awareness which observes and transcends conflicts at the level of ego and personality. This transpersonal self does not have the same sense of a strict boundary as does the existential self. And the continuing search for inner truth means a commitment to this transpersonal self and a confidence in it as a path to the deepest level of self-awareness that can be attained. It has also been called the guidance self (Whitmont, 1987), the entelechy self (Houston, 1987), the higher self (Heery, 1989), the deep self (Starhawk, 1989), the transfigured self (Heron, 1988), the soul (Hillman, 1990) or the guardian angel (Bendit, 1990).

But this means that it is a serious error to attempt therapy solely on a transpersonal basis. The work at this level must be grounded in the life of the person, which means doing justice to the earlier selves of the person, nested within one another. If this grounding is not achieved, then we might get a spiritual person whose life still does not work. If it is achieved, on the other hand, we get a person who can genuinely make contact in all areas of life.

So this approach is neither a complete therapy in itself, nor is it an adjunct to other forms of therapy: it is a dimension which underlies all psycho-therapy and can either be ignored or attended to. Petruska Clarkson (1993) has well said that it is one of five relationships which are always present in therapy.

But two standard mistakes have often been made by people working in the transpersonal field. The first of these mistakes is in thinking that there is just one thing called 'the transpersonal'. It has been shown by Ken Wilber (1995) that there are half a dozen different stages within the transpersonal: let us just look at three of them. First, there is the centaur stage: this is on the borderline between the personal and the transpersonal, and is the location of the first peak experiences, the discovery of existential authenticity and bodymind unity, and self-actualization. This is what we called just now the existential self. Secondly, there is the subtle stage: this is where we open the third eye (as taught in Yoga), realize that there are no real boundaries between us and other people, commit ourselves to some spiritual discipline, discover our higher or deeper self, contact the divine in an authentic way, use symbols rather than words, and so on. Thirdly, there is the causal stage: this is where we give up all our symbols, and launch out into the deep water of spirituality (the absolute, the void, the final god, the deepest truth, and so forth), usually using some form of meditation to do so. Most of the spiritual work in psychotherapy seems to take place at the subtle level. But there is a persistent attempt by people in the transpersonal field to promote their work to the causal level, which is actually much less useful, in spite of its depth, because it is so abstract.

The second of these mistakes is mixing up the mythic and magical levels, which are prepersonal, with the subtle level, which is transpersonal. People have often taken up the perfectly valid religious ceremonies of indigenous peoples, translated them into their own languages, and assumed that they were working at the subtle level. They are not. These rituals are prepersonal, and the way we tell is by asking whether they deny ordinary rational and logical thought, or whether they go beyond it. Joseph Campbell, the great writer on mythical themes, and Jung were both in the habit of promoting mythic-membership material to subtle status, and they misled many by doing so. We do not enter the transpersonal realm simply by talking about myths.

Transpersonal psychotherapy has to be very careful to observe these distinctions. If this is not done, we drop into ways of talking like this:

> Alongside this people gradually discover a sense of inner confidence that rests not on human achievement but on the presence of who one really is. What could inspire greater trust and sense of worth in the long run than realizing one's true identity to be the source? As the Buddha said, 'I alone am the Honoured One above and below the heavens'. He was talking about his true identity, not his human one.
>
> (Lang, 1994: 91)

This does seem rather to suggest that people who have been through Lang's 'Headless Way' workshop are in some sense equal to the Buddha, which seems presumptuous and unlikely. Ecstatic experiences of the real self are quite common at the centaur level, and it is quite easy to confuse these with experiences at the causal level, because they are both experiences of being alone. In other words, beyond the limited self of the mental ego there are a number of different realms, and we have to make proper distinctions between them if we are to make sense and not to go in for improper inflation.

The dangers of ego inflation are very great in this realm, and have been warned against by Jung (1992), Bragdon (1990), McNamara (1975) and others. If we begin to take personal credit for actually being the transpersonal self, instead of letting it be something transcending the ordinary ego (and therefore not owned by the ego), we are liable to fall into the trap of inflation.

So the transpersonal is difficult to handle and deal with, but it is something essential to dealing with the whole person, because it is an aspect of every human being. It is a dimension which we ignore at our peril. Of course we cannot help the client at this level unless we have experienced the subtle level ourselves. Wilber (1986) makes the point that our own contractions, our own reluctance to open up to the transpersonal levels, can hold back clients who come to the point where they need to explore such realms of their own experience. And nowadays these are not just people in the second half of life (Jung, 1930). They can come to us at any age.

There is one question which is worth considering because it concerns an error which I have made myself. I used to say (beginning with my essay on Holistic Listening of 1986, reprinted in Rowan, 1992) that there was a subtle-level experience called 'the self open to others' where the therapist could actually identify with and completely enter the world of the client (Rowan, 1993: 54–8). This has been well described by Nathan Schwartz-Salant: 'A realm that is felt to be outside normal time sense and in a space felt to have substance. This space, long known as the subtle body, exists because of imagination, yet it also has autonomy' (Schwartz-Salant, 1984: 10–11). He uses the term *conjunctio*, taken from alchemy. Elsewhere he speaks even more deeply of this experience, in discussing a particularly difficult client of his:

> The process is difficult to describe because it exists within an imaginal reality in which one's attention flows through the heart and out toward another person. In the process imaginal sight emerges, a quality of consciousness that perceives the presence of the archetypal level. This sight can be experienced through the eyes, the body or the emotions, but it is a level of perception that gently penetrates in ways that a discursive process fails to achieve. To the abandoned soul, knowledge without heart feels like abandonment. The heart offers a way to connect without violating the soul.
>
> (Schwartz-Salant, 1991: 211)

But it now seems clear to me that although this is legitimately described as a transpersonal experience, something very similar can be experienced at the personal and at the prepersonal levels. At the personal level we have the work of Alvin Mahrer, who says things like this:

> Experiential therapy rests on the assumption that altered states are available

wherein the therapist and patient can integrate with one another. The personhood and identity of one can assimilate or fuse with that of the other. The therapist can become a part of the personality of the patient.

(Mahrer, 1983: 138)

He gives clear instructions as to how to achieve this state, and uses it regularly in his work, and teaches it to others. So it clearly is possible to conduct such work at a personal level.

Similarly, it is possible to get into such states through the process of regression, taking us into a prepersonal state of consciousness. Margaret Little, a well-known psychoanalyst, has this to way: 'The analyst has to be willing to feel about his patient, with his patient, and sometimes even for his patient, the sense of supplying feelings which the patient is unable to find in himself, and in the absence of which no real change can happen' (Little, 1986: 58). This is not claiming any transpersonal status, but simply saying that in regression the barriers between therapist and client can fall away – not by being 'gone beyond' (in the transpersonal sense), but by primitive merging.

Donald Winnicott said much the same thing. Interestingly enough, he analysed Little. Here is the Winnicott view:

What is important here is the process of becoming, of developing a sense of division rooted in unity of being. He [Winnicott] speaks of 'giving room', of making space for what is not overly restrictive, room to breathe and move, an area of freedom. One comes through union, distinction, distinction-in-union, in order to link up with the experiencing that is fed by, yet transcends, dualistic categories.

(Eigen, 1991: 71)

At first blush, this may sound like a statement of the transpersonal, but it is clear in the context that what is being talked about here is a reproduction of the original mother-and-baby symbiosis. Winnicott allowed his clients to regress to a boundariless oneness with him so that the wounds of early trauma could be healed. This is work at the prepersonal level.

This seems to me an important clarification, which I only achieved by reading an interesting draft dissertation by Rosemary Budgell.

Besides any subjective preference for your chosen approach, is there any objective (research or other) evidence or rationale which you consider compelling in its favour?

The transpersonal is also transrational and transegoic. This means that the ordinary methods of empirical research will not work with this approach. If the work is genuinely transpersonal it will not fall within the range of convenience of standard research paradigms. If someone says they have had a glimpse of their transpersonal self, there is no way in which we can apply personality tests or the like to see if it checks out. Take, for example, the experience which opens this chapter – how could this be subjected to research processes?

Some writers have suggested that these areas can be researched, and

Alister Hardy (1979) collected several thousand accounts of mystical experiences. This tells us little, however, about the actual content of such experiences. The point is that such research gives us the impression of telling us all about mystical experiences, but in fact does not. All it can give us is the illusion of knowing.

The reason for this is that mystical experiences are experiences. In the same way as we cannot convey to another person the taste of a strawberry or the feeling of falling in love, if they have not themselves experienced such things, so we cannot convey the mystical experience to someone who has never had one.

As Wilber (1983) has well argued, from the everyday standpoint of the average researcher the prepersonal and the transpersonal cannot be distinguished. They are both equally alien. And what ordinary consciousness does is very often to reduce the transpersonal to the prepersonal, or even to the depersonalized. So an experience described as 'oceanic bliss' can be dismissed as regression to the womb or as a manic state of psychosis. An experience described as 'mystical union with God' can be dismissed as an unconscious wish for reunion with the parents. Nona Coxhead (1985) has a very full discussion of all these matters.

The *Journal of Transpersonal Psychology* often publishes research studies. But they have titles such as: 'Clinical psychologists' religious and spiritual orientations and their practice of psychotherapy' – in other words opinion surveys. One piece of research collected and analysed 293 samples of artwork drawn in response to a request for children to draw a picture of God. Another one developed a 'Spiritual Orientation Inventory', another a 'Spiritual Well-Being Scale', and yet another an 'Intrinsic–Extrinsic Religious Orientation Scale'. Quite a useful piece of research asked about therapists' attitudes to mystical experiences of their clients.

What we have to say, therefore, is that all sorts of things around transpersonal psychotherapy can be researched very well, but the innermost essence of it cannot be conveyed to anyone outside the experience. You can't lay your trip on someone else, as we used to say in the 1960s.

Do you think this approach is particularly suited to certain clients or client problems more than to others?

Jung (1930) used to say that people became more interested in spirituality in the second half of their lives. This may have been true once, but today it seems that there is a much greater interest in spirituality, and this interest is much more widespread than it was before. Ten years ago one could hardly mention the word without being looked at askance, but today most people will admit some concern with this area of life.

This is no doubt because of the New Age revival, which has influenced so many people. Shirley Maclaine, in a series of books, has been particularly influential in introducing people to this sort of thinking. More seriously, people like Fritjof Capra, Jean Houston, Marilyn Ferguson, Louise Hay, the Findhorn Foundation and so forth have come on television to tell of their involvement with new spiritual traditions.

The spiritual emergencies which are now becoming more common may emerge from this kind of interest. So quite young people are now coming into therapy with an interest in near-death experiences, or reincarnation, or in ecstatic experiences, or in the study of Tantra, or Yoga, or Buddhism, and wanting to relate those interests to their problems. Hence we see helpful books such as Button and Bloom (1992) appearing specifically to guide such people, and including references to transpersonal psychotherapy.

Having got the interest in a quite indiscriminate way, they may then begin to discriminate. One useful distinction is that between the transpersonal and the extrapersonal, as we saw in the first section. This makes it clear that there are certain things we are not concerned with, and do not need to explore, if we are to enter the realm of the transpersonal. The transpersonal always has some close and direct connection with the divine, whereas the extrapersonal does not need to have such a connection.

If people come to a transpersonal psychotherapist, these confusions and questionings can be explored in a sympathetic atmosphere, where they will not be labelled as strange or peculiar.

Which criticisms of your approach by other therapists do you believe contain some validity?

One of the most important criticisms was that put forward by Rollo May (1986) in a letter to the *APA Monitor*. He accused transpersonalists of trying to go beyond humanness, of trying to achieve peace at the expense of reality. But in 1992 he engaged in a discussion with Stanley Krippner and Jacqueline Larcombe Doyle, two transpersonally inclined members of the Association for Humanistic Psychology (of which he was a founder member), and made his position much clearer. He explained that when he had written the letter, he had been angry with Ken Wilber after an unproductive meeting, and had perhaps said too much. This discussion is so interesting that it seems worth quoting at some length:

> Stanley Krippner: For me Transpersonal Psychology is a psychological perspective or framework which assigns primary importance to experiential reports of concern or contact with entities, beliefs or realms greater than oneself, using them as a basis for conducting and interpreting psychological theories, intervention and research. When I say theory I mean development theory, motivational theory, personality theory. When I say interventions I mean psychotherapy, counseling and education.
>
> Jacqueline Doyle: I appreciate your definition of Transpersonal Psychology because it doesn't delineate Transpersonal Psychology as a total psychology but one which is additive to other forms of psychology such as Ego Psychology. It explores a realm beyond what is presumably covered within ego psychology. And I think the difficulty arises when it's implicitly viewed as supplanting or being

hierarchically arranged with other psychological concepts. In other words of greater value or of a merit above and beyond. Then a contest is set up . . .

Rollo May: I was very surprised, and very hurt by the responses to my letter published in the *APA Monitor* [May 1986] several years ago. It was completely misunderstood. You know I am very interested in the primitive and the spiritual . . .

Ken Wilber (1983) says we were all growing toward Eden. We will be happier and happier. We will be freed from our problems. This is impossible and undesirable. We would cease to be human. This is what I fight against. . . . I am against the belief that this comes automatically. . . . Progress is not automatic; we do not become better every day without effort . . .

Jacqueline Doyle: Transcendent development is accomplished through the individual struggling with the forces internal to personality rather than waiting on the sidelines for transcendence to fall upon them.

Rollo May: Very good. . . . A very important point that is often covered over by transpersonal psychology is that anger, for example, can be a very constructive emotion. . . . An example is a case of mine in *Power and Innocence* that shows the constructive use of anger: 'Mercedes' [See, May, 1972: 81].

Stanley Krippner: I think that anger can serve very important purposes, both personal and social purposes, if it is directed and used wisely. There are many people in Rio de Janeiro who are very angry about the destruction of the rain forest, and they are taking that anger and channeling it in very worthwhile social directions.

Jacqueline Doyle: Exactly.

Stanley Krippner: Without the anger, they might just be sitting at home and saying 'well, this is just the karma of the planet'. Or 'this is just fate' or 'this was meant to be' . . .

Jacqueline Doyle: Last night you [Rollo May] said that you understand the impulse toward the transpersonal theory, because people are always trying to escape the narrowness of human life. You went on to say that the spiritual impetus is always there, but it is effective only when people have covered, beforehand, the steps of developing the ego and the personality so that there's a good base for embracing the spiritual, for pursuing the spiritual impetus. Then it's no longer an escape from the problems of the daily life or of the personality. I'm quoting Rollo May. (Laugh)

Rollo May: Yeah, I know this. [laughter] It's so good there's nothing I can add.

(May, Krippner and Doyle, 1992: 308–15)

Most people in the transpersonal area would welcome this correction, and thank Rollo May for clarifying matters so well. There is nothing here to reject, only a valuable warning as to what traps not to fall into.

The criticism of Ernesto Spinelli (1994) is again more of a caution. After allowing that there is 'much to be gained in allowing the therapeutic process to acknowledge and address the "experience of duality dissolving"', he worries that the transpersonal approach is too 'open to tendencies bordering more on religious conviction than on therapeutic encounter' (Spinelli, 1994: 281–2). Again the transpersonal practitioner would regard this more as a warning of where to be careful than as negative criticism.

The most trenchant criticism comes from Albert Ellis. He starts off by naming 35 tenets of transpersonal psychology. Each one of them is presented in a negative way, and followed by between one and fourteen references: the unwary reader might think that each one is backed up by scholarly research.

But when we look more closely, we find that:

1 Each 'tenet' is phrased in the most extreme way possible, so that it is made to sound more like a neurotic compulsion than any reasonable belief.
2 Many of the 'scholarly references' are not to the books or papers where transpersonalists lay down their tenets, but to newspaper and magazine articles by critics of the transpersonal.
3 Some of the 'tenets' are simply misquoted. I was so amazed to see my own work mentioned that I actually went back and checked what I had said: it was nothing like what Ellis said I had said.
4 The transpersonal and the extrapersonal and the religious fringe are mixed up and confused with each other, as if there were no difference between mysticism and fortune-telling, meditation and spoon-bending, sacred psychology and Scientology, authentic spirituality and religious fanaticism, therapy and cults. A specimen quote:

> More importantly, devout transpersonalists and devout religionists are often almost identical in their absolutistic beliefs; and both groups (if, indeed, they are two) have a strong tendency to promote, or at least excuse, violence, torture, terrorism, and wars directed against their dissenters and opponents.
>
> (Ellis and Yeager, 1989: 62)

A great deal of the Ellis book is devoted to showing that his own brand of therapy, Rational Emotive Behaviour Therapy, is better than any other, and, in fact, of the references at the back no less than 68 are authored or co-authored by Ellis himself.

Perhaps the most annoying thing about Ellis is that he claims to be humanistic. He lets the façade down, however, when he talks about secular humanism as if it were the same thing as humanistic psychology. One of the standard misunderstandings which humanistic psychologists continually have to correct is the belief that they are secular humanists. The big difference is that humanistic psychology has a place for spirituality, and secular humanism does not. The best-known name in humanistic psychology is Abraham Maslow, and he was noted for his open-minded stance in this respect. This is so well known that a Roman Catholic volume warning against secular humanism (which I saw once on a bookshelf and never noted down) does not mention humanistic psychology at all.

The Ellis and Yeager book therefore seems to me a self-serving work not worthy of respect and quite impossible to answer in any sensible way.

Which other psychotherapeutic approaches besides your own command your respect or strike you as especially effective or promising?

There are four which I think are worthy of attention. The first of these is primal integration. Primal integration is a form of therapy brought over to

Britain by Bill Swartley, one of its main originators, although it was also pioneered here by Frank Lake. It is not to be confused with primal therapy, coming from Arthur Janov; it is a parallel development occurring at about the same time. It lays the major emphasis upon early trauma as the basic cause of neurosis, and enables people to regress back to the point in time where the trouble began, and to relive it there. This often involves a cathartic experience called 'a primal'. But some people using this approach do not like this language, and instead call what they do regression–integration therapy. It is strongly influenced by the research of Stanislav Grof, who pointed particularly to the traumas often associated with the experience of birth (Rowan, 1988).

In primal integration therapy the practicioner uses a variety of techniques taken from body therapies, feeling therapies, analytic therapies and transpersonal therapies, because a lot of stress is laid on the unity of body, feelings, thought and spirituality. Grof has recently written very well about this, and his holotropic therapy is close to what we call primal integration.

Obviously the main technique is regression – that is, taking the person back to the trauma on which their neurosis is based. Laing has argued that we should also talk about recession – the move from the outer to the inner world. Primal integration agrees with this, and finds that recession and regression go very well together. One of the clearest statements of the case for doing this comes from Grof: he talks about the COEX (Condensed Experience) system, a set of emotional experiences which hang together for a person and appear or disappear as a whole. It is a Gestalt which keeps on reappearing in the person's life. This is a common concept, being called 'restimulation' in co-counselling and 'reintegration' in social psychology. The basic idea is that anything which is associated with a traumatic experience may henceforth be attended to with great sensitivity, so that 'a whisper becomes a shout' and a strong reaction is provoked. But Grof is the best exponent of this theory.

The centres which deal with primal integration usually say that they deal with the early material and the transpersonal material, and I think this is a good direction to take (Brown and Mowbray, 1994). The image is of a spiral staircase on a mirrored floor: every step up (into the higher unconscious) is a step down (into the lower unconscious), and every step down (into the depths) is a step up (to the heights).

The second one I think is of interest is the process approach of Arnold Mindell (1985). Mindell is a native New Yorker, trained in Jungian analysis and with degrees in physics and psychology. He has worked in Zurich, and also in the USA. His way of working, however, goes far beyond what most Jungian analysts would consider proper.

His emphasis throughout is on process: 'The therapist's only tool is his ability to observe processes' (Mindell, 1985: 9). This enables him to see the importance of nonverbal communication, and to pay attention to the body and the actions of the client.

An important concept for him is the dreambody: 'The dreambody is a term for the total, multi-channeled personality. It expresses itself in any one or all of the possible channels I mentioned. It can also use the telepathic channel and can manifest itself in dreams' (Mindell, 1985: 39). He says that with the discovery of the dreambody, dreamwork and bodywork become interchangeable. 'I find that if I start working on the dream, it invariably switches to the body problem and vice versa' (Mindell, 1985: 39).

Perhaps his best book is *Working with the Dreaming Body* (1985). This could be a key book for the transpersonal psychotherapist working today. It exemplifies a way of working which the practitioner can aim at, and gives copious examples of how the author actually does it in practice.

The third approach I think a lot of is encounter, particularly as expounded and practised by Jim Elliott, Will Schutz and Elizabeth Mintz. Encounter is a form of group therapy which allows all aspects of the human being to come forth and be recognized and dealt with. It is strong on the regressive end of things, often using cathartic methods; it is strong on the existential side of things, often encouraging direct expression of meaning, and direct confrontation with others in the group; and it is strong on the transpersonal end, using ritual and imagery to access spiritual realities of one kind and another. I have written at length about this elsewhere (Rowan, 1992).

The fourth approach is somatotropic therapy, as expounded, for example, by William Emerson. His aims are close to my own, as stated for instance in the following quote:

> When this resolution is attained, the result is the emergence of the true Self, and simultaneous contact with the psyche at the most profound level, unencumbered by coaxial, coexistent presence of traumatic memories or energies. This brings with it the capacity for the unfolding of full human potential. Ultimately, the quintessential outcome is contact with one's essential being, unencumbered by traumatic and/or conditioned experience.
>
> (Emerson, 1994: 32)

Emerson works with children as well as with adults, and his approach is heartening and positive.

In general, I would be interested in any approach which admits that human beings exist on many levels – at least body, mind, soul and spirit.

Which approaches do you find particularly unhelpful, unappealing, ineffective, misleading or dangerous? Why?

The approach of Rational Emotive Behaviour Therapy, if Albert Ellis is anything to go by, is dangerous because of its intolerance. As we saw in an earlier section of this chapter, Ellis denounces the transpersonal in a way which is quite ignorant and prejudiced. He tries to save face in the end by saying that 'transpersonal psychology and psychotherapy do great harm and present enormous dangers. We do not, of course, advocate that they thereby be censored or abolished . . .' (Ellis and Yeager, 1989: 153). However, since everything in the book shrieks against the appalling dangers and excesses of anything transpersonal, this seems quite a lame conclusion, and not really very convincing.

It is interesting to see the response which Ellis makes in the book to a criticism of his position put up by Ken Wilber (1989), who replied to an earlier article (Ellis, 1986) along the lines mentioned earlier in this chapter. The key passage goes as follows:

> Wilber says that I do not understand the crucial difference between regressive pre-rational states (which presumably include the dangers I have accused transpersonal believers of fomenting) and 'higher development *trans*-rational states'. No, I don't quite understand this difference, though I have read his well-written paper on 'the pre-trans fallacy' (Wilber, 1983). As far as I can see, both states are equally mystical, magical and transpersonal.
>
> (Ellis and Yeager, 1989: 147)

Someone who cannot see the difference between prerational and transrational, even after reading a 45-page essay on the subject, just does not want to see it. It is this not wanting to see it which I think is the most objectionable part of Ellis's position.

To different degrees, I object to any form of psychotherapy which reduces people to something less than human beings. The radical behaviourism of Skinner (1953) and his colleagues and followers seems to me to reduce human beings to the level of a machine, and the behaviour therapy advocated by Eysenck (1992) is no better in this respect. The more recent cognitive-behavioural approaches (Dryden and Golden, 1986) still seem to adopt mechanistic models of the person.

Equally, I object to some of the attempts of therapists in the psychoanalytic field to codify and control their practice, so that the person who wants to go into foetal imagery is firmly told that this is oral material, and that anything else must be 'psychological anachronism' (Malan, 1979: 167). Or that the patient who wants to raise the issue of changing the times of sessions must be firmly faced with either silence or a suggestion that the patient continue to say whatever comes to mind (Langs, 1982: 421). In these instances it is the therapist who has become like a machine.

How do you account for the research which suggests that no one approach seems more effective than any other?

In long-term counselling there are normally three phases, as Kopp (1977) has pointed out rather elegantly. In phase one, the initial symptoms are dealt with, and a reasonable degree of success is achieved in disposing of them. This has to do with the immediate alleviation of pain.

In phase two, deeper issues are tackled, which might not have been evident at all at the beginning, but which now seem to be important. For example, in the course of counselling, some clients discover that they were sexually abused as children, which they were not consciously aware of at all when they came into counselling. To leave the client at this point because the contract did not anticipate such an eventuality seems abusive to me. Similarly, but much more frequently, many clients discover that their childhood was not the idyllic or bland experience they had previously thought, but was in fact a hotbed of emotions and decision-making. During this phase the client may at times feel worse rather than better, and any crude attempt to measure improvement can go astray at this point. Research designs on the whole do not even attempt to do justice to this phase, perhaps sometimes being funded by organizations intent on saving money.

Thirdly, there is the phase of working through the implications for daily life of the discoveries made during the therapeutic experience. This bridging activity, between new self-concepts and action in the everyday world, is often a lengthy process, where there may be setbacks and errors which need to be dealt with.

It seems to me that brief counselling or therapy ignores the second phase, and in effect cheats the clients of the potential hidden within their crisis. It sticks to the easy part, the part where some immediate results can be seen, and ignores the more demanding parts, where there may be difficulties with the therapeutic relationship itself. It is in the second phase that higher levels of skill and deeper levels of self-knowledge are called for on the part of the counsellor.

Research is so difficult in this field that it is no surprise when assiduous researchers like Greenberg say things like this: 'After decades of research the amount of well-established knowledge about what affects therapeutic outcomes is disappointingly meagre. Research of the sort done in the last decade, although approaching clinical relevance, still has not offered much to practising clinicians' (Greenberg, 1981: 30). Similar conclusions are offered by Beutler et al. (1986) and by Greenberg and Pinsof (1986). The real deep research, comparing long-term results in terms which are convincing to practitioners, still has not been done.

How do you account historically for the vast number of differing approaches and for their continuing proliferation?

All evolution is a process of differentiation and integration, and we have seen in the past 35 years an enormous differentiation and proliferation of psychotherapies. The fat book edited by Herink (1980) contains details of more than 250 different therapies: of these approximately 34 per cent come from the 1970s, 36 per cent from the 1960s, 17 per cent from the 1950s, 6 per cent from the 1940s, 5 per cent from the 1930s, and 2 per cent from before 1930. This shows the remarkable increase over the 20 years from 1960 to 1980. If a similar book were produced today, my belief is that the growth would have slowed down considerably. Today we are in a period, I believe, of integration rather than differentiation.

In the earlier periods, so much was left out of the picture that we were dealing with quite small parts of the person. The body, for example, was usually left out. It was not until the advent of the body therapies, beginning with Reich and considerably enhanced by the work of people such as Ola Raknes, Alexander Lowen, Stanley Keleman, Ida Rolf, Jack Painter, Gerda Boyesen, John Pierrakos, David Boadella and so forth, that justice was done to this important level of work.

Similarly, the spiritual level was often ignored, until the work of Jung, Assagioli, Gordon-Brown, Wilber, Vaughan, Houston and others showed how it might be approached. So many of the new therapies were simply showing how these gaps might be filled. But now that the whole field is reasonably well covered, it is more a case of refining and eliminating what is unnecessary, and putting together the good work from various angles.

One important distinction which has to be made is that between forms of therapy which try to do the whole job – the three stages we mentioned earlier – and forms which only try to deal with the first stage – the initial relief of symptoms. Obviously it is much easier to research the latter, and obviously such limited efforts are much more able to fit into the requirements of the National Health Service and other areas where there is a shortage of money and resources. The transpersonal approach, dealing as it does with some of the most subtle and sensitive issues of all, is never going to fit in to such a restricted box or cage.

How would you advise distressed people seeking therapy to choose a therapist and therapeutic orientation?

As suggested earlier, there are different phases in therapy. If the person has a problem which clearly falls within phase 1 – in other words, if it is a short-term problem suggesting a fairly clear goal – then it would be best to go to someone who specializes in short-term work. Sometimes a problem can be solved in one session, and if so who wants more?

If on the other hand someone is looking for liberation from the bonds of neurosis, and freedom from long-term compulsions, then it would be best to go to someone skilled in dealing with phase 2. It would be important here not to be seduced by short-term promises, because they would be false. This kind of work cannot be done on such a limited basis.

And if someone has been through various kinds of therapy, and has perhaps even had a training in some form of counselling or psychotherapy, and feels that there is more – that there is a next step of some kind beyond self-actualization – they would be strongly advised to go to someone who deals with spiritual matters.

This would be even more true if the person were experiencing a crisis having to do with ultimate questions – a spiritual emergency – because it is only a transpersonal psychotherapist who could handle such material in the right way (Grof and Grof, 1990).

Most clients, however, have some spiritual issues which occur to them sooner or later, so it is valuable for all therapists to have some acquaintance with the transpersonal approach.

What are your views on eclecticism and integrationism?

This seems to be a period of time where integration is the most important thing. The old ways of the past, where we studied one approach in great depth, and made that do for the rest of our lives, are not enough any longer.

The whole idea of integration, it seems to me, is that either therapists can do the whole job – covering the whole range of body, feelings, intellect, soul and spirit – or can refer people to other therapists who cover the missing bits in their own approach. At least all therapists could find out what the complementary facilities are to what they are offering themselves. That is something I am entirely in favour of.

I have written at length elsewhere (Rowan, 1992) about the way in which encounter is very naturally an integrative approach to therapy, and how it teaches us a great deal about how to handle an integrated psychotherapy. It is enormously flexible in practice. And in general, I believe that the humanistic approaches generally offer a matrix within which all that is necessary may be accommodated.

Can you hazard a guess as to what the field will look like in, say, 50 years' time? Which approaches will thrive and which will decline?

At the moment the field seems to be dominated by accountants and NVQs (National Vocational Qualifications – a system which operates by specifying testable elements and combining them in various patterns). There is a version of science, dominated by empiricism and cognitive psychology, which says that cost-benefit analyses can always be conducted. Everything worthwhile can be measured at the level of ordinary consciousness. There is no need to worry about the unconscious or the spiritual. As for the oppressions of class, race, gender, age, disability, sexual orientation and the like, all that can be taken care of within the NVQ.

In the USA the same thing is happening. Under the heading of 'managed care', some companies are asking therapists for symptom checklists and therapeutic intervention reports after every single session. The American Psychological Association has embarked upon a project to create a diagnostic manual of its own, distinct from the psychiatric manual (DSM–IV) which is now so well known. This will enable clear distinctions to be made between acceptable care and substandard care. Humanistic training is under threat because of changes in the requirements of licensing boards. Some humanistic and transpersonal psychologists have already been charged with ethics violations and malpractice for using experiential or shamanistic practices.

There is a tendency towards manualization, by which is meant teaching psychotherapy or counselling by the use of a manual which is strictly adhered to in practice. The therapist follows the manual at all times. This obviously makes research much easier.

Now there is in statistics a thing called the Gompertz curve, which applies quite regularly to innovative practices. After a slow start, the innovation speeds up and starts an exponential period of growth, such that if the trend continued, the whole world would be totally taken over by it. But at a certain point, the curve inflects, making it more like an S – in fact, it is sometimes called the S-curve. At that point the phenomenon slows down, and some new innovation comes on the scene. I assume that the process of progressive control and centralization, of which some examples have been given above, will also go the same way. How far it still has to go is uncertain.

After it I suspect there will be a period of fragmentation, very much in tune with the postmodern ideas which at the moment are only popular in the universities. In this more postmodern atmosphere, humanistic and transpersonal approaches would fit very well. In fact, the transpersonal, with its full appreciation of the multiplicity of things, might be more at home in such a world than most others.

References

Bendit, L.J. (1990) The incarnation of the angels. In M. Parisen (ed.), *Angels and Mortals*. Wheaton, IL: Quest.

Beutler, L.E., Crago, M. and Arizmendi, I.G. (1986) Therapist variables in psychotherapy process and outcome. In S.L. Garfield and A.E. Bergin (eds), *Handbook of Psychotherapy and Behavior Change* (3rd edn). New York: Wiley.

Boorstein, S. (ed.) (1996) *Transpersonal Psychotherapy*. Albany, NY: State University of New York Press.

Bragdon, E. (1990) *The Call of Spiritual Emergency: From Personal Crisis to Personal Transformation*. San Francisco: Harper & Row.

Brown, J. and Mowbray, R. (1994) Primal integration. In D. Jones (ed.), *Innovative Therapy: A Handbook*. Buckingham: Open University Press.

Button, J. and Bloom, W. (eds) (1992) *The Seeker's Guide*. London: Aquarian Press.

Clarkson, P. (1993) A multiplicity of psychotherapeutic relationships. In P. Clarkson, *On Psychotherapy*, London: Whurr.

Coxhead, N. (1985) *The Relevance of Bliss*. London: Wildwood House.

Davis, J., Lockwood, L. and Wright, C. (1991) Reasons for not reporting peak experiences. *Journal of Humanistic Psychology*, 31 (1), 86–94.

Dryden, W. and Golden, W. (1986) *Cognitive-Behavioural Approaches to Psychotherapy*. London: Harper & Row.

Eigen, M. (1991) *The Psychotic Core*. Northvale, NJ: Aronson.

Ellis, A. (1986) Fanaticism that may lead to a nuclear holocaust: the contributions of scientific counselling and psychotherapy. *Journal of Counselling and Development*, 65, 146–51.

Ellis, A. and Yeager, R.J. (1989) *Why Some Therapies Don't Work: The Dangers of Transpersonal Psychology*. Buffalo, NY: Prometheus.

Emerson, W. (1994) Somatotropic therapy. In W. Dryden (ed.), *Innovative Therapy: A Handbook*. Milton Keynes: Open University Press.

Eysenck, H.J. (1992) The outcome problem in psychotherapy. In W. Dryden and C. Feltham (eds), *Psychotherapy and Its Discontents*. Buckingham: Open University Press.

Gordon-Brown, I. and Somers, B. (1988) Transpersonal psychotherapy. In J. Rowan and W. Dryden (eds), *Innovative Therapy in Britain*. Buckingham: Open University Press.

Green, E.E. and Green, A.M. (1986) Biofeedback and states of consciousness. In B.B. Wolman and M. Ullman (eds), *Handbook of States of Consciousness*. New York: Van Nostrand Reinhold.

Greenberg, L.G. (1981) Advances in clinical intervention research: a decade review. *Canadian Psychology*, 22 (1), 25–34.

Greenberg, L.S. and Pinsof, W.M. (eds) (1986) *The Psychotherapeutic Process: A Research Handbook*. New York: Guilford Press.

Grof, S. (1975) *Realms of the Human Unconscious*. London: Souvenir Press.

Grof, S. (1988) *The Adventure of Self-Discovery*. Albany, NY: SUNY Press.

Grof, C. and Grof, S. (1990) *The Stormy Search for the Self*. Los Angeles: Jeremy P. Tarcher.

Hardy, A. (1979) *The Spiritual Nature of Man*. Oxford: Oxford University Press.

Heery, M. (1989) Inner voice experiences: an exploratory study of thirty cases. *The Journal of Transpersonal Psychology*, 21 (1), 73–82.

Herink, R. (1980) *The Psychotherapy Handbook*. New York: New American Library.

Heron, J. (1988) *Cosmic Psychology*. London: Endymion Press.

Hillman, J. (1990) *The Essential James Hillman* (introduced and edited by Thomas Moore). London: Routledge.

Horne, J.R. (1978) *Beyond Mysticism*. Waterloo, Ontario: Wilfrid Laurier University Press.

Houston, J. (1987) *The Search for the Beloved: Journeys in Sacred Psychology*. Los Angeles, CA: J.P. Tarcher.

Jung, C.G. (1930) The stages of life. In *Collected Works Volume 8*.

Jung, C.G. (1992) The relations between the ego and the unconscious (para 143). In C.G. Jung, *Two Essays on Analytical Psychology* (original 2nd edn, 1966). London: Routledge.

Kohlberg, L. (1981) *Essays on Moral Development* (Vol. 1). San Francisco: Harper & Row.

Kopp, S. (1977) *Back to One*. Palo Alto, CA: Science & Behaviour.

Lang, R. (1994) The headless way. In W. Dryden (ed.), *Innovative Therapy: A Handbook*. Buckingham: Open University Press.

Langs, R. (1982) *Psychotherapy: A Basic Text*. Northvale, NJ: Aronson.

Little, M.I. (1986) *Transference Neurosis and Transference Psychosis*. London: Free Association Books.

Loevinger, J. (1976) *Ego Development*. San Francisco: Jossey-Bass.

Mahrer, A.R. (1983) *Experiential Psychotherapy: Basic Practices*. New York: Brunner/Mazel.

Malan, D.H. (1979) *Individual Psychotherapy and the Science of Psychodynamics*. London: Butterworths.

Maslow, A.H. (1968) *Toward a Psychology of Being* (2nd edn). New York: Van Nostrand.

Maslow, A.H. (1970) *Religion, Values and Peak Experiences*. New York: Viking.

Maslow, A.H. (1987) *Motivation and Personality* (3rd edn). New York: Harper & Row.

May, R. (1972) *Power and Innocence*. New York: W.W. Norton.

May, R. (1986) Transpersonal psychology. *APA Monitor*, 17 (5), 2.

May, R., Krippner, S. and Doyle, J.L. (1992) The role of transpersonal psychology in psychology as a whole: a discussion. *The Humanistic Psychologist*, 2 (3), 307–17.

McNamara, W. (1975) Psychology and the Christian mystical tradition. In C.T. Tart (ed.), *Transpersonal Psychologies*. London: Routledge.

Mindell, A. (1985) *Working with the Dreaming Body*. London: Routledge.

Piaget, J. (1977) *The Essential Piaget* (H. Gruber and J. Voneche, eds). New York: Basic Books.

Rowan, J. (1988) Primal integration. In J. Rowan and W. Dryden (eds), *Innovative Therapy in Britain*. Buckingham: Open University Press.

Rowan, J. (1992) *Breakthroughs and Integration in Psychotherapy*. London: Whurr.

Rowan, J. (1993) *The Transpersonal: In Psychotherapy and Counselling*. London: Routledge.

Schwartz-Salant, N. (1984) Archetypal factors underlying sexual acting-out in the transference-countertransference process. Wilmette, IL: Chiron Publications.

Schwartz-Salant, N. (1991) The abandonment depression: developmental and alchemical perspectives. In M.A. Mattoon (ed.), *Paris 89*. Einsiedeln: Daimon Verlag.

Skinner, B.F. (1953) *Science and Human Behavior*. New York: Macmillan.

Spinelli, E. (1994) *Demystifying Therapy*. London: Constable.

Starhawk (1989) *The Spiral Dance* (2nd edn). San Francisco: Harper & Row.

Whitmont, E. (1987) Archetypal and personal interaction in the clinical process. In N. Schwartz-Salant and M. Stein (eds), *Archetypal Processes in Psychotherapy*. Wilmette, IL: Chiron Publications.

Whitmore, D. (1991) *Psychosynthesis Counselling in Action*. London: Sage.

Wilber, K. (1980) *The Atman Project*. Wheaton, IL: Quest.

Wilber, K. (1983) *Eye to Eye*. Boston, MA: Anchor.

Wilber, K. (1986) The spectrum of psychopathology. In K. Wilber, J. Engler and D.P. Brown, *Transformations of Consciousness*. Boston, MA: New Science Library.

Wilber, K. (1989) Let's nuke the transpersonalists. *Journal of Counselling and Development*.

Wilber, K. (1995) *Sex, Ecology, Spirituality*. Boston, MA: Shambhala.

Appendix 1: Questions to Contributors

1 What were the factors leading you to choose, found, or adapt the approach you currently espouse and practise?

2 Do you consider this approach to be simply one among many others, and equally valid, or more effective, elegant or comprehensive?

3 Besides any subjective preference for your approach, is there any objective (research or other) evidence or rationale which you consider compelling in its favour?

4 Do you think this approach is particularly suited to certain clients or client problems more than to others?

5 Which criticisms of your approach by other therapists do you believe contain some validity?

6 Which other therapists and approaches command your respect or strike you as especially effective or promising?

7 Which approaches do you find particularly unhelpful, unappealing, ineffective, misleading or dangerous? Why?

8 How do you account for research which suggests that no one approach seems more effective than any other?

9 What are your views on eclecticism and integrationism?

10 How do you account for the vast number of different approaches and their continuing proliferation?

11 How would you advise people seeking therapy to choose a therapist and a therapeutic orientation?

12 What would you guess the field will look like in, say, 50 years' time? Which approaches will thrive and which will decline?

Appendix 2: Different Psychotherapeutic Orientations

This list is intended to give a flavour of the current range and proliferation of psychotherapies. It must be acknowledged that no attempt has been made to ascertain just how current all these approaches are, although to the best of my knowledge they are all currently being practised. Some may object that certain therapies listed here are merely variants of others (e.g., redecision therapy is a kind of transactional analysis) and might be better described as schools within a particular approach. On the other hand, I have not included, for example, creative novation therapy or other varieties of non-classical behaviour therapy, nor the different schools of Jungian or post-Jungian therapy. Family therapy (and its many variants), group and couple therapy, sex therapy, child psychotherapy, and so on, have all been omitted. I have not included the many burgeoning forms of brief therapy, such as short-term anxiety-provoking psychotherapy, not to mention different approaches to crisis intervention. Nor have I included all humanistic therapies and complementary or alternative medicine approaches to psychological/emotional/holistic problems or concerns, such as polarity therapy, postural integration, shamanism, est, Alexander Technique, Sufi dancing, acupuncture, homeopathy, Bach flower remedies, and so on. Dianetics (scientology) has been similarly excluded, although many would classify this as therapy. Meditation, yoga, LSD therapy and the many varieties of traditional and non-traditional religious practices have likewise been excluded.

Adlerian Therapy (Individual Psychology)
Art Therapy
Behaviour Therapy
Biodynamics
Bioenergetics
Biofeedback
Biosynthesis
Body Psychotherapy
Clinical Theology
Cognitive-Analytic Therapy
Cognitive Behavioural Therapy
Cognitive-Interpersonal Therapy

Cognitive Therapy
Communicative Psychotherapy
Contextual Modular Therapy
Daseinanalyse
Dialogical Psychotherapy
Dramatherapy
Encounter
Existential Therapy
Experiential Psychotherapy
Feminist Therapy
Focused Expressive Psychotherapy
Focusing
Gestalt Therapy
Hypnotherapy
Implosive Therapy
Inner Child Advocacy
Integrative Psychotherapy
Intensive Short-term Dynamic Psychotherapy
Interpersonal Psychotherapy
Jungian Analysis (Analytical Psychology)
Kleinian Analysis
Lacanian Analysis
Lifeskills Training
Logotherapy
Micropsychoanalysis
Morita Therapy
Motivational Interviewing
Multimodal Therapy
Narrative-Constructivist Therapy
Neuro-linguistic Programming
Object Relations Therapy
Past Lives Therapy
Personal Construct Therapy
Person-centred Therapy
Primal Integration
Primal Therapy
Process-oriented Psychotherapy
Psychoanalysis
Psychoanalytically-oriented Psychotherapy
Psychodrama
Psychosynthesis
Rational Emotive Behaviour Therapy
Reality Therapy
Rebirthing
Redecision Therapy
Re-evaluation Counselling

Reichian Therapy (Orgone Therapy)
Rolfing
Single-session Therapy
Social Therapy
Solution-focused Brief Therapy
Stress Inoculation Training
Systemic Therapy
Transactional Analysis
Transpersonal Therapy
Twelve Steps Therapy
Will Therapy

Index